LADY IN THE LORDS

LADY IN THE LORDS

Jane Ewart-Biggs

Best wishes —

Jane Ewart-Biggs

Weidenfeld and Nicolson · London

First published in Great Britain in 1988 by
George Weidenfeld & Nicolson Limited,
91 Clapham High Street, London sw4 7ta

Copyright © by Jane Ewart-Biggs, 1988

ISBN 0 297 79321 7

Printed in Great Britain at The Bath Press, Avon

To my mother

Contents

List of Illustrations

Foreword

This book was never intended to be a study of the function of the House of Lords. There are many better qualified than I to write a scholarly account of the historical background and constitutional significance of Britain's Second Chamber. My intention is to give the reader a glimpse of what occurs behind those stately walls as its members go about their daily business. Through describing my own experiences in the Upper House, I wish to guide the reader down its corridors to marvel at the many architectural beauties and then lead him into the Chamber to eavesdrop on debates and become acquainted with some of the outstanding characters. In this way I hope to make known how intense a life is lived in the House of Lords, and the strength of the bonds drawing together those who serve it.

My narrative often goes into a wider orbit, leaving the Palace of Westminster far behind. The reason for these digressions is to describe how – lacking a ready-made constituency – I have become involved with the activities of groups throughout the country which make me aware of what goes on among ordinary families, and how social and economic changes affect them.

Drawing on these encounters, I recall with admiration and affection the many men and women whose work is devoted to enabling the less fortunate to lead fuller and happier lives. Yet the narrative throughout never for long departs from my central preoccupation, which remains my family, home and friends.

I found it difficult to finish this book. Right up to the end so much was happening in the Lords. The exceptionally heavy load of business, the expectation that Their Lordships should take decisions on fundamental issues going wider than the House's normal constitutional role of scrutiny, and the arrival of active new colleagues; all this made it harder to bring my narrative to an end.

I am indebted to many people for their help and encouragement while I was writing this book. I am grateful to all the colleagues

who shared with me their views about the Upper House, as I am
to all those who provided information and advice to help me get
my facts right. As in my earlier volume of memoirs, I once again
had the benefit of discussing and arguing out many of the ideas with
Kevin O'Sullivan, which was of infinite value. The book certainly
would never have reached the finishing post without the encouragement, support and advice given to me by my editor, Alex
MacCormick, and my agent, Xandra Hardie. I am most grateful to
them, as I am to Liz Travis for her heroism in deciphering my inexcusa-
bly bad handwriting.

I have mentioned many people by name in recounting events and
I hope all of them – not least my own children – will take these
references in the benign and friendly spirit in which they are intended.
I have dedicated the book to my mother. For although – sadly –
she died before *Lady in the Lords* was completed, she was so happy
and proud when her daughter became one.

CHAPTER ONE

The Making of a Lady

ONE GREY EVENING in April 1981, just after I had been nominated for a peerage, I was at the Royal Festival Hall with some friends. It was pouring with rain, but across the Thames the blurred outline of the Palace of Westminster was just visible.

'I wonder what exactly goes on over there,' I said to Kevin O'Sullivan, my particular friend.

'But you know a bit about it,' he replied. 'You've been there a few times. You said how impressive it was and you liked the friendly atmosphere. I can't help feeling it will suit you really well and that you'll be very happy there.'

Until a few weeks before that evening the possibility of becoming a peer of the realm had never occurred to me. Like so many other people in Britain I knew little about the Upper House and it seemed remote. I realized there was a lot of expertise there and it did a good job as a revising chamber. I thought it looked interesting from the outside and confessed to a guilty admiration for titles. So, on the whole, I was typical of many other people in the country.

It is true that after my husband Christopher was assassinated by the Provisional IRA in 1976, while he was Ambassador to Dublin, there were a few hints in the press that I might be given a peerage in recognition of his distinguished diplomatic career and of my own work towards reconciliation in Ireland after his death. But it did not happen and I did not expect it to, because after Christopher was killed I became gripped by a pessimism which took away any belief in good luck. In any event the political party to which I belonged, the Labour Party, disapproved of a second chamber in Parliament and Michael Foot, himself a committed unicameralist, had not made one single nomination to the House of Lords during his leadership.

Nevertheless, coming back to Britain in 1976 after sixteen years of diplomatic life mainly spent abroad, I was determined to try to enter into the political life of my country. *Pay, Pack and Follow,*

my first book, is about the world of diplomacy and the intense interest
I shared with Christopher in the affairs of countries where we lived
and served. We had witnessed the coming of independence to war-
weary Algeria in 1962, the 1971 negotiations in Brussels leading up
to Britain's entry into the European Community, and the honeymoon
period between France and Britain in the 1970s. I believed that by
being a working diplomatic wife, I had in a sense served an apprenticeship. In 1978 friends pointed out that direct elections for the
European Parliament the following year might be my way in. So,
with a mixture of naïvety and bravado, rather than any experience
or expertise, I launched myself into preparations.

Painstakingly I recorded what I saw as my life's high points and
achievements for a curriculum vitae: details of my education, marriage, knowledge of foreign countries and languages. I showed it to
David Lipsey, previously one of Tony Crosland's young political
advisers, who without saying a word but with great sensitivity, pen-
cilled through all the entries which reflected an image of the kind
of person least likely to appeal to Labour Party selection committees.
First, there was my education. Downe House in Cold Ash, near New-
bury, looked wrong and had to go, but the course at Grenoble University in France was relevant. The pencil hovered longest over the
evidence of my Euro-enthusiasm: chairman of Kensington and Chelsea for Europe, member of the European Movement and Labour
Committee for Europe – all anathema to the Labour Party in 1978.
Entries which concerned Ireland escaped his pencil for they were
non-controversial and at least showed I had done something positive.
In the end, committees choosing prospective candidates for EEC election learned from my c.v. – and were probably bewildered to know
– that I had been awarded an Hon. D.Litt. from the New University
of Ulster, had set up a Literary Prize in memory of Christopher and
become President of the Women's Peace Movement in Northern Ireland. But not much else.

Once typed, my c.v., in spite of its imperfections, gave me some
confidence. It defined my new identity. In my old life I had identified
myself as the wife of a diplomat, and I had been proud of that.
After Christopher was killed my status should have been that of a
widow. But – still feeling so firmly married to Christopher – I rejected
that, so was left with no identity at all; none except the one provided
by motherhood, and my pride in that took a serious knock when,

one day, I overheard a child upbraiding her mother for a long list of shortcomings, culminating with the sobering truth, 'And you're only a Mummy because of me'. So after the c.v. was despatched around the Euro-constituencies, I felt as if I had acquired a status again. I was a politically concerned person, mother of three children, seeking adoption to fight a seat in the European elections.

I remember those days so well. The letters from constituency groups inviting me to appear before them, the terrifying trauma of presenting myself, and the minimal prospect of being chosen. But I was glad at least to be asked. I always awoke on those mornings feeling rather sick and then, for the umpteenth time, re-wrote my speech. I knew it should last ten minutes and be followed by five minutes of questions. I tested the length on my tape recorder and never enjoyed playing it back because of the unnatural voice I heard. It was hard to present membership of the European Community as beneficial to people from the Inner London area. The common agricultural policy, aid pro-grammes to the developing countries, political co-operation or any other EEC policies seemed far way from their lives.

The selection committees usually met in a pub. Once in Kentish Town I tracked down The Pineapple, parked my car far away because the red Triumph Stag, given to me by Christopher, fell into the same undesirable category as my upper class voice and January suntan, and went into the bar. Other aspiring candidates were easily recogniz-able, nervously buying each other drinks, waiting their turn to climb the little narrow staircase to the room above where the selectors were gathered. When at last my turn came, I looked apprehensively at the committee: several young women dressed in jeans talking poli-tics in classless voices, a couple of oldish men looking as if they represented the traditional Labour movement, a young West Indian, several old ladies, a pin-striped 'liberal' businessman and a couple of Militants.

The chairman – or rather 'chair', as they are called in Labour circles (I have never been in favour of 'furniturism') – invited me to speak. Out of nervousness I set off at quite a rate, but I noticed gratefully that one of the old ladies was nodding her head in a seem-ingly appreciative manner, giving me courage to continue. I ended up with my favourite peroration about the EEC being our generation's collective effort to build a safer, fairer, more prosperous world. Then a new apprehension came with the questions which, as usual, revealed the rift between my selectors and me. I was asked how membership of the Community could possibly make a jot of difference to local problems of residents of Kentish Town, why had I been the only candidate to speak in favour of Britain's continued membership of the Community; and then the old lady who had seemed to be my only ally, turned on me to repudiate all my arguments – proving that far from agreement, her nods had signified dissatisfied sleep.

I turned to her: 'From what you say, perhaps you would prefer Britain to withdraw her membership from the Community?'

'Not at all,' she replied furiously, 'I want to stay in and go on grumbling.'

Agonized occasions happened often, like the meeting near Swindon, where I decided to give my speech from a sitting position and even thought it had gone quite well until, just as I was leaving the hall, an icy voice said, 'Never address a Labour party meeting sitting down.' The worst of all was in Hammersmith, when my ignorance was revealed in such a way that remembering it still makes me feel hot. I had not much liked the look of the group round the table, a feeling which they evidently reciprocated. I launched nervously into my speech and after a stony silence, the first question came: 'If you became a member of the European Parliament, what would you do about Clause 4?' I longed with all my heart that, instead of boning up on the EEC aid programme under its Lomé Convention, I had done the same regarding the application of Clause 4 to an integrated European economy. One of my tormentors moved a motion, immediately and gleefully seconded by a fellow torturer, to prolong question time by five minutes. I have never known five minutes last so long.

Failure, here and elsewhere, came as no surprise. Indeed I was more than satisfied to have been shortlisted twice. And I did not blame myself for losing at Sidcup – my last hope – when my rival, and NUM official, was asked by the selection committee, 'Can you give one good reason why Britain should remain within the Community', and he answered, 'No'. I was grateful that the experience provided me with a group of new friends, gave me the opportunity to learn a little about Labour politics and proved my commitment to the Party. A year later I tried to be adopted for the GLC elections, but my lack of experience was shown up even more and I promptly and discreetly withdrew before losing face.

The penny had dropped. The hustings were no place for me. My whole background, experience and life style were totally opposed to my ever being a standard bearer for the Labour Party. Sixteen years of diplomatic life, with all the exaggerated politeness that went with it, had not been a good apprenticeship for holding definite views and sticking to them; it schooled you, rather, in tentative and qualified discussion and in being a good listener. Electioneering required a dogmatic – even aggressive – stance which I was unlikely to acquire.

Reconciled, I took up constituency work. Though I had little in common with the political views of some of the members of the East Chelsea Branch, I went to the monthly meetings in the top room of The Blenheim in Cale Street and listened to the often acrimonious discussion. In the 1979 general election I engaged in the hard slog of stuffing envelopes, canvassing, running errands, and on one occasion I spoke at a public meeting. The Labour candidate was Mr Pandy, a dustman by trade, who twice a week had the doubtful honour of emptying Mrs Thatcher's dustbin at her home in Flood Street.

But there were some Labour Party events I really enjoyed when I met people I felt happy with. There was the evening in 1979 that I spent with friends, members of the women's section of the constituency party in Ilford. I had got to know them at my selection panel for the European elections and, although I failed to get the nomination, I knew the women had wanted me. They were warmhearted and straight, and I realized then that I felt more at home with them than I had done with many of the people I met in my diplomatic life. After tea and sandwiches, they sat themselves down on the rows of chairs in the hall whilst I stood in front of them at the table which had a glass of water on it and gave my speech. I compared the 1945 watershed election. Labour's great post-war emergence, to the one we faced that 3 May. 'The decision next Thursday will be whether to continue with Labour policies which have brought stability and a fairer way of life, or to change to a new style of radical and divisive Conservative policies. These may reverse so much of what has been done since the end of the war to bring about a fairer and kinder system and a less divided and stratified society. We may see the old divisions return and with them a sense of grievance and bitterness.'

The election results were a grave disappointment. Soon afterwards the new Social Democratic Party emerged from a torn and uncertain

Labour Party. I might have joined it, for I shared a strong commitment to the European Community with its founding members. But I have never liked giving up on things. Anyhow, it would have meant walking out on people in the party I admired, people like my friends at Ilford, and I didn't feel I could do that. So I stayed with Labour.

The telephone call which was to herald such profound change in my life came on a Friday in February 1981. The children were at home and we were all sitting down to supper. When the bell rang, one of them answered. It was someone called Llewelyn-Davies.

The name did mean something to me, but I couldn't place it. 'This is Pat Llewelyn-Davies, and I'm Labour's Chief Whip in the Lords. We met briefly at the Wembley Conference last month. You may remember.' A pretty dark-haired woman with brown eyes came into my mind. The voice went on. 'I am ringing to tell you that your name has been suggested as one of the Labour nominations for the House of Lords in the next political honours list.' At that point, my mind went spinning off and I stopped listening. When I could concentrate again I heard her say, 'Before going any further I thought I had better talk to you to see what you felt about it, if you want to be considered and, if appointed, whether you would be able to attend regularly and take part in the work of the House. As you probably know, the Party tends to see a peerage as a working appointment rather than purely an honour.'

I could hardly believe my ears, but tried to respond intelligently. Yes, I said, I certainly was very interested and would be able to attend regularly. I explained that since leaving the Savoy Hotel, where I had worked on my return from Dublin, I had not had a full-time job but was doing freelance work: lecturing, journalism, broadcasting and television. Then my usual self-doubt intervened. 'But do you think I'd be any good at it? I have no experience of parliamentary work.'

'A lot of people have spoken highly of you.' The conversation ended in some confusion with me muttering something about it being such an honour but such a surprise, and I had better talk to the children, and might I ring her after the weekend.

She said, 'Yes, of course. But don't tell anyone else.'

I went back to the kitchen. The children were still eating their supper and looked up expectantly as I came in. Perhaps they felt there was a significance about that telephone call which distinguished it from the others that flooded into 31 Radnor Walk.

They reacted in different ways. The eldest, Henrietta, remembering that what happened to her parents – singly or collectively – always seemed to rub off on her, was pleased. She obviously welcomed the possibility of this strange, unexpected development bringing with it a sense of security; a return to the days when the family had a position in life. So although not said in so many words, her reaction was, 'OK Mum, why not?' Her sister Kate, then aged about thirteen, also seized on what seemed the positive side. She remembered with pleasure an excellent tea she had in the House of Lords when on a tour of the Palace of Westminster with her school. With the prospect of a long succession of teas unfolding before her, she too conceded a cautious welcome to the news. But Robin, then in his last year at school, made no comment whatsoever. Embassies had been bad enough for him, with the formal and – to him – artificial life that went with them. And now something which sounded even worse had appeared out of the blue. He was suspicious and said nothing. But in the end his kind heart prevailed. His first letter home from school read, 'Dear Mum ... I don't think I was enthusiastic enough about that news of yours. But, in my heart, I'm really very glad for you and – if you want – I'll come to your coronation or whatever ...'

On Monday morning I telephoned Lady Llewelyn-Davies and said I was happy to have my name put forward. 'Good,' she said, 'that's fine. I'll put things in motion and see how it goes.' She repeated her warning not to go around telling people. 'If news of a possible peerage gets around, it has a funny habit of stopping it happen.'

So of course I didn't tell a soul. And after a few weeks, having heard nothing further, I started to think I had imagined the whole thing. But I have since learned more about the whole procedure. There are three routes to a life peerage. First, there are the New Year and Birthday honours lists made up of 'the great and the good', men and women from all walks of life elevated as a reward for services to the nation. Next, there is the dissolution honours list at the end of a Parliament containing a mixture from all Parties of those who have lost their seats or retired from the House of Commons after occupying cabinet rank or prominent positions. (Some Prime Ministers have seemed to misuse their power in this respect; Harold Wilson ennobled not only colleagues from his cabinet but also members of his personal entourage.) And last there is the political honours list which comes out at irregular intervals and is made up of nominees from each political party. These are the 'working peers'. Their numbers are calculated to maintain a party balance, and my name was under consideration for this list. Pat Llewelyn-Davies and other Labour Party leaders had been wishing to replenish their stock of active working peers for some time. In spite of the party's abolition policy, Pat argued, 'While the Upper Chamber is part of the system we need a sufficient number of Opposition peers to make it work.'

The Prime Minister is responsible for the next stage in the process. He (or now, she) reviews the entire list of Conservative, Labour and Liberal nominees and makes any desired changes before passing it to the Political Honours Scrutiny Committee, though obviously changes made by either the PM or the Committee are unlikely ever to be made public.

It was not until late in March that the postman brought evidence that I had passed through all the hoops except the final one. On the doormat one Saturday morning lay a very official-looking envelope. As I had a headache I opened it listlessly. 'Dear Mrs Ewart-Biggs, I am writing to let you know, in strict confidence, that I have it in mind to submit your name to the Queen with a recommendation that Her Majesty may be graciously pleased to approve that the dignity of a Barony of the United Kingdom for life be conferred upon you. I hope that you will be able to let me know as soon as possible that this would be agreeable to you.' Marked 'In Confidence' and signed 'Yours sincerely, Margaret Thatcher'.

Headache miraculously gone, my first thought was, 'Surely the Queen couldn't have anything against my going to the House of Lords.' But even while I wrote my letter of acceptance, the doubt lurked. Liz Travis typed the letter. She had been coming every Friday morning to help me with correspondence, form filling, appointments, and had brought order out of chaos for several years. She was married with three children; each a little older than mine. This meant she had preceded me in the different stages of children's needs and knew, for example, when child benefit stopped, how to fill in university entrance forms, where holiday jobs could be found, and so on. The number of knots she had undone for our family was enormous, and we all depended on her. Her one idiosyncrasy during those early years was that she never called me Jane. (It is true the longer one puts off calling someone by their Christian name the harder it becomes to do so.) She either called me nothing or, if I was out of sight, attracted my attention with 'Hello'.

The manner in which I received final confirmation of my ennoblement was bizarre, to put it mildly. The Easter holidays arrived and soon after posting the letter we set off on one of our return visits to France, the country in which we had spent five happy years safely tucked up in the bosom of the Paris Embassy. To me France is our second home. So, with Henrietta away visiting an old school friend in Canada, Robin, Kate plus her school friend Sophie and I drove off to Courcheval in the Alps for a week's skiing. We stayed in the miniscule studio we had rented in previous years, and just managed to squeeze in. The days were magical – sun, snow and mountains make a powerful combination. One morning around eleven o'clock we decided to take a break from skiing for some hot chocolate in a café in the village, and sitting over the steaming cups I noticed the family at the neighbouring table. They were English and the mother was reading the *Daily Telegraph*. 'Look,' she said rather blankly, 'they've put some new people in the House of Lords. Wonder who the old codgers are?' Reading aloud down the list she said, 'Well for goodness' sake look at this. You'd never believe it. There they are, always chivvying that poor Ronald from pillar to post, and now they've gone and put his wife in the Lords. Wonders never will cease.' I sat there bemused. Out of the corner of my eye I could see my photograph in the paper and there, by my name, I could just spot the figure giving my age. (I had always been a bit economical with the truth about that, so hoped the children wouldn't mind discovering the reality.)

Before coming out of my state of shock my mind slid over the other occasions when we have basked in Ronald Biggs's glory. At the time of the great train robbery itself when we were *en poste* in Algeria and, to our surprise and for the first time, found ourselves suddenly the focus of admiration from the sons of the revolution, who much admired the coup. And then there was another occasion when I was on my way to the BBC in a hired car. All of a sudden the driver, without turning round, said to me, 'Are you *the* Mrs Biggs?' For a split second it seemed a remote possibility . . . and then . . . 'No-o-o,' I said sadly.

I will always remember the remainder of that day in the mountains.

It was 14 April and the sky was that particular dark blue only to be found on a clear day in the Alps. I needed to be alone to disentangle what was going on in my mind, so I went and skied by myself for a time. What I felt was more complicated than the normal sense of pleasure people might experience on receiving an important honour. That was part of it, but not all of it. There was something more. The news also provided an antidote to the sense of bitterness, anger and injustice which, although not allowed to dominate everything, had lurked around inside me for the five years since Christopher had been murdered, the voice in my head which had said, 'why should it have happened to us? Why him – why me – why is life so cruel and unfair?' So my sense of liberation from that voice was so strong it was as if my skis never touched down but swooped effortlessly just above the surface of the snow. I felt that for both Christopher and me the balance sheet had, in a small way, been adjusted. Previously the entries were weighted on the paying out side. First the years he had dedicated to the Foreign Office, followed by his death in the service of his country. There was the sacrifice of a gifted life, the destruction of peace and happiness of a family, and so on. But my peerage, coming as an entry on the other side of the sheet, went some way towards redressing the balance.

I knew Christopher would have thought so too, and I could imagine him grinning away on hearing the news, screwing his monocle in with the look of rather shy amusement he sometimes wore.

We went home next day, driving the long route from Chambery to Calais and then over the Channel and back to London. We did not go into Paris but skirted it around the Boulevard Peripherique. But I couldn't resist sharing my news with someone in that beloved city. We stopped for petrol and from the telephone kiosk I rang Nicole Hébert, one of the girls we so often invited to bring glamour to our dinner parties, and told her: 'Nicole, I'm going to the House of Lords.'

'Pour quoi faire, Jane?'

'To be a member of it.'

'Mon dieu, tu vas être un Lord – comme tu vas être importante.'

On the ferry I read some press reports. A *Daily Telegraph* leader was not very kind. Starting with, 'The abolition of the House of Lords has been a Labour aim for almost as long as even peers themselves can remember,' it ended, 'Mr Foot's impeccably unmemorable half dozen would happily vote for their own abolition'! There was already a pile of telegrams and letters waiting in Radnor Walk, and the tape on the answering machine was so full it had run out. It was the best homecoming I could remember. Kevin was there to say well done. He and I had been going round together for several years and had formed a very strong attachment. The circumstances of our past lives were very different. For me a happy marriage with three children, and for him a short, tumultuous marriage and no children. But we have become very entangled with each other. I recognized how complex his reactions to my news must be. On the one hand happiness for me but, on the other, fear that the House of Lords might draw me away or create a barrier between us. He was worried, but did everything he could to show his pleasure and gave a wonderful party for all my friends to celebrate.

With the first euphoria over, there were a lot of more mundane things to be done. First and foremost, Robin and Kate had to go back to school (Henrietta was in her year off between school and Durham University). Then there were letters of congratulation to be answered and the arrangements made for taking my seat. The children were apprehensive of the effect the new label indirectly attached to themselves might have on their school friends. Remembering my own longing for complete anonymity at school, I felt worried for them. However, with the same fortitude they had shown through the eruptions and crises of their lives, they survived my ennoblement. 'Whew,' said Kate after her first day back from school, 'it was alright. A few of the teachers said "Well done" about it, but the other children didn't say anything. I don't think they know very much about the House of Lords.' And she looked as if she very much hoped that state of affairs might continue.

The letters of congratulation taught me something about human nature I had not known before. It was the second time in my life the postman had arrived at our door so heavily laden. In the first case the letters had been written to convey condolences and sorrow. Now they were about joy and good fortune. On both occasions they revealed hidden characteristics of the people writing them. When Christopher was killed, there was a common thread of horror and profound regret. They differed only in expression. The more introverted and inhibited writers expressed their feelings without much emotion. I suppose the best way of protecting their own sensitivities was to write in a way which diminished the tragedy; otherwise their own emotions might have been affected. Others who were more open and courageous took the risk of exposing their innermost sensitivities by reflecting the true measure of the tragedy.

So, although on the first occasion, I certainly learned something about my friends, the second time around I was surprised to find this repeated. For instance, the letters revealed the degree of generosity necessary to feel and express genuine pleasure at other people's good fortune, and the difficulty for unhappy people to do so. I had myself experienced this after Christopher was killed. I had found it impossible to congratulate a former colleague on a promotion or a good new job. 'Why should *he* be posted to x,' I used to agonize, 'when Christopher's last posting led to his death?' So as the letters rolled in they told me more than their authors had perhaps intended.

An example of generosity and genuine pleasure came from an old Foreign Office friend, Nigel Clive, who wrote: 'What a marvellous ascent. It brings you half way to Heaven. This splendid news will make all your friends rejoice and you need no telling how enormously pleased and proud Christopher would have been.' But there was a slight edge to the good wishes from another old friend: 'A thousand congratulations on your peerage. Will you speak up in the House of Lords? Ben [the son] who has just been on a school visit there says that eveyone was asleep all afternoon.'

Some members of Christopher's family as well as my own could not refrain from showing their political prejudice. 'Dear Jane, It would be ungracious of me if I did not congratulate you on your elevation. I think of course you've achieved it with the wrong Party... But enjoy what it is whilst you can! And do make sure that when Benn takes over, you all get a jolly good pension...' Another included among the good wishes, 'I must add that we were rather shattered and surprised to see the party that you support. I always thought and hoped that everyone connected with us would be Tory supporters.'

Doubts about the institution itself were expressed even by some already there. Barbara Wootton, who was one of the first women to sit in the Lords, wrote, 'As I am now the "Mother of the House" I send this note as an expression of pleasure at the latest addition to my "family". I am sure that we shall be enriched by your company and I much hope that you will find this anomalous institution in some ways rewarding, even though it has its tedious and exasperating moments...' Michael Foot, well known for his antipathy to a second chamber, ended his letter, 'So congratulations and good wishes from all of us in the House of Commons which may last a little longer than the House of Lords.'

I was particularly pleased that the letters and messages came from people I had known in all the different stages of my life. For instance a letter from the Foreign Office ended, 'When I do the answer to one of your Parliamentary Questions I will put three kisses at the bottom of the draft, and hope it gets delivered that way.' But others obviously had found it easier to deal with me when in adversity rather than in triumph. This was proved by an astonishing conversation I had with a very old friend – she and her husband had served in Paris at the same time as we had. Although only a couple of days after the honours list had been published, she made no mention of it. Finally, thinking she did not know, I asked her if she had heard about my peerage. Her reply was devastating in its lack of generosity. 'Oh yes,' she said with a note of simulated interest. 'And is that a good thing?' However, another couple from the days at the Paris Embassy rang from Harvard, where he was on a sabbatical, and their voices were full of pleasure and shared happiness.

A letter from the Principal Private Secretary at 10 Downing Street was on a different subject. It told me of the arrangements to be made. One was to visit Garter King of Arms (known as Garter for short) to settle my name. It was not easy to decide what it should be. Some new life peers change their names; either out of taste or to avoid confusion. For example, Ted Bishop, who was in the same intake as me, called himself Lord Bishopston to save becoming confused with the ecclesiastic Bishops; Diana Neave adopted the Christian name of her assassinated husband and became Baroness Airey. A second option was to retain existing surnames whilst appending a territorial designation. Heads of family businesses have sometimes taken a different name when ennobled to prevent the peerage being discredited if their company were to go bust. In the cases of Lord Heyter (Chubb locks) and Lord Nuffield (Morris motor cars) this proved unnecessary.

It did not take me long to decide to keep my own name. For although Christopher often made jokes about his surname it did belong to him and as such had the first right to ennoblement. But what about the required territorial name? The choice is simple for new peers. For example, there were those whose title had originally been won for some deed of valour. Monty became Viscount Montgomery of Alamein, and there was Lord Alexander of Tunis. But diplomats don't win battles; they negotiate treaties. And it would have been presumptuous to adopt for myself names such as Versailles, Venice, Rome, etc. So that was no good. The decision for a member of the House of Commons who is elevated – or 'kicked upstairs', as it is generally called – is also clearcut. He or she invariably uses the name of their old constituency. A further option is to use the name of one's birthplace.

None of these solutions seemed quite right for me. Of course, having been born in India made Ewart-Biggs of Simla a possibility – but I did not much care for the Kiplingesque flavour. I had been brought up in a small village in Somerset which provided the somewhat poetic-sounding title of Baroness Ewart-Biggs of Queen Camel. But the alarm spreading over the faces of all three children at this idea made me drop it immediately. Liz Travis eventually hit on the solution. 'What about Ellis Green?' she said thoughtfully. The minute the words had left her mouth, the choice seemed obvious. Ellis Green was our beloved little cottage in Essex, the setting for so many happy family scenes over the years. Tucked away in the middle of the fields, without road or electricity. In the first place it had provided Christopher and me with an idyllic pre-marriage love nest. His friends had told him when he bought it, 'You can use it to invite a whole lot of girls to see which you like best', but in the end I was the only one he ever took there. In the winter we were forced to abandon the car on the other side of the field and walk; and, as events developed, carry Henrietta in her carry cot through the mud. And then, after lighting all the fires and the oil lamps, we would test the temperature with our breath. It was usually not until Sunday evening, just before returning to London, that the 'breath test' was passed as the thick clouds from our mouths thinned down.

If Alamein had been central to Monty's life, then Ellis Green certainly provided a pinnacle of contentment and family union for us. So on the appointed day I arrived at the College of Arms with my mind made up. Sir Colin Cole was sitting at his desk waiting for me. On the walls above him hung the coats of arms of many of Britain's great families and the atmosphere was distinctly feudal. I began to wonder if Ellis Green was quite adequate. However, grasping my courage with both hands I put it to him, and after minutely examining the ordnance map to prove it existed, he acquiesced.

I learned that I should not be addressed as Lady Jane Ewart-Biggs – although over the years I have often been called this, doubtless an echo of Lady Jane Grey – for the addition of the Christian name would make me the daughter of a duke. My correct style should be Lady Ewart-Biggs or Baroness Ewart-Biggs. Later on I found that many of my female colleagues in the Lords prefer to be called Baroness as it makes it unequivocally clear that the title is their own, but I prefer the more modest version.

Next, Garter asked, 'What about a coat of arms? If you provide a family crest, a motto and ideas for the two supporters on each side of the shield, I will have one designed for you.' As I pondered this amazing suggestion he added, 'It is fairly expensive, but less expensive for a baroness than a baron.' (This was the first time I recognized that the makings of a full-blooded feminist were lurking inside me.) In reply, I said I thought I had better think about it and see what the children felt.

Finally there were the robes. Would I like to order a set of parliamentary robes from Ede & Ravenscroft in Chancery Lane? They were the robe-makers who produced ceremonial gear for peers, academics, diplomats and so on. I was tempted. The idea of the long heavy red velour garment with its white ermine collar and lapels was attractive. I asked Garter when they were worn. 'For your introduction, of course, and also for the State Opening of Parliament. No peer is permitted into the Chamber for that ceremony unless robed.'

I felt I was letting Garter down when in the end I declined both coat of arms and robes. But after all, I had the sensitivities of my children to consider. Already the visit had transformed me from an ordinary mum into what seemed almost like a supernatural being: The Baroness Ewart-Biggs of Ellis Green in the County of Essex. If on top of that they were asked to swallow the elaborate fancy dress and a mark of privilege such as a coat of arms, they might rebel.

I still had a little time to wait before the day of my Introduction. This was a period when I was neither one thing nor the other; a period to acclimatize myself to being different, and to register other people's reactions to the difference. There was again a faint echo to the state of limbo in which I found myself following Christopher's death. A time when suddenly I was perceived in a new light, when letters arrived no longer addressed to Mrs Christopher Ewart-Biggs but – alarmingly – to Mrs Jane Ewart-Biggs. When filling up the never-ending forms, the marital state which drew my tick had to be 'widow'. There is little doubt that suddenly being addressed in a different way has a bewildering effect. In this instance, when first visiting the House to meet some of my future colleagues, I felt distinctly shaken – although happily so – when one of the attendants called me 'My Lady'. Who was this new person? For after all, whatever the changes or crises which erupt in a person's life, that person remains the same inside. Their ideas, fears, hopes, values are unchanged. So it is disconcerting when the outside world seems to want to disprove this.

During those next few weeks, I began to learn about people's attitudes towards the House of Lords, and realized how little they know about it. 'Don't worry, Jane,' one said, 'you'll be fine – just treat it like a good club.' But I had never belonged to a club; so that was no comfort at all. People also seemed to divide its inmates into two distinct and separate categories; 'Congratulations,' said a friend in a slightly doubting voice when we met outside Habitat in the King's Road. 'You've just become a Labour peer, haven't you'. This made me realize there was a distinction between peers and Labour peers, the second category presumably being an ersatz version of the first. (I have since discovered there is a more accurate breakdown, i.e. hereditary peers, life peers, Labour peers and working peers.)

There was also, inevitably, evidence of people's entrenched views about the role of women. 'What's your mother do?' Henrietta was asked by the mother of a friend.

'She's going to work in the House of Lords,' said Henrietta.

'What as? A secretary?' came the response.

On the day of my Introduction, 3 June 1981, I gave a formal lunch at the House for family, some friends – including Susan Crosland and Tilli Edelman, who had both helped me take the first steps in my political career – and those taking part in the ceremony. Reading the guest list just before, Henrietta exclaimed, 'Black Rod, Garter, Chief Whip – sounds like a bunch of perverts to me!' (Henrietta has a mordant turn of phrase.) Despite her misgivings, the lunch was most enjoyable. Afterwards, having put on the robes I had borrowed from Lady Sharples, my supporters and I were shepherded by Garter into our places in the procession.

There was complete silence in the Chamber as we entered. The assembled peers sat silently on the benches, looking towards the door, waiting to see what I looked like.

I paused at the entrance. I took in the magnificence of the Chamber. At the far end was the Throne covered by the richly decorated canopy which represents the Cloth of Estate. In front of the Throne was the Woolsack stuffed, I knew, with wool from England, Wales, Scotland, Northern Ireland and the countries of the Commonwealth. Lord Hailsham, the Lord Chancellor, was in his place on the Woolsack. In front of him I saw the two other Woolsacks and the Table of the House occupying the whole centre of the Chamber. The despatch boxes were placed one on each side ready for Government ministers and Opposition spokesmen to make their speeches. At the end of the table nearest to where I stood, sat the Clerks in their wigs, high white collars and bow ties. Theirs, I knew, was the responsibility of calling and recording the business of the House. Behind them, the *Hansard* writer, his pencil at that moment lying idle but who, during debate, I knew would be recording all that was said. And finally between them and the Bar of the House, which designates the limits of the Chamber, sat the crossbenchers facing the centre of the Chamber and with their backs to where I was standing on the other side of the Bar. In the benches on the left sat the Government supporters and in the centre of the front bench, in his capacity of Leader of the House, I saw Christopher Soames smiling at me reassuringly. Beyond them the bishops brought a dash of white to the dark red benches sitting in their ecclesiastical robes. My eyes still circling the Chamber, I saw the Liberal and SDP peers sitting on the benches on the right nearest the Throne and finally my own benches, the opposition party, closest to me on my right.

My gaze returned to the red-clad back of Lord (Denis) Greenhill in front of me. He was moving forward; I quickly followed. As we entered the Chamber I felt self-conscious rather than nervous because of the extreme formality of the occasion. The procession of which I was the central figure was as follows. First came Black Rod, followed by Garter King of Arms, looking substantial and sumptuous in his red tunic heavily encrusted in gold. Behind him came Denis Greenhill, my junior supporter, impassive but resplendent in his parliamentary robes. I came next and, instead of the long fore-and-aft Nelson-type hat of my two supporters, I wore a small black tricorne. Goronwy Roberts, Deputy Leader of the Labour peers and my senior supporter, took up the rear. He looked ill and frail, and I had asked him before-hand if he was all right. 'If I don't look well,' he had replied, 'then the reason must be my worry to see everything right for the Introduc-tion of an important young lady.' Dear, kind Goronwy; he must have known by then that he had cancer.

Once we were in the Chamber, Black Rod stood aside to allow Garter to lead the procession, and we went through the ceremonial Introduction of a new peer. After entering the Chamber at the Bar the procession moves toward the Woolsack; each member pausing in turn first at the Bar, then the Table to bow to the Cloth of Estate. As I arrived at the Woolsack, remembering the rehearsal I stopped and knelt on my right knee whilst presenting my Writ of Summons and Letter Patent to the Lord Chancellor. (My peerage had been granted by Letter Patent and the Writ was the method of summoning me to Parliament.) I then rose and moved towards the table where the Clerk read out the Patent and the Writ. This was the first time the deep silence had been broken.

ELIZABETH THE SECOND by the grace of God of the United Kingdom of Great Britain and Northern Ireland and of our other Realms and Territories Queen Head of the Commonwealth Defender of the Faith To all Lords Spiritual and Temporal and all other Our Subjects whatsoever to whom these presents shall come Greeting Know Ye that We of our especial grace certain knowledge & mere motion in pursuance of the Life Peerage Act 1958 & of all other powers in that behalf Us enabling do by these Presents advance create & prefer Our trusty and well beloved FELICITY JANE EWART-BIGGS widow of Christopher Thomas Ewart EWART-BIGGS Esquire Companion of Our Most Distinguished Order of Saint Michael & Saint George Officer of Our Most Excellent Order of the British Empire to the state degree style dignity title and honour of BARONESS EWART-BIGGS of Ellis Green in Our County of Essex And for Us Our heirs & successors do appoint give and grant unto her the said name state degree style dignity title & honour of Baroness Ewart-Biggs to have & to hold unto her during her life Willing and by these Presents granting for Us Our heirs & successors that she may have hold & possess a seat place & voice in the Parliaments & Public Assemblies & Councils of Us Our heirs & successors within Our United Kingdom amongst the Barons And also that she may enjoy & use all the rights privileges pre-eminences immunities & advantages to the degree of a Baron duly & of right belonging which Barons of Our United Kingdom have heretofore used & enjoyed or as they do at present use & enjoy In Witness whereof We have caused these Our Letters to be made Patent Witness Ourself at Westminster the twenty-second day of May in the thirtieth year of Our Reign

BY WARRANT UNDER THE QUEEN'S SIGN MANUAL

The Clerk then invited me to take the Oath of Allegiance. Holding the Bible, I declared, hoping my voice sounded natural, but doubting that it did: 'I, Jane, Baroness Ewart-Biggs do swear by Almighty God that I will be faithful and bear true allegiance to Her Majesty Queen Elizabeth, Her Heirs & successors according to the Law. So help me God.' I signed the Roll upon the Table. At that moment I looked up and saw my children in the gallery. They looked suitably impressed and Kate gave me one of her biggest smiles. Dragging my eyes away, I took my place again in the procession which had been reformed to continue with the ceremony. Led by Garter, we proceeded across the Chamber, each of us bowing to the Cloth of Estate on the way, and up to the uppermost bench, one of those usually occupied by the crossbenchers. There Garter, like the conductor of an orchestra, stood facing us and, whispering, led us through the most bizarre part of the whole ritual. This consisted of four motions, repeated three times. First, we rose to our feet, next my two supporters removed their hats and bowed towards the Lord Chancellor, replaced their hats and sat down again. The origin of this was to confirm the true identity of the maiden peer whose face could be more clearly seen once his head was uncovered.

As we went through this part of the ceremony I suddenly remembered an anecdote – possibly apocryphal, but most certainly relevant – about the misadventure of a maiden peer who had borrowed his Nelson hat from a colleague of many years standing. The hat, perhaps in common with its owner, was feeling the passage of time and when the maiden peer went through this part of the time-honoured ritual he clasped the brim so firmly that it became detached from the crown which on each of the three occasions remained firmly on his noble head. I cast a furtive, hurried look to my right and left to make sure a similar disaster had not befallen either of my colleagues.

The Lord Chancellor having acknowledged these salutations from the Woolsack, our procession reformed and moved down the side of the Chamber occupied by the Opposition and, having bowed twice more to the Cloth of Estate, I finally found myself before the Woolsack. Here I knew the proceedings would end on a less formal note by me shaking hands with the Lord Chancellor. I did this smiling broadly but to the accompaniment of a strange, dull roar. I traced this as coming from the throats of Their Lordships, but was unable to understand its meaning (It was not till later that the sound was interpreted to me as the words, 'Hear, hear'. It was their welcome.) I left the Chamber, divested myself of Lady Sharples' robes and was given my Letters Patent. This was an immense handscriven scroll with a big glossy seal, contained in a red leather box as big as a coffee table.

For a short time I returned to sit on the Labour benches to listen to the debate. It was on an EEC subject and had been introduced by Denis Greenhill, who was having a busy afternoon. Before long I noticed a mild disturbance in the visitors' seats just beyond the Bar. To my dismay it was none other than my mother causing it. Deathly pale, she was being escorted out by one of the tail-coated attendants with a somewhat flurried Henrietta, who had been put in charge of her grandmother, hurrying along behind. Abandoning my newly acquired parliamentary career, I followed them out and found the old lady sitting in the Peers' Lobby feeling much recovered and quite pleased with herself for having caused such a stir.

The family was then reunited round the tea table in the Peers' dining-room; a beautiful room with its Pugin wallpaper and hanging tapestries. Although afternoon tea may have dropped out of many people's lives, in the House of Lords it still holds an important place. Robin and Kate appeared from the Gallery with my brother and his family and several other relatives and friends. Robin had made an important concession for the occasion and was wearing a tie. The fact that it was knotted at half mast inevitably brought a wrinkle to the brows of the attendants whose own appearances are of meticulous smartness (I later learned they graduate from the ranks of warrant officers.) To bring an end to the proceedings and by way of congratulation, Kate gave me a small parcel.

It was a present: a white T-shirt with the words, 'I'm Lady Jane' printed in large blue letters on the front. She told me later that asking for this inscription in the King's Road shop had caused her embarrassment. But it did the trick. From that moment on, I felt I really was a Lady in the Lords.

CHAPTER TWO

Learning the Ropes

'MY LORDS, I AM deeply conscious of the privilege of addressing Your Lordships for the first time, but...'

Whose was the disembodied voice droning away in the distance? Mine, of course: in fear and trembling and with a parched mouth, I was making my maiden speech. I had taken the decision to make it as soon as possible after my Introduction. For realizing how little I knew of the parliamentary process, panic had seized me. Just as the longer a swimmer hesitates on the top diving board the harder it will be for him to dive into the pool, I knew that the longer I sat awestruck in my seat in the Chamber, knowing virtually nothing of the parliamentary process, the more I would fear to rise and speak.

Not only did I find the proceedings mystifying, but I could not even understand the vocabulary used. What was the difference (I asked myself despairingly) between the committee and report stages of a bill? Whenever there was a problem, 'The usual channels' was the answer. But what did that mean? And what would a Starred Question turn out to be – not to mention an unstarred one? And then there were Consolidation Orders, and Hybrid Bills, and where on earth could this 'other place' be to which speakers regularly referred? The more I sat in on debates, listening with all my might, the more confused and frightened I became. Yet again I realized how inappropriate my whole background had been for a political life. It's all very splendid working out the seating arrangements for a dinner party, stage-managing the conversation and being a good listener. These are all commendable qualities, but passive. To become qualified to take part in the cut and thrust of debate I needed to go on the offensive.

During this listening period – before my maiden speech – I made certain discoveries, one of which put to rest an anxiety which had consumed me from the very first day. This was about how some of the more elderly peers occupied their seats. (Although there are some sprightly young hereditary peers, the average age of the life barons and baronesses is quite high.) To say they were reclining would not have been correct. They were positively slumped; leaning sideways at an angle of approximately 45° from the seat, their heads drooped against upright backs. The first time I noticed this alarming situation I wondered frantically why the nurse was not being summoned and why the tail-coated attendants were not registering alarm. Resisting any expression of panic on my part, I decided to wait until the next day to see if those who had been most slumped reappeared. If they did not, I would only have one conclusion to draw. The discovery removing my worry came quite inadvertently when, feeling tired one day, I allowed my head to droop sideways against the back of the bench. Immediately, the vastly magnified voice of the speaker booming into my ear made me realize that the amplifiers were set at intervals in the thickly upholstered seat-backs and the peers whom I had taken to be at death's door were merely those anxious not to miss a word of the debate.

I became good at matching-up speakers with their former professions. For instance, those who come to the Lords from academic life speak without notes, articulate clearly and cover their subject extensively. They stand either with their hands behind their backs and bodies swaying slightly or clasping the back of the bench infront of them. Lord (Max) Beloff of academic distinction – he came to the Lords at the same time as me – is an example. Standing in his usual place in the centre on the Tory benches opposite, he lucidly proclaims his firmly held hard-line views with eyes fixed on a point just above our heads, as if he still wants to avoid his students' eyes. The lawyers speak with equal, or even greater, confidence and clarity, and some of them at inordinate length. Prefacing their remarks with 'I would suggest...' they explore every legal aspect of the subject, and as the vast majority sit on the opposition or crossbenches, a Government Minister without legal training is often left perplexed and cut off from the discussion. Those who have been kicked upstairs from the House of Commons are easily distinguishable. They present their arguments from a party political angle and speak in a challenging tone. Having to adapt themselves to the good-mannered style of the Lords, however, they very soon drop all insulting language. Lord Molloy on our benches was a bit fiery when he first arrived. Having lost his seat at Ealing North, he came to the Lords with a mission. Small, Welsh and very articulate, he lashes the Tories about the miners, the health service, the poor. This brings on mutters of, 'Doesn't he realize he's not in the Commons any longer?' from every side of the House. I recognized several ex-trades union leaders on my benches. Old campaigners like Hugh Scanlon and Len Murray, both ex-TUC bosses, still speak with fire and their style is one for open-air rallies. Leaning forward, they jab the air with their index fingers and sweep their eyes round 180°. The hereditary peers – many of them land-owners or farmers – adopt the opposite style. Speaking quietly, some of them read their speeches from extensive notes, they state facts rather than seek to win support. Their traditional place in society has been to take the lead and command rather than persuade or cajole. They have traditional, rather exaggerated upper-class accents and wear well-cut double-breasted suits with waistcoats. The former civil servants have spent lifetimes persuading governments to do the right thing. Their speeches, delivered with authority, sometimes sound like thoroughly sensible briefings. Although if Lord Allen, ex-Permanent Under-Secretary at the Home Office, treated his Ministers in the same robust way as he does Their Lordships, he must have left a few rather flattened Home Secretaries behind him.

In general I would say that women speakers, regardless of their backgrounds, are more brief than their male colleagues. Fearing they may lose the attention of the House, they plan what they have to say more painstakingly and appear to require the encouragement of an attentive audience. They are more easily put off by all the coming and going: peers leaving or arriving during speeches, others talking to each other, others asleep, front bench speakers with their feet up on the table, and so on. (There is the story of how one day as a distinguished peer is making his speech, a voice from the other side of the House interrupts: 'Speak up, we can't hear you over this side.' 'Oh, I'm so sorry,' comes the apologetic answer, 'I had no idea anyone was listening.') Finally there are those peers who like myself have come from the listening professions; social workers, doctors and nurses. Right from the start I could see they were to be my only comfort, for some speak hesitantly, lacking the confidence and flair of many of the others. Whenever they lift their gaze, intending to stress a point, it is as if a magnet drags their eyes back to the security of the written notes held in their not too steady hands. Baroness Cox, originally a nurse, is an exception as her speeches are strong and forceful. But her previous profession is reflected in the rapid

walk of a Ward Sister and whenever she bustles into the Chamber
– the ghost of a crisp white cap nestling in her hair – I feel reassured,
as if suddenly I may find a thermometer slipped into my mouth and
my pillows tidied.

Eddie Shackleton made me decide to take the plunge. It was he
who had been one of the leading proponents for my nomination
to the Lords, and he felt responsible for me. So, seeing me in the
lobby one day only about a week after my Introduction, he said,
'When are you going to make your maiden speech, Jane?'

'Heaven knows – I just don't seem to know enough about anything.
Everyone here speaks out of such a wealth of experience and knowledge. I don't think I shall ever dare make a speech at all.'

But I knew I had no choice. The Labour Party's view of the House
of Lords is, to put it mildly, equivocal. The official policy is abolition
but, in the meantime, while the second chamber still exists, the people
it appoints are expected not to treat it as an honour but to do some
serious work on behalf of the Party. The Conservatives ennoble those
who have served their Party well either in the Commons or as outside
benefactors. Both ways Tory appointees consider it as an honour
rather than a job, and their Whips have an uphill job persuading
them otherwise.

'Why don't you put your name down for Lord O'Hagan's motion
about Britain in the EEC? It's in about ten days' time,' Eddie went
on. 'You must know quite a bit about Community matters from
your time in Brussels and Paris and from when you tried to be adopted
for the European elections. I would have thought it an ideal subject.'

This decided me, and next morning saw me racing off to the Foreign
Office to ask advice from my old friends. David Hannay, then Head
of the European Community Department, had spent longer dealing
with EEC matters in Brussels than anyone else in the Foreign Office
and he was the great expert. 'David, do you think you could help
me with my maiden speech? It's on a European theme. It should
not be longer than ten minutes, or be controversial. Ideally it should
contain a joke and a quotation.' Even the outstanding David Hannay
looked slightly daunted. However, after talking with him for a little
while, the skeleton for my speech started to take shape. Every morning
until the day of the debate, I wrote it and rewrote it; tried it out
on a tape recorder, to test the length and the voice. I eventually got
the time right, but the voice plunged me into despair. There was

a bit of the Queen in it – but the wrong bit. And it did not sound at all natural. Loyally, on hearing the recording, Kate said, 'Very good, Mum.' Then speaking gently she added, 'But you've got your funny voice on. The one you use to make speeches.'

I felt distinctly sick when waking up on the morning of 17 June and on arriving at the House I might have been facing the guillotine. But in keeping with the friendliness there – everyone cares for each other regardless of party – several people wished me luck. As I had made even more alterations to my speech, I thought I should get it retyped. The St Stephen's secretarial service in the House use type-writers with a big script; I didn't at that time use reading spectacles but the day was not far off. Holding the notes carefully I went into the Chamber and sat down on the seat I usually seemed to occupy. (Although in fact no one, except front bench speakers, have particular seats). Prayers, conducted by one of the bishops, always precede the afternoon's session, and agnostic as I am I did not normally attend them. However, on that day I was hypocritical enough to take the opportunity to call on the Lord to help calm my nerves. The occasion itself presents a somewhat humorous and endearing picture. For after the bishop has read the prayer, the assembled lordships kneel down but, instead of facing the centre of the Chamber, they turn around and kneel on or lean against their benches facing the outside walls. In this way the clerks sitting at the Table get a view of row upon row of noble backsides.

My name was sixth on the list. The Lords system for establishing the order of speakers is different from the Commons where Members catch the Speaker's eye. With us, where there is no Speaker, the Government Whips office issue lists of speakers prior to debates. Mai-den speakers are put high in order to keep their period of anxiety to the minimum. So there, after Lord O'Hagan, the front bench spok-esmen, and Lord Home, who ranked high through being an ex-prime minister, came my name: Bns. Ewart-Biggs (M). As I sat frozen with terror I began to realize what it must feel like to be a parachutist waiting to make his jump. As each one disappears, the rest shuffle up one place nearer to the hatch. So it is with us. Every time a speaker sits down the rest metaphorically shuffle up a place. And finally as the bearer of the name just ahead on the list sits down, there is abso-lutely nothing for the next to do but to stand up and speak.

I don't know what got me to my feet; some inner force I never knew existed. While I spoke, my mind was blank. The voice – although uttering vaguely familiar phrases – seemed to belong to somebody else. My mouth and lips went as dry as parchment. Out of the corner of my eye I could see peers entering the Chamber and standing by the Throne or at the Bar. They had seen from the closed circuit TV annunciator screens, scattered through the House and showing what is going on in the Chamber, that I was speaking, and out of interest and consideration for a new member had come to listen. As a further measure of consideration to Maiden speakers and to avoid putting them off their stride, no one is allowed to be on their feet in the Chamber during their speeches.

Turning the pages of my carefully typed notes, I realized with infinite relief that I had almost reached the end. This gave me sufficient courage to raise my eyes for a moment to sweep them confidently – I hoped – round the Chamber as I had seen other speakers do. However, this turned out to be a mistake as doing so only served to remind me of my awe-inspiring audience. My mind turned to stone again, I lost my place and instead of the peroration culminating in a wave of idealism and triumph as intended, it merely trickled sadly to an end. The ordeal at last over, I sank down in my seat and started work immediately to restore the inside of my mouth to its normal state. First something had to be done about the hard, flat wooden wedge which was normally my tongue. Whilst embarking on this I heard first the comforting purr of the assembled 'Hear, hear' and then, as music to my ears, words of praise from the following speaker. Lord Kennet, the SDP foreign affairs spokesman said, 'I am pleased to be the first to congratulate the noble Baroness Lady Ewart-Biggs on her maiden speech. I do so not only with the usual sense of pleasure but also, fortunately, in complete agreement with everything she has said. I know that, bearing in mind what has happened to her and what she herself has done about it since then, she will be a more than usually welcome recruit to this House...' From a later speaker there were more compliments. I straightened my back with pride, waggled my stick-like tongue once more round the inside of my mouth and decided that perhaps all was not lost and there lurked the makings of a parliamentarian inside me yet. Alas, I did not at that stage realize that to compliment maiden speeches is a matter of routine and the speakers who follow vie with each other to bring out more and more extravagantly phrased accolades.

For the rest of the debate, – it was as if I had entered paradise, so great was my sense of relief. The next morning brought two trophies. First, a recorded extract on BBC Radio 4's *Yesterday in Parliament*; but why had I gone at such a lick? And *The Times* published a photograph and a few lines of the speech. But what almost pleased me most was that below the photograph was printed, 'Ewart-Biggs said...', just as if I were an old hand.

Once peers have made their maiden speeches they are entitled to participate fully in the work of the House, take part in debates, table questions and motions. Yet it is not unknown for peers, in particular hereditary peers, to postpone making their maiden speeches for as long as thirty years. For my part, with this hurdle behind me, I knew the time had come to do some serious boning up. I needed to know the origins of this incongruous second chamber; one which differed from all its counterparts in Western Europe.

Burke contemptuously referred to it as 'The weakest part of the Constitution', and later Lord Rosebery compared it to 'a mediaeval barque stranded in the tideway of the nineteenth century'. A more democratic modern statesman declared that the only legislative qualifications of peers consist of their being the first-born of persons possessing as few qualifications as themselves. Another cynically observed that they represented nobody but themselves and enjoyed the full confidence of their constituents. Furthermore it was argued, rightly, that talent is not hereditary. No man chooses a coachman, as the first Lord Halifax once remarked, because his father was a coachman before him. On the other hand it is undeniable that the descendant of a long line of coachmen is likely to know more about the care of horses than the grandson of a pork butcher; similarly the scion of a race of legislators is at least as fully qualified for the duties of a legislator as many a politician whose chief reason for entering Parliament is the desire to add the letters MP to his name.

Although few of the most ardent admirers of the hereditary system will pretend that a perfect bicameral system is achieved by the present House of Lords, they would admit the necessity for a second chamber of some sort if only to prevent the other House from being exposed to what Cromwell called 'the horridest arbitrariness that was ever known in the world' and what John Stuart Mill called 'the corrupting influence of undivided power'.

The hereditary principle had clearly been under constant attack since its inception; which begs the question of how the system was established in the first place. The origin of parliament consisted of councils whose members were summoned by the English kings to advise them and occasionally to make special financial grants. These assemblies were attended by archbishops, bishops, abbots, earls, barons, etc. By 1236 some of these councils were being called 'parliaments' and it is recorded in A.F.Pollard's *The Evolution of Parliament* that in 1295 a special writ of summons to the Model Parliament entitled its recipient and his successors to an hereditary peerage, and consequently to a special writ of summons to every succeeding parliament until his lineage was extinct. Later, during the 13th century representatives of the 'communities of the realm' from counties, cities and boroughs were summoned with increasing frequency to assist; their attendance in Parliament becoming unvarying after 1327. By the end of the 14th century they formed a separate house, the House of Commons with its own Speaker and Clerk. The lords similarly acquired identity as a separate House of Parliament, usually known as 'the lords spiritual and temporal' or 'the upper house'. It was not until the 16th century that the term 'House of Lords' became normal. The Lords Spiritual consisted of the bishops and certain abbots and priors whose membership lasted as long as they held their office. The membership of the Lords Temporal became almost entirely hereditary by the 15th century, and to indicate their equality among each other they were called 'peers'. However, in effect they became increasingly divided in rank; there eventually being – as there now are – five degrees. The most ancient are those of Earl and Baron, the more recent those of Duke, Marquess and Viscount. In addition, from 1302 the Prince of Wales was summoned to Parliament.

Oliver Cromwell's impact on the House of Lords was the most profound, for the suppression of the monasteries meant that abbots and priors no longer sat; for the first time the majority of the House's membership became secular. In 1642 things got even worse when the remaining Lords Spiritual were excluded from Parliament. This was followed in 1649 by the suppression of the House itself. However, the existence of a second chamber was obviously missed because in 1658, only eleven years later, an upper house was restored under the title of the 'Other House' as a secular body. Eventually in 1661 the Clergy Act restored bishops to the House of Lords.

Although it was as late as 1958 that the Macmillan Government brought in the Life Peerages Act, the concept of life peerages was much older. For example, a peerage for life was conferred on Sir James Parke in 1856 to strengthen the judicial membership of the House. But in this case, the House resolved that such a life peerage did not entitle the grantee to sit and vote in Parliament. It was therefore left to Harold Macmillan to bring about this radical reform; namely, that the new legislation enabled the sovereign to grant by Letters Patent baronies for life without limit of number. Women were also eligible for elevation, which meant that for the first time they took their place in this exclusively male establishment. In 1963 they were given yet another concession through the Peerage Act which allowed women holders of hereditary peerages the same right to be members of the House as men.

Membership of the House is made up of four distinct groups and totals 1,195 at the present time. First there are the Archbishops of Canterbury and of York and twenty-four bishops of the Church of England. The Bishops of Durham, London and Winchester are always entitled to a seat in the Lords, but the others sit by virtue of their seniority of appointment. Next come the hereditary peers, about 762 at present, including twenty women; the number attending varies, depending on how many have not received a writ of summons without which they may not take their seats and how many are on leave of absence (this is granted for the duration of a Parliament to lords who are unable or unwilling to attend the House, and at present stands at 186). There are also twenty-seven hereditary peers of the first creation (including the Prince of Wales and Prince Andrew). The third group consists of the twenty-one salaried Law Lords, life peers created under the Appelate Jurisdiction Act of 1876 to carry out the judicial work of the House as the final court of appeal. Lastly there are the life peers, 359 of them including forty-seven women. The daily attendance at the House, counting peers of all these categories, stands at between 250 and 350.

This list makes it clear that the old days of parity between State and Church representation in the House are well over. It is for this reason that the bishops are no longer described as the 'Lords Spiritual', which has become the appelation for the Government of the day, while the Opposition are now described as the 'Lords Temporal'. As a reminder of the past, the two benches nearest the Woolsack on the Government side are still reserved for the bishops. The front bench has elbow rests and the present Archbishop of Canterbury, Dr Robert Runcie, can often be seen sitting there waiting to make his speech, his arm on the elbow rest.

I realized how much there was to learn about the procedure of the House and how to make the best use of the forum it presented. It was not like becoming part of a machine with clearly defined roles for each person. Each one of us represented a separate unit and could work either independently, or as part of a team.

It was the end of June, so I still had time before the recess to continue my education. Parliament usually rises around the end of July and the summer recess lasts till October or November with short breaks at Christmas, Easter and the Spring Bank Holiday. But if the Lords have not finished all their business before the summer recess, they return before the Commons in October to complete what is called 'the spill-over'. It did not take long to discover how much good will and friendliness there exists between peers. Regardless of party barriers they all care for each other and I had met with a great deal of warmth since my arrival, but I soon learned about some of the 'house rules'. The first occasion brought me great discomfort. I had already noticed that sometimes an offended rumble would go through the assembled House but I did not know what triggered it. The expression they used to express this disapproval was 'Order, order', and one or two peers acted as chorus masters – although I did not know if this was an official or unofficial appointment – by shouting the word loudest. One afternoon, to my infinite horror, I found myself the target. I had risen from my seat to leave the chamber, and was walking past the Liberal front bench when suddenly the usual ringleader set off the chanting. Then I felt two arms coming up and encircling me from behind, drawing me down to a sitting position. In my ear the Liberal peer on whose knee I was by that time sitting told me what my offence had been: to be on my feet when the Lord Chancellor was himself standing. That it was a misdemeanour of vast proportion he made clear before releasing me. To my way of thinking, though, my sitting on his knee with his arms round me in the august setting of the House of Lords seemed even worse.

I suppose it is in the order of things that most people only find things out the hard way; through experience. This was the case with my first starred question. Each day Question Time takes place at the beginning of business at 2.30 p.m. and is made up of four starred questions, as they are called. The object is to provide an opportunity for the House to cross-examine a Minister on the activities of the Government. These questions develop into mini-debates, for once the Minister has replied, and the peer whose question it originally was has exercised his right of asking a supplementary, then the whole House can participate. But, in order to prevent long-winded interventions, each point must be phrased in an interrogatory manner: Is the Minister aware... Can the Minister assure the House... Will the Minister give a commitment that... Does the Minister not agree... and so on.

Feeling bloated with pride, with the major step of my maiden speech behind me, I thought I would put down a question while my confidence was still high. The subjects of the questions are very varied; usually reflecting a peer's special interest or a particular preoccupation he has, or in order to raise a topical issue. Lady Sharples, for example, 'Asked Her Majesty's Government whether there are any plans to provide prisoners' wives on supplementary benefit with free travel for their visits to prisons every 14 days instead of every 28 days as at present'. Lady Young, with her interest in education, 'Asked HMG what plans they have for the training of school governors'. An interest in animals is usually shown: Lord Gainford asked 'what action is being considered to deal with the damage being done to livestock by dogs?'; or a preoccupation with death – 'to ask HMG if they have given consideration to a review of the law relating to euthanasia?'

I had become concerned about the harm to children's health from lead in petrol. My first question was: 'To ask HMG what consultations they are having with our EEC partners with a view to reaching agreement on a date for phasing out lead in petrol?' The first stage is comparatively painless. With the question printed on the order paper, the peer is only required to stand and say, 'My Lords, I beg leave to ask the question standing in my name on the order paper', and sit down again. I tried hard to take in the Minister's reply, hoping that the supplementary question I had prepared beforehand would tie in with it. I then again rose to my feet and, mindful of the rule that supplementaries must not be read out, tore my eyes away from my notes, and requested the further clarification. While speaking that rumble came again but it didn't have the right note to it (I had at least learned to distinguish between a congratulatory rumble and a disapproving one). Had the rumble contained the words 'Reading, reading', I would have understood that my eyes had inadvertently dropped towards the notes but, led by the usual ringmaster, they seemed to be saying, 'Question, question'. How could they be so stupid, of course I was asking a question. I stumbled on, my mind growing more blank all the time and my mouth devoid of spit. Then just as I was about to come to a halt and burst into tears, the ringmaster suddenly changed the piece and led them all into the much appreciated chorus of 'Hear, hear'. I could not understand what had brought on the volte-face.

'What did I do wrong?!' I asked Kevin, who had come to give me support.

'I think you didn't use the proper interrogatory style,' he said. Again I had committed one of the cardinal sins.

But it isn't downhill all the way for the Minister replying either. At best he may be desperately searching through his looseleaf folder to find the relevant answer prepared by the civil servant or, at worst, falling back on native wit. Ministers unable to respond to a point made during debate on a bill look despairingly towards 'the box' in the corner of the Chamber where a civil servant hastily scribbles the required answer. But I best like the story of a Minister who was determined to make no mistake and, when an interruption forced him to sit down – only one speaker is allowed on his feet at any one time – he kept his finger firmly on his place in the brief despite the fact that this was on the despatch box well above his head, which left him in a most ungainly position.

The memory of my first question haunted me for days. I realized I was trying to run before having learned to walk, so I decided to take up a passive role for the following weeks and not launch myself into any new initiatives.

Each Thursday I attended the Party meeting. At 2.15 the Labour peers taking the whip (i.e. those attending regularly and agreeing to being disciplined) congregate in Committee Room 4 and sit on rows of chairs facing the top table where the officers of the Party sit. In the centre there is the leader, who at that time was Fred Peart; later to be replaced by Cledwyn Hughes. On his right sat the Chief Whip, Pat Llewelyn-Davies, and Deputy Whip, Tom Ponsonby. On Fred's left the deputy leader, Goronwy Roberts, and at the end there was Elwyn Jones, previous Lord Chancellor in the Labour Government.

The Chief Whip goes through the business of the following week, explaining which front bench speakers will be taking the various debates, and what degree of whip will be imposed: A three line whip says 'Your attendance is required'; a two line whip, 'Your attendance is requested', and a single line is to draw attention to a particular debate. Private Members' bills carry a free vote as do Government bills representing matters of principle or morality. Following on this, backbenchers may ask questions and inform themselves on any point of disagreement or misunderstanding. There then follows a part of the meeting which always has and always will bring a lump to my throat, when the Chief Whip gives his report which usually includes the health of absent, ailing colleagues. 'Barbara Wootton (at ninety) is now in a very nice nursing home. She is better there – they make her take her medicines – rather more lucid. Even a return to some Barbara-like jokes. But what she really needs is some intellectual stimulation. Then there's Jack Crook. He's fed up. He's been stuck in the same place – the same chair – and likes hearing from us. Joe Stone has had a setback – he's confined to his room. I don't think we can expect much change from him. Dora Gaitskell has also had a setback. She finds it difficult to negotiate stairs, and her speech is affected. Frank Beswick is not at all well; but much enjoys postcards or letters.' There is, of course, the humane consideration in this catalogue of frailties, but there is another side, as put forward one Thursday meeting. A member of the group stood up at the end of the report and asked Cledwyn Hughes whether he realized these peers represented some of the most regular voters of the Party in the Lords. 'Yes,' said Cledwyn, 'we think of this day and night.'

Some meetings include the announcement of the death of a colleague. I remember Cledwyn Hughes, as Leader, speaking of Frank Beswick's death. He reminded us that it had been Frank's debate which had been the first to be televised in 1985: 'His compassion and sincerity shone right through his speech; many people wrote in to me about it. I shall think of him always sitting on the Privy Councillor's Bench putting his penetrating questions. He would go on until he got his answer – he was frightened of no one ... He was one of the nicest of men ....' Once the tribute is over, we all stand for a moment's silence, and I think of the lives of such stalwart old campaigners; lives so often devoted to fighting the cause of social justice. Lives so often started in the humblest fashion and, unaided by privilege of any kind, had been devoted to representing the interests of those least able to do so for themselves. I often feel a wave of pride to be among them, although so often the accusation of being a 'drawing-room socialist' is levelled against me.

Some years later the Labour leader, Neil Kinnock, came to talk to the group. At the end of the meeting, just as he was completing his remarks, in walked the recently ennobled James Callaghan. 'It's your timing Jim – that's what I love about you – you've got it wrong again,' laughed Neil, alluding to the previous Labour prime minister's disastrous choice of date for the 1979 election.

The Parliamentary Labour Party meeting, held at six o'clock on Thursdays in a Committee Room in the House of Commons, is a very different affair to the Lords. Strident and noisy with members holding forth according to their position on the right or left of the Party and arguing with a great deal of banging the table. I crept in and sat at the very back one Thursday soon after joining the Lords. I hoped not to be noticed but within minutes one of them, obviously puzzled, asked me who I was. Having told him, he said he felt there should be some recognition of my arrival in the circle. My heart sank even further. He then went up to the top table and whispered to Michael Foot, then the leader, and Jack Dorman, who chaired these meetings. They looked across the crowded room and having located my shrinking figure, Jack Dorman shouted out, 'I have just been informed that one of our new members in the Lords, Jane Ewart-Biggs, is here among us. So give her a welcome...' I stood up, feeling *extremely* self-conscious, and then there was an enormous amount of banging on the table – presumably their equivalent of the Lords' discreet 'Hear, hear'.

I hoped I might join one of the House of Lords European Community sub-committees. Soon after Britain joined the EEC each House of Parliament had appointed a Select Committee to consider procedures for scrutinizing Community proposals. So, when Baroness White, the chairman, approached me and said, 'It was obvious from your maiden speech that you're interested in Community affairs. Would you like to work with one of our committees?', I immediately agreed. There were seven of them, each dealing with a particular policy area. We discussed the different subjects and it was easy to discard the inappropriate ones. For instance there was Sub-Committee E which considered the legal implications of every European Community proposal, and A which dealt with finance, economics and regional policy; D covered agriculture, and F energy, transport, technology and research. I could not see myself as experienced enough to contribute very much to any of those. So finally we agreed that I should join Sub-Committee B which was responsible for considering proposals relating to external relations, trade and industry. What made it better still was that my old friend Denis Greenhill was its chairman.

I attended my first meeting the following week. As I entered the room I felt inadequate and lacking in confidence. I reflected again on the irony of my having to occupy a position for which Christopher, with his education and professional expertise, would have been so eminently qualified. I sat down at the horseshoe table in the high-ceilinged room overlooking the river. Oak panelling around the walls reached up to join the luxurious, ornate wallpaper still copied from the original Pugin designs and which are used in so many House of Lords apartments: the room we occupied had bold royal motifs in dark red, gold and green. In front of each one of us, facing the shorthand writers in the centre, were cards with our names printed in big letters. Paper and pencils were laid out in front of each place. Our subject was the changing pattern of trade since Britain's entry into the Community, and witnesses from different professional fields like the British manufacturing industry, the European Parliament, the Commission or the Foreign Office, were invited to give evidence. Some of the information they gave us was so technical as to be boring; at other times what they said – if I had been listening carefully enough – brought a sudden shaft of understanding.

It was then up to the members of the committee to cross-examine them to extract information. These exchanges would contribute to the eventual report and were recorded by the shorthand writers so that the chairman of the committee, with the help of the clerk and the specialist adviser, could compile a draft report with recommendations for the committee's final meeting and agreement. Then it would be printed and made available to the European Civil Commission, the Strasbourg Parliament, the House of Commons, Service Departments and so on.

I cannot claim to have made much of a contribution at my first meeting, but, for my own benefit, I observed and saw, firstly, the sense of awe manifestly felt by the witnesses themselves, and next, how astute and expert were the members of the committee. Seemingly frail and somewhat somnolent, they never missed an opportunity of firing off questions directed towards the very heart of the subject – sometimes leaving the witness looking stunned from the unexpected onslaught. I remember a later meeting when John de Courcy Ling, an old friend from our days in the Paris Embassy, came as a Member of the European Parliament to give evidence. Wanting to put him – and myself – at ease, I prefaced my question by telling him how interesting I had found his presentation and the pleasure with which I remembered our time together in Paris. He looked pleased. With relief I came to realize that a layman's view, together with the application of common sense, could be of value to the work of the committee.

It was not until several years later, on the committee dealing with environmental issues, that I came very near to making a fool of myself. The subject under consideration was Community restrictions on the use of lead in petrol. Representatives from the motor industry came to give evidence and were extremely preoccupied by the prospect of re-designing engines to run on lead-free petrol, referring constantly to 'Leanburn' engines. I didn't think twice about what this meant, I was so sure it concerned a chap called Mr Lean (probably short for Leonard) Burn who had invented this remarkable engine. Luckily at no point did I give myself away, but it took quite a few meetings before I realized that Leanburn was the name for a particular motor which, to minimize the poisonous exhaust fumes, ran on very little fuel. But it had been a near squeak.

By this time the children were used to my being in the Lords. Henrietta was at Durham University, Robin about to go there and Kate still at her day school in London. I made a priority of everything to do with them. I even went, in fear and trembling, to speak in a debate at the Durham Union, with all three of them in the audience. And then there were important events at Kate's school like carol services, school plays and the parent/teacher sessions. '*Please* don't be late,' Kate always pleaded. But once, having duly presented myself to discuss her ability at maths, chemistry, physics, history and so on, the teachers left me with the distinct impression that Kate was not doing much work.

'But I think she's very happy here,' I said when finally talking with the headmistress. 'I wonder what makes her so eager to come in the mornings.'

'Purely and simply so that she can see her friends,' came the rather chilly reply.

I never ceased to be grateful for the pure luck of where we had chosen to buy our home in 1960. We could never have foreseen the necessity to live so close to Parliament. It has made it possible for me to hurry back to have supper with Kate in the dinner break starting at about 7.30, when short pieces of legislation are taken. (If there are none, the annunciator screens display the rather startling message, 'The House has adjourned for pleasure until...' giving the time.)

One evening I was due to speak in a late debate, so, instead of hanging around, I asked one of the attendants in the Peers' Lobby if he would ring me at home in good time for me to get back for Lord Allen's debate on Telephone Bingo?' He promised to do so when the Minister rose to sum up the previous debate, giving me, he estimated, a good twenty minutes to get back.

Just as I was finishing a relaxed supper with Kate the telephone rang. 'You had better hurry, My Lady. Everything has been quicker than we expected and I have heard the Minister will only speak for a few minutes.' To Kate's bewilderment I dropped everything and fled. After driving furiously along the Embankment, I rushed into the Chamber to find my debate had started and the reproachful eyes of both the Government Whip and my own were fixed on me.

'If any of you would like to visit the House of Lords next time you're in London, I'll be happy to show you round' – a rash offer made at the end of my talk to the Cleethorpes Ladies' Luncheon Club. When, a few days later, I received a letter from the chairman gleefully taking me up on my offer, I found that here too I needed to do some homework.

Edmund Burke could not have realized how long his phrase 'England is the Mother of Parliaments' would endure or how it would be universally applied to the Palace of Westminster itself. The magnificent structure created by William Barry and Augustus Pugin in the mid-nineteenth century is known the world over, while the pinnacles of the Victoria Tower and the dominating round face of Big Ben have become London's universal symbol. The original building, with the exception of the Hall, had burned to the ground on 16 October 1834. The 'dreadful calamity', as it was described, originated in the House of Lords where an attempt had been made to dispose of the tally sticks which, in earlier times, were used as receipts for sums paid to the Exchequer. The wood used was usually hazel or willow and the short rods were notched to indicate the sums paid and then split, one piece being given to the debtor as a receipt, and the other kept by the Exchequer as a record.

Charles Dickens, then a young reporter, who witnessed the fire, gave a humorous account to an audience at Drury Lane Theatre. 'In 1834 it was found that there was a considerable accumulation of these sticks; and the question then arose, what was to be done with such worn-out, wormeaten rotten old bits of wood? The sticks were housed at Westminster and it would naturally occur to any intelligent person that nothing would be easier than to allow them to be carried away as firewood by the miserable people who lived in the neighbourhood. However, they never had been useful and official routine required that they never should be. And so the order went through that they should privately and confidentially burn. It came to pass that they were burnt in a stove in the House of Lords. The stove, over-gorged with these preposterous sticks, set fire to the panelling; the panelling set fire to the House of Lords; the House of Lords set fire to the House of Commons; and two Houses were reduced to ashes...'

From all accounts, with the unpopularity of the Government, there was very little mourning at this passing of the Houses of Parliament. But, although the mob cheered each collapse of masonry, the saving of ancient Westminster Hall was universally acclaimed.

So the Palace which I showed to the ladies of Cleethorpes was of a very different order. The State opening by Queen Victoria had been in 1852 and its creators, Barry and Pugin, as instructed, had designed and built it following the Gothic style. In my new role of tour operator, I decided to follow the route the Queen takes when she comes to read the speech from the throne at the State Opening of Parliament. I met my fifteen ladies in the Peers' Lobby and led them back to the top of the Royal Staircase, at the very southern end of the building, where the Norman Porch serves as an ante-room to the Royal Robing Room. This room is considered one of the finest examples of Gothic art and, as we stood admiring the spendidly ornate ceiling, I told the ladies how, after the destruction of the Chamber of the Commons in an air raid in 1941, the Lords gave up their Chamber to the MPs and met instead for the next ten years in this Robing Room. Thus it had come about that some of Churchill's greatest speeches had been made in the House of Lords' Chamber.

We moved on to the Royal Gallery, one of the grandest and most imposing rooms in the whole Palace. One hundred and ten feet long, forty-five feet wide and forty-five feet high, it acts as a grand processional hall between the Robing Room – where the Queen puts on her Crown and robes of state – and the Chamber of the Lords. I explained to my ladies how, for the State Opening, each peer is allowed to invite one relative or friend to watch the procession from the Royal Gallery. On my first occasion I had given my ticket to Kate who was thirteen at the time. When the procession passed by, Kate noticed the worried look and pale face of the Princess of Wales, on one of her first major public appearances, and smiled at her. The Princess, doubtless much relieved at seeing someone closer to her own age, smiled back.

The Gallery is also the setting for visiting Heads of State to address the members of both Houses, and I had been entirely taken in by President Reagan when I heard him speak there in the early 1980s. I had been most impressed by the way he appeared to have memorized his whole speech. 'Well, after all, he was an actor and must be very practised at learning lines,' I said to my neighbour, Lord Sainsbury, who was equally impressed. It took a less gullible colleague to point out the ultra modern device whereby obscured screens reflected the words for him to read. On another privileged occasion we listened to the President of the Federal Republic of Germany who impressed me so much that I wrote down his phrase, 'In England life is not governed by ideas, ideas are born from life', which to my great pleasure appeared in the *Observer* 'Sayings of the Week'.

The ladies and I passed between two enormous frescos on each side of the gallery which show the most dramatic moments of Britain's victories against the French at Trafalgar and Waterloo. I told them how these might have had a bad effect on President Mitterrand, who read his speech from notes in the old-fashioned manner and although the content was excellent, he delivered it in such rapid French that bewilderment soon appeared on the faces of the not particularly Francophone parliamentarians and his message failed to get through.

We went through the Prince's Chamber – a small ante-room which contains the two magnificent Pugin octagonal tables at which peers can sit and open their mail – and into the Chamber. Here one feels a sense of awe at the beauty and grandeur of Pugin's lofty masterpiece with its fine oak panelling, brass lattice work and rich red and gold decoration. It is a fact that when designing the House of Lords Barry and Pugin considered it 'not a mere place of business nor even a mere House of Lords – but as a Chamber in which a Sovereign, surrounded by the Court, summoned the three estates of the realm'. And so it was. The effect was unmarred even by the scaffolding covering the rich ceiling, there because a few years earlier a large area of plaster had dropped onto the benches below, falling on the place where Lord Shinwell habitually sat. When the restoration work was set in hand, the whole ceiling was discovered to be suffering from dry rot brought on by the gas lights hanging from it, and a promise was made to complete it for Manny Shinwell's hundredth birthday.

I pointed out some of the beauties of what is generally agreed to be the most richly appointed legislative chamber in the world. And together we marvelled at the exquisitely carved and gilded canopy above the Throne which is surrounded by a brass rail. Privy Councillors, members of the Commons and the eldest sons of peers are allowed to sit on the steps leading up to the Throne or stand at the Bar when the House was in session. The ladies asked if Robin, my son, had ever done so, but unfortunately the absence of a necktie disqualified him even from entering the Chamber, so for the present he was unlikely to take up his right. I also told them what Frank Dobson, a cheerful Labour MP, had once said standing at the Bar. Listening to the debate on homosexuality, he muttered to his companion, 'It could only be in England that you'd find this subject being debated in a place where there is a chap in a white wig and black silk stockings presiding'.

We moved slowly past the red leather benches, the great Pugin table carrying the two despatch boxes from which Ministers and Opposition spokesmen give their speeches, and at which sit the three Clerks in their wigs and black gowns, past the crossbenches where the Royal Dukes and others not wishing to proclaim any party allegiance sit, and then out at the Bar of the House and into the Peers' Lobby. From this lovely apartment with its beautifully tiled floor I showed the ladies the voting lobbies on each side of the

Chamber. Peers vote 'Content' or 'Not content' merely by passing through one or other of these lobbies and having their names registered as they do so. By tradition Black Rod or his deputy, the Yeoman Usher, has to be present in the Chamber at every division to separate any explosive peers who, as a result of the vote, have started a fight.

I also told them the story – possibly apochryphal but certainly funny – of a moment rendered immortal during the Lord Chancellor's procession. Each day this occurs prior to the commencement of business and is made up of the Sergeant-at-Arms bearing the mace followed by the Lord Chancellor with an attendant holding up his train and Black Rod bringing up the rear. This ritual is watched by many visitors and tourists. The story relates how one day a peer explaining the ceremony to his American guest is suddenly diverted by the sight of a colleague he wants to see. 'Oh, Neil . . .' he calls walking towards him. Then remembering his guest he stops and looks back, only to find the American, obviously overcome by the pomp and ceremony, down on his knees with eyes reverently following the receding figure of the Lord Chancellor.

By this time it was nearly one o'clock, when tours of the House have to end, so I accompanied my group to the Central Lobby from which they could find their way out by the St Stephen's public entrance and back to their coach. But along the Peer's Corridor, which runs from one lobby to the other, I pointed out the abrupt change in the colour of carpets and furnishings. Here the rich red of the Lords, traditional colour of royalty, changes to the rather dingy green used in the Commons. This is a great help to newcomers to the Palace of Westminster for when they are lost they only have to look down at the carpet to discover whether they are in the Commons or Lords end.

There are four great archways leading out of the Central Lobby, and I told my visitors one last story, which Cledwyn Hughes had thought up. 'Above each of the doorways a mosaic panel depicts one of the four patron saints. The way in which they are placed is highly relevant. First, above the archway leading to the House of Lords we see St George with the dragon at his feet; this makes sense for the well-known reason that every Englishman is a dreadful snob. We then pass on to the Scots, and their patron saint is appropriately placed over the passageway leading to the bar and a good whiskey. Next St David, patron saint of the great orators, the Welsh, is well placed over the doorway to the chamber of the Commons. And finally we get to St Patrick. His statue wearing the robes of a bishop with the shamrock at his feet is over the West Door which is the way out; and that is the route which the Irish chose to take'.

The ladies laughed and thanked me profusely, saying they would never forget the visit, but I wondered whether the part they would best remember might be Cledwyn's anecdote.

CHAPTER THREE

New Friends

I SOON DISCOVERED how much talent and character there was amongst my new colleagues. First I made friends with some of the other women in the Earl Marshal Room. This accommodation on the principal floor is for the exclusive use of women peers of all parties and comprises two comfortable rooms, each containing desks with telephones (calls are free), armchairs, hanging cupboards, long mirrors, very old-fashioned electric fires and some filing cabinets. Next door there is a loo with 'Women Peers' written in big letters on the door. It used to strike me as odd that whereas there are loos all over the country with 'Ladies' on the door, here in the only place where the genuine article exists, it is labelled 'Women'. However, I soon learned from one of the more emancipated Baronesses that a female member of the House of Lords is not a peeress – that's the wife of a peer; she must be called a peer or, when precision is necessary, a woman peer.

When I had first been taken the rounds by Pat Llewelyn-Davies, she explained the Earl Marshal rule that anyone using a desk must clear all their papers away when vacating it, even if only temporarily, to allow someone else the use of it; she added that I might one day get a desk of my own if I rose to the dizzy heights of becoming an Opposition spokesman or whip. She also mentioned another suite on the first floor, made up of a room with a bed, an adjoining bath-room and an ironing board: a great help if you had to go straight to a dinner after a late debate.

The Earl Marshal Room is not ideal for working as there is a constant background noise of women on the telephone or engaged in lively conversation. But it is excellent for making friends. My first was Dora Gaitskill. She had already endeared herself to me for life when I overheard her in the Bishops' Bar one day remark to nobody in particular, 'Have you met that lovely girl Jane Ewart-Biggs yet?' After that, my fifty – and a few more – years held no more terror.

44

It is true that everything is relative. During the following months the Earl Marshal Room was the setting for many a long conversation, when she recounted to me episodes from life with her husband Hugh, one of the famous post-war Labour leaders. There is a strong romantic streak in Dora, yet she believes in calling a spade a spade, so the high points of drama in the Gaitskell household were described to me with great clarity.

But Dora had two problems: she was a diabetic and also suffered from poor eyesight which made her wear glasses with thick lenses. The combination of these disabilities, plus her eighty odd years, had made her rather absent-minded. But, in the days when she attended regularly, there were two subjects which drew strong reactions from her. The mildest reference to the Israelis produced a verbal stampede, from under which I have seen many a battered-looking contestant emerge; her other idiosyncrasy was a limpet-like attachment to her seat in the Chamber. This was despite the fact that in the House of Lords – unlike other debating chambers – there are no designated places for members, although most of us usually drift to the same seat out of habit. But for Dora there was a sanctity about the last seat nearest the throne, on the second row of the Labour benches. I can still see her entering the Chamber – tiny, dressed in a suit with matching round-brimmed hat and steering her way along with the stick that she carried not so much for physical support but more for visual aid. After inclining her head towards the cloth of gold above the throne, as convention demands, her eyes would swivel round and became transfixed on 'her' seat. And if there was anyone sitting in it, or even too close to it, woe betide them. Advancing threateningly, the tirade was let loose.

'That's my seat – will you please move.'

Some people – poor ignorant fools – trying to cling to the realities, would remonstrate, whispering loudly, 'No, Dora, it's not your seat. We don't have particular seats.'

But this got them nowhere. The small, angry lady gesticulating with her stick, even using it to make a few stabbing motions towards the offending colleague, would then raise her voice. 'Will you please go. I've already told you. You're sitting in *my* seat.'

With the attention of the whole House magnetized towards the exchange and feeling the heat of the determined old lady's growing indignation, there were not many stalwarts who did not concede defeat and shuffle disconsolately along the bench out of reach. Dora, immediately appeased, then sat down, perched on the edge of her seat, and looked around for approbation.

One of my most vivid memories of Dora was during a debate in the committee stage of the Female Circumcision Bill. She was attentive in her seat – all intruders having been repulsed – listening to Lord Kennet introducing the Bill. The objective of the Bill was to make the primitive and cruel operation illegal in Britain. Entailing the removal of the tip or the whole of the clitoris, the physical pain caused to the young girls was horrendous and the effects on their future sexual lives devastating. The medical facts were laid bare by Lord Rea, a practising GP on our benches.

It could be argued, of course, that this operation was hardly likely to be much carried out in Britain. Only two cases were known for sure, although true numbers would never be revealed as neither the surgeon nor the girl would be likely to volunteer the information. The danger lay in the fact that the reformers in the countries where the operation was carried out – Sudan, Kenya and so on – were making headway in stamping out the primitive practice. This meant those families still demanding it, as the tradition was so firmly entrenched among primitive communities, might come as far afield as Britain to have it performed on their daughters.

As the debate continued with all its horrendous details, Dora suddenly took to her feet. She delivered a strong denunciation of the cruelty of the practice and spoke movingly about the devastating effect it would have on women throughout their lives. The moment which is engraved on my memory was when Lord George-Brown entered the Chamber, looking calm and detached, and took his seat on the crossbenches. He knew nothing of the subject or even the aim of the Bill, and as Dora continued with her tirade, his face took on a look of incredulity and profound shock which reached a peak when she came to the point in her speech which ran: '. . . The problem is that some men in other countries will not put up with any kind of infidelity. I know that this operation is undertaken to keep their women faithful to themselves. It is one of the strongest reasons for getting it performed. The fact that the women came here to have it done is simply shocking. It is terrible. It is the most cruel operation possible. One thing about it is particularly cruel. The clitoris is the organ which gives women pleasure. That is another reason for men

being thoroughly chauvinistic and why some of them may not wish
to support the Bill ... I feel that this idea of keeping women faithful
by performing this absolutely savage operation is a great indictment
against men in countries where it is done for that reason.'

Unable to bear it any longer George-Brown hurried from the
Chamber looking positively shell-shocked.

Dora lived in Hampstead in a house which she and Hugh had
bought and which, after his death, she had split up into three parts
in order that she and her two daughters should each have a flat.
Sometimes – to our worry – she would take the Underground home.
Other times she took a taxi. Her telephone conversations with the
car hire service were most endearing. 'Hullo, hullo – can you hear
me?' (This meant she could not hear them.) 'This is Lady Gaitskell
speaking. Could you send a taxi to the House of Lords to take me
to Hampstead. Yes, the HOUSE OF LORDS, PEERS' ENTRANCE (arti-
culated very slowly). What, what's that? There is already one ordered
for me? Oh how very kind. Thank you so much. Yes, Yes I'll be
down waiting at the Peers' Entrance – do you hear that, the PEERS'
ENTRANCE at 7 o'clock.' Putting the receiver down she would then
turn to me and say in a very satisfied way, 'Such nice people. It's
a new taxi service I'm trying out.' But I knew that the daily routine
was for a member of Mr Scott's staff in the mail room to order
a taxi for her from the firm who had for years been ferrying the
old lady back to Hampstead. 'Well, I'll be off now and perhaps have
something to eat at the Strangers' Cafeteria on the way. Just a bowl
of soup or something like that'. And then suddenly worried, 'But
Jane, do you think it's all right for me to go? Are you sure there
are not going to be any more votes? I feel so useless here.'

'Dora, you're not useless at all. You made a very good speech during
yesterday's debate. I thought some of your points were excellent.'

She was still not totally convinced. 'Well, I do hope what you
say is true. But I felt I was getting into a bit of a muddle and reckoned
Hansard would probably have to tidy it up a bit to make it sound
better.' (I was reminded of the words of my friend Mary Villiers,
the editor of *Hansard*, when I once asked her how on earth the shorthand writers kept up when people spoke fast. 'It's not the speed
that worries them,' she said. 'It's working out what some of Their
Lordships actually mean.') With Dora it was not the specific details
of her speech which mattered; it was the expression of the deep

and genuine concern she felt for her fellow beings.

I miss Dora so much now that she doesn't come to the House any more. I miss those potentially explosive situations on the benches. I miss the remarks – perhaps slightly adrift from the subject, but delivered straight from the heart. The debates have never been quite the same since. And I miss the cosy chats in the Earl Marshal Room about Dora's past sex life. But we get news of her when the Chief Whip gives his report about absent colleagues at the Thursday afternoon party meeting, and that's some comfort.

The two major pieces of legislation passing through the Lords on their way to the statute book at the end of my first session were the Nationality Bill which restricted the right to claiming British nationality, and the Transport Bill. 'This Bill,' intoned Dr Runcie, the Archbishop of Canterbury, during the Nationality Bill debate, 'will be seen by future generations as a bad bill.' This drew some dirty looks from the front bench Government Ministers – relations between the State and Church were decidedly under pressure – yet there was little doubt that the Right Reverend prelates, as they are referred to in debates, were fully justified in speaking out. Their work in their dioceses brought them much closer than other peers to the lives of ordinary people.

The Transport Bill contained the controversial reform over the wearing of seat belts. The move to include this requirement in the Bill while it was in the Commons was defeated and feeling ran high between those defending personal freedom and others wishing to safeguard life and limb. In the Lords, Lord Nugent, a long-standing campaigner on this issue, moved his amendment with conviction and persuasiveness at the appropriate point during the committee stage. The debate which followed was lengthy and complex, and when the time came to vote we did so out of our own convictions rather than under the constraints of a party whip. Those of us in favour of seat belts won by a good majority. (I have been trying ever since to remember to wear my own belt and thereby not break the first law I was ever involved in making!)

These first two major debates gave me great opportunities to listen and to learn, but I did not know enough about the subjects to participate. I had hoped to divorce myself from Irish affairs, but realized that this was the area where I was sufficiently knowledgeable to speak with a little authority. The reason I wanted to cut the bonds between Ireland and myself was not from lack of interest but because of the unnatural way it had entered my life. Tragedy had brought it in and then, although my only other experience of Ireland was living there for three weeks after Christopher was killed, I got lumped with it. I remember talking to Frank Longford about it one day.

'You're stuck with Ireland in exactly the same way that I got stuck with pornography,' he said. 'That's what people associate me with, and it's not even as if I'm interested.'

'If only we could swap,' I said, laughing but meaning it.

Yet I realized that involving myself with Northern Ireland might be useful because there are so very few people interested in the Irish saga who genuinely are unbiased. Moreover I had a longing to continue the work Christopher would have done and as I was not imprisoned by any 'tribal' affiliation I could keep my mind open. So I decided to take part in debates about the administration of the Province. The legislative procedure for Northern Ireland is quite different than for the rest of the UK because in 1974, when the Stormont Parliament was prorogued, all its powers were taken over by Westminster. This means that measures affecting Northern Ireland go through Parliament by Orders in Council with no amendments, no voting, no chance to affect the outcome. Moreover, these Orders are invariably taken through during dinner-time with very few peers present ... just as on the first time I spoke about Northern Ireland, towards the end of June in 1981.

The debate was the Appropriation (No. 2) (Northern Ireland) Order 1981, which laid out the distribution of funds (sometimes this budget can consist of £3 billion) in the Province. I must have been feeling very brave that evening for I opened my speech on a reproachful tone and – on looking back – I now admire the courage I must have built up to do so. I started with the customary politeness: 'I would like to thank the noble Lord, the Minister, for his clear presentation of this draft order.' I then went on: 'However I must object to the timing of this debate. We are discussing the economy of a very sensitive area and I think a full discussion would have been helpful as a means of informing the Northern Irish people about the issues under review. And, at the same time, I cannot believe they find it very complimentary to see the debate squeezed into the dinner hour to be dealt with as briefly as possible. ...' I went on to speak about the provisions of the Order and followed up by making two main points. The first was about the importance of funding projects concerned with the Province's 21% unemployed, and the second a plea for greater support for women whose lives in Northern Ireland's particular circumstances face so many extra problems.

I knew enough about what was going on over there both through contacts in Belfast and also from the spasmodic visits I made across the water. One I remember well was brought on by an invitation from the Soroptomists, the organization of professional women. They asked me to be the guest of honour at their annual dinner at Belfast's City Hall. I have always admired these organizations made up of resolute and highly motivated women, intent on furthering the interests of their sex. In this case the President was called Miss Lark and she was more than adequately supported by her mother; a fact I recognized when spending the night with them afterwards.

During the afternoon I had been to visit Hugh Frazer and my other friends at the Northern Ireland Voluntary Trust, an organization financing work going on in the Province at community level, work designed to rectify some of the social and sectarian ills from which people in Northern Ireland suffer. He took me to see some of the projects which the Trust supported and the memory of two of them still stands out vividly. The first was in Divis Flats – a very deprived Catholic area – where we went to visit a little school set up especially to deal with children who were regular truants. Having negotiated the mud and puddles in the Divis wasteland, we walked up the narrow stairs of a small house which looked as if it was on the verge of demolition. But the scene which greeted us at the top of the stairs was infinitely reassuring. The room was warm with brightly coloured curtains across the window and children's paintings covering the peeling walls. In the main part of the L-shaped room there were about seven or eight small desks with children sitting at them. In the adjoining part about a dozen boys, who looked as if they were in their late teens, sat on benches round the edge of the room, holding reading books. The teacher was called Ealanor.

'What actually happens here, then?' I asked her.

'The younger children are here because they ran away from every school they were ever sent to, so now no schools will take them. The bigger boys have all left school but failed to learn anything at all. So now they're here to learn to read.'

'But what is it that makes them want to come here when they rejected all these other schools?'

Ealanor turned her very large dark eyes on me and said, 'Well, they're all waiting outside the door when I arrive in the morning. They see this as their own little school and they trust me. I come from Divis myself and although I didn't have a job, I am a trained teacher. I teach them English, maths and handicrafts. I can't manage any more because the children are of different ages. They are all pretty insecure. It's hardly surprising when you think of the violence in this area. They need to be made to feel safe, and Crazy Joe's – that's what they call this place – makes them feel that way. I asked them to write a composition about the school. One little girl wrote: "I didn't like being at St Theresa's (one of her previous schools from which she had run away) because there were so many people. There were 35 girls in my class but no one to talk to ... Crazy Joe's is nice because it's small and very close to home". So I know I'm giving these kids something they couldn't get anywhere else.' She smiled at us and went to help one of the girls with her sums.

Hugh and I left the warm little room and went to see another project that had been set up to cope with Belfast's 'joy-riders'. These young people, often only twelve or thirteen, indulge in a particularly devastating form of delinquency: stealing a car, they drive it at top speed through the streets of Belfast defying army and police check-points on the way. The risks to life and limb both for themselves and others are easily imagined. One way of dealing with them was to lock them away in some corrective establishment, but social workers had thought up an alternative, a form of remedial treatment based on the fact that the obsession claiming these young people was undoubtedly motor cars and that the best way of curing them of the delinquency was to provide a constructive framework in which to channel their obsession. An old unused hangar had been taken over, a motor mechanic engaged and large numbers of old battered cars collected. When Hugh and I arrived that afternoon the scene was one of great industriousness. Some of the young offenders were banging away at bent exhaust pipes, long spindly legs sticking out from beneath dilapidated cars, others were bent double under open bonnets.

'Can you sustain their interest during the whole week without pro-viding some reward or fun?' I asked the project organizer. 'Well, on Fridays they get a break.'

'What happens on Fridays?' I asked.

'They race the cars against each other,' he said calmly.

'Isn't that rather dangerous? What do their parents think?'

'We do it on a race track and surprisingly enough there never seem to be any prangs. And as for the parents, they know there are so many dangers for their children in Belfast that a risk like this one pales into insignificance.'

My visit to these two projects had a profound effect on me. First it brought home to me the importance of devising special ways of channelling destructive energies back into positive avenues. And also I perceived clearly, for the first time, the emergence of two separate groups within the community. One made up of the traditional nuclear family consisting of a father in work and mother primarily concerned with looking after the house and children; families who may own their homes and rely on earnings from relatively secure employment, whose children are unlikely to get into trouble with the law, and for whom our old laws, services and system of provision are adequate and appropriate. Then there are the new and rapidly expanding second group made up of people who for reasons outside their control no longer conform to the old pattern of life. Families, led by single-parent mothers, with inadequate revenues or houses; children, brutalized by their home environment, growing up with no respect for property; heads of households denied the opportunity to work; and so many old people living longer and longer, often in poverty and loneliness – all the members of this second group require a new set of arrangements. They are the people who occupy the emerging and fast-growing 'alternative Britain'. Seeing some of them that afternoon, I realized that many of the solutions were coming from a growing band of workers in the voluntary organizations and in charities. This is a subject which has engrossed me more and more.

Hugh Frazer dropped me at the City Hall, the magnificent and imposing building at the centre of Belfast which seems to give the lie to the reputation of insecurity for which sadly Belfast is known. I met my hostess of the Soroptomists at the entrance and put my suitcase in the ladies' cloakroom. We took our place in the receiving line and whilst shaking the several hundred hands I realized I wasn't looking smart enough. I was wearing a not quite smart enough dress, and the rain had made my hair go limp and straight, but the long stream of ladies were all friendly and warmhearted. Those who have never visited Belfast can have no idea how much enthusiasm and energy its inhabitants inject into everything they do.

I can remember little of what I said in my speech: the shock the conversation with my neighbour at dinner gave me blotted out everything else. I was sitting on the right hand of the Lord Mayor of Belfast, and we were talking about rates and the merits and disadvantages of the system. 'It's very simple,' he said, smiling amiably, his gold chain of office appearing to give credence to his words. 'It's the people who pay rates who get the rights. The two go together. So those who can't pay don't get any rights.' It was shattering to hear such a sentiment expressed in the 1980s. I turned away to speak to the person sitting on my left, but could just overhear the Lord Mayor's voice – suddenly anxious – saying to the President, 'Oh dear, I think I've upset the Baroness.'

Her retort was sharp: 'But you've no business to upset the Baroness. She's our honoured guest.'

The more I became involved with the work of the House, the more I recognized the difficulties confronting professional women who try to be parent and worker at the same time. My children were all teenagers by then and certainly required a lot of parental time and attention, all of which had to come from me alone. Their lives had not been easy. Starting with the nomadic life diplomatic children are unwillingly forced to lead, they then had lived through the trauma of their father's violent death. On our return to England, their hopes for a calm and obscure life never quite came off. The combination of the tragedy itself and the unusualness of the name Ewart-Biggs made the incident memorable to many. Often on being introduced a hazy look entered people's eyes. 'Ewart-Biggs,' they would say pensively, 'the name reminds me of something – but what?' Trying to deflect them didn't usually work and invariably it all ended with embarrassment on both sides and muttered apologies.

Then, when obscurity was again within reach, their mother had to go and cause a fuss by becoming a baroness. (This – to Robin's profound disgust – entitled them if they wished to call themselves 'The Honourable ...', which brought on an avalanche of teasing.) The subject of embarrassing mothers brings to mind my favourite story, told me by Stewart Steven, editor of the *Mail on Sunday*. The agonizing incident happened when he was at boarding school and his mother, apparently a lady who was not the sort of woman who faded away into the background, had promised to come down to his Speech Day. He was taking part in the ritual cricket match, but being the kind of person she was she arrived late as he had feared she would. The match had already started and Stewart was fielding when he saw her hove into view in an outfit – the hat in particular – which sent a shudder down his back. She spotted him immediately and without hesitation came up to kiss him. 'But Mum,' he said in a tortured voice, 'I'm playing at the moment.' She was outraged. 'Well, if you'd rather stand around playing than greet your mother, I just don't know ...'

My two elder children were now at university, with only Kate living full time at home. She was about fourteen years old and suffering quite seriously from asthma. In my efforts to be a responsible mother and because I did not like to leave her to get back to an empty house, we had returned to the old system of having au pair girls. With the House not sitting until 2.30 – a hangover from when MPs carried out their professions in the mornings – there was no hope of my returning home to greet her from school by 4.15. However, each girl seemed less acceptable to Kate than the one before, so, eventually, I confronted her with the choice of either being pleasant to the poor creatures or doing without them. And I demanded a promise that, were she to choose the second option, she refrain from making me feel guilty for not being at home all the time. Already she had scored some direct hits with her bedtime notes laid out on my pillow: 'Dear Mum ... I hope your speech went well. And now will you be a proper mother ... My gym things need ironing for tomorrow and I have to get to school a bit earlier. Will you wake me up at ... Kate.' Nevertheless she was coping well with her new life, but even better when a solution emerged and the last au pair was routed.

'Don't you see,' she said, 'the last thing I want when I get home is to make conversation with those silly girls. I'm too tired.'

'But surely you don't want to be a latchkey child?'

'I don't mind a bit. I just want to be left alone.'

So we agreed on a formula which suited her perfectly. The final departing au pair was not replaced, and instead of finding a garrulous girl Kate returned to an entirely silent house. Her tea, laid out on a tray by me before leaving for the House, awaited her, accompanied by a note of welcome composed by me before leaving.

The child would then settle down in front of the television with her tray and after eating her sandwich, apple, carrot, cake and tea, she went to sleep. By the time I got back – around seven thirty or eight – she was rested, happier and ready to do a little homework.

However, the 1983 election messed things up again. This time it was not so much due to my being a peer but in particular a Labour peer. By then, I had moved her from the French Lycée – where the academic demands on someone like her, who missed so many days through asthma, were insupportable – to a small day school within walking distance from home. But the trouble for us both was that it was a private school. This put my principles in a state of disarray and caused her considerable embarrassment if forced to admit I was in the party hell-bent on abolishing that particular system.

'Mum, what on earth shall I do?' she asked one evening. 'They all came in to school this morning wearing enormous blue rosettes – even the little tiny girls in the kindergarten. One could hardly see them for the rosettes.'

'That doesn't matter. You don't have to say anything.' I said to her.

'But you see, I'd like to tell them what you think – but I'm not brave enough.'

Thinking that I wouldn't be brave enough either – not in her school – I suggested she should, if necessary, explain she hadn't decided which political party she supported. She should say she was still too young and didn't yet know enough about each party's policies to take a position. She seemed relieved with this rationalization.

But next day she came back looking still more axious. 'Now things have got even worse,' she groaned. 'The Current Affairs teacher wants us to have *a debate* about the election with each party represented. She says I'm the only one to speak for the Labour Party as everyone else is against it.'

The prospect was appalling. 'No, of course, you mustn't do it. All the others know is what they've heard from their parents, so they'll just bombard you with the views and attitudes they have picked up from them. You must tell the teacher you can't do it.'

Kate then remembered what I had said before, 'All right, and anyhow none of us is old enough yet to know what we really believe.'

The final occasion – I hope – for Kate to suffer from having me as a mother came several years later through the televising of the House of Lords. The major pioneers behind this move were Willie Whitelaw and Christopher Soames. They believed it was high time the cameras were let into the House of Commons, not only to enable the public to watch their own elected representatives at work, but also to impose a discipline on those MPs whose behaviour they considered a little rowdy. They thought that by setting the scene in the Lords, the Commons would then follow suit. The decision to make the experiment was taken through a lengthy procedure. First there was a debate to set up a Select Committee to examine the question of televising proceedings. A majority having voted in the affirmative, the Select Committee deliberated and duly made its report. The final stage was a debate on the report, which resulted in an experimental period of six months during which the proceedings of the Upper Chamber should be filmed and extracts chosen to televise each evening. I hadn't followed the affair very closely and somehow Kate had the news before me. 'Oh God, Mum, you'll never be televised, will you? It would be so embarrassing,' she complained.

As the time drew nearer, although I had not been all that interested I found myself drawn into discussion about the pros and cons of the new development. Journalists rang me up insistently: 'What do you think about televising the Lords, Lady Ewart-Biggs?'

'I don't feel strongly either way,' I would say.

'But you must be for or against,' came the insistent voice. (Having for so long occupied that central grey area made up of doubt and seeing things both ways, I hate being dragooned into making black or white decisions.)

'I think people should have the right to watch what's going on in their own Parliament from their own sitting-rooms if they want to,' I then responded.

'But do you think the peers will play to the camera and take advantage of the opportunity to make some party political points?

I said I thought the British public were too sensible to be taken in by that sort of thing and would switch off pretty quickly if it happened.

I realized the House of Lords was being plunged into the limelight. We were constantly interviewed by newspapers and magazines on the subject. A very serious young woman reporter from *City Limits* cross-examined me closely. The result was rather more than I had bargained for; huge banner headlines on the front page, 'Wanna be a Lord?' But the strangest question came on the morning of the day the experiment started. 'Lady Ewart-Biggs,' said the voice with its unmistakably *Daily Express*-ish note to it, 'I understand you are taking part in the debate this afternoon. What will you be wearing?'

Exhausted from having grappled nervously with my speech since an early hour that morning, I said rather snappishly, 'Wouldn't your readers be more interested in what I am going to say rather than what I'll be wearing?' He seemed astounded at this suggestion. But, having extracted the disappointing answer that it would be a thoroughly conventional suit plus cream coloured silk shirt, he persisted, 'And what perfume will you be using, do you think?' I said I had no idea and in any case had not known modern technology was so far advanced that my eventual choice could possibly affect the audience.

Panic seized Kate when she realized I was speaking in the first televised debate. I kept trying to excuse myself by telling her, quite untruthfully, that when I had put my name down to speak, some weeks earlier, I had not known it was to be televised, and anyhow, I assured her, the cameras were to be switched off at seven o'clock and it was unlikely that I would have spoken by then. She was slightly reassured. However, when the list of speakers was issued at 2.15 on the day, I saw to my horror that my name was seventh and therefore sure to come up before seven o'clock. My speech immediately appeared inadequate. I hurried off to the Earl Marshal Room to have a last go at it, staying there through Question Time feverishly crossing little bits out, polishing the grammar and settling on a peroration.

I entered the Chamber at 3 o'clock. (I found out later that some peers had arrived as early as 11 o'clock that morning to get a good seat. Such vanity about the camera seems surprising from people who have attained positions of eminence.) The television lights were very bright and the Chamber felt much warmer than usual. The motion moved by Lord Beswick, on our side, was asking for social and economic policies to unite the nation. Viscount Whitelaw replied for the Government and Frank Beswick made a moving speech, but, when the Earl of Stockton rose, it became obvious who was going to be the star of the afternoon. His speech contained all the right elements. It was spoken and not read (by that time he was nearly blind and notes would have been of little help), contained personal reminiscences, humorous anecdotes and, best of all for our side, it poked fun at the Government.

It was a masterpiece and heaven-sent for the cameras. But from my point of view, it had two effects. First, by holding my attention it helped me forget my own impending ordeal and, second, it provided the possibility that viewers might then switch their sets off, content with having watched the great master himself.

My speech was horribly serious, all about the place women hold in the workplace. I had done a lot of research; going through much dross to find the most relevant statistics to support my arguments. I never feel women's issues are Their Lordships' favourite topic. For although they regard their female colleagues in the House as equals, their views about women in general tend to be reactionary. The place for women, as many of them see it, is distinctly in the home and their role to support men. Proof of this came at the end of my speech when the Viscount Massereene and Ferrard rose to his feet saying: 'My Lords, before the noble Baroness sits down, does she consider that a married woman with young children, who has a husband in lucrative employment, should go out and get a job; or does she consider she should remain with the children?'

From the depth of my soul I answered, 'My Lords, I think there should be no discrimination of job opportunities between men and women who have the same qualifications.'

But as far as my speech went, the cameras did not in the least increase my nervousness because it is so high at the best of times; and the theme worked out quite well. It was about the importance of offering women a wider choice in life and adjusting the system to support them in their dual role of worker and mother. I also pointed to the irony for women of the arrival of Britain's first woman Prime Minister on the scene. '... Would it not seem a strange paradox when in years to come we look back at the present coincidence of the first ever government led by a woman and the continued undermining of working women's opportunities? It must be recognized that at no point does the Government's record display enough sympathy for the Prime Minister's peers and contemporaries who, like her, also happen to be working family women ...' And finally, the peroration: '... I have spoken specifically to the part of the motion before us calling for policies which encourage motives of social responsibility. These are the policies which bring out the best in people; policies which, so to speak, touch the nice bit of Britain. And it is the Government's failure through their attitudes, values and priorities to do this which we on this side of the House so deeply deplore.'

Well, it wasn't Macmillan, but it was the best I could do. I felt moderately pleased but regretted going on for so long. I had aimed at nine minutes; as I sat down the digital clock on the wall opposite showed I had spoken for twelve.

I had tried not to think about Kate and the suffering caused to her by my unwelcome appearance on television. However, when I reached home that evening – rather late as many of the speakers had erred in the same direction as me and made lengthy speeches – I was totally unprepared for what she had to say on the telephone from school. 'Well done, Mum, it was great.'

'What do you mean? Did you actually watch some of the debate?'

'Not some of it – all of it,' said Kate. 'The teacher decided we should watch the whole programme for our Politics/Current Affairs period. I was in such a panic and then you came on and, after you had finished, everyone said how good you were. They didn't seem to mind a bit about your being Labour. Our Housekeeper was very pleased you talked about single parents because she is one. I'm so relieved it all turned out alright.' I could not believe the complete turnaround.

I must admit that I was, and still am, very easily put off by other people's reactions to what I say. The effect which the interest and appreciation of my audience has on me is magical. It makes me feel elated and provides the confidence to rattle along happily. If, on the other hand, I sense disapproval, I start drying up. My sensitivities have become so acute that the smallest things put me off. For instance, if I notice two peers talking to each other sitting on their bench, I imagine their conversation to be more or less on the lines of: 'What *is* she talking about? Entirely off the point and going on too long. It was a mistake letting women in here; the place has never been quite the same since they arrived.' This inhibition has a dreadful effect on my presentation. On the one hand, I am tempted to sit down promptly, bringing my remarks to a premature end, but on the other I do not want to waste the hours of toil put into the speech. So I usually settle for the compromise of rushing headlong with the sole aim of getting it all done with. I know that the deficiencies in style and delivery won't show up in *Hansard*. I also know that the number of people reading *Hansard* will be infinitely greater than those sitting in the Chamber with slightly glazed looks. So sometimes I address my remarks more towards the shorthand writers than towards the audience.

So I have concluded that there is a fundamental difference between men and women speakers. For example, women seem to be much more reliant on their audiences than are men; they tend to speak more briefly, perhaps because of the fear of losing the attention of their audience; they are more easily put off by lack of interest or disagreement. A man appears to speak for his own satisfaction; he provides his own stimulus and his audience becomes a secondary factor. So he is less affected by whether they are listening or not, agreeing or disagreeing.

CHAPTER FOUR

All about Their Lordships' House

THERE IS ONE day in the year when the House of Lords takes precedence over the Commons. This is when the Queen comes to read the Speech from the Throne at the State Opening of Parliament. The second chamber has Charles I to thank for this moment of glory, for since his regrettable attempt to enter the Commons to arrest two members of his Parliament, no living monarch has ever been permitted to set foot in that Chamber.

So when on 4 November 1981, as I arrived at my first Opening of Parliament, I was very conscious of what the day meant to us underdogs in the Lords. I had put my name down for the ballot of robes. A small stock is held by the Secretary to the Lord Great Chamberlain for peers not owning their own but wishing to attend. Having never won anything in a raffle in my life, I was pleasantly surprised to learn I had been successful. A set of robes, I was told, would be ready for me in the Moses Room from 9.30 a.m. on the morning of the Opening.

It was considerably later when I arrived as I had been unable to extricate myself from home in time to get to Westminster before all the roads leading to it had been closed. (The major reason for my unpunctuality, I know, is an inability to break out of one capsule in order to go and join another. My home sends out tentacles which hold me back just at the critical moment; the telephone rings, things need tidying away, a child needs me – the tentacles are numerous. Departures from an office or a party or a restaurant are also often blocked. In fact the only occasions which allow instant release are those with a clear-cut beginning and end: a film, a conference, a wedding, a funeral, and so on.) The sticker on my windscreen should have allowed me free passage but the police were not convinced by the sight of me and my rather dirty and ageing car. Perhaps this was another proof of what the popular image of a peer really is; namely rich, chauffeur-driven and male. My borrowed robes were the last ones hanging on the improvised rail in the Moses Room. 'That is the lady who pressed your robes for you, My Lady,' the attendant whispered to me nodding towards one of the maids in her black dress and white apron. I thanked her and then turned my attention to getting into the complicated garment. It was rather like a knight having his armour put on, as two of the attendants lowered the heavy velour and white ermined garment over my head. Tying the black ribbon into a bow at my throat and hitching the flying panel on one side round my left wrist, I looked at myself in the mirror. What I saw was an unreal sight and it gave me little confidence.

The Chamber was very full indeed when I entered it, for a lot of Their Lordships had been there for an hour or more. Conscious of presenting a very conspicuous figure, as one of the few left standing, I feverishly started looking for a space. Fortunately the age of chivalry still thrives in the House of Lords. Soon two peers made room for me, and I gratefully sat down. But doing so reminded me of the limited space I had learned that Pugin allowed each peer when he designed the Chamber. This was only two foot – which is not much when taking the voluminous folds of their robes into account.

The sight presented by the assembly on the day of the State Opening elicits conflicting feelings. You can see it as a vision of unparalleled ceremonial splendour and lavishness, or as a scene providing the ultimate incentive for the uprising of the masses. But let us take it as Barry intended, 'not a mere place of business nor even a mere House of Lords – but as a Chamber in which a Sovereign surrounded by the Court, summoned the three estates of the realm', and few would question his accomplishment in translating vision into reality.

Looking round from the rather compressed position between my substantial neighbours, I first recognized the group of ambassadors sitting on the benches to the left of the Throne usually occupied by Conservative peers and the bishops. The diplomats – all male – were either in national dress or morning suits. They could hardly have looked more multi-racial with each differing so fundamentally in colouring, features, shape of head, type of hair and so on. I recognized my friend Bobbie de Margerie, the French Ambassador, and waved discreetly. On the benches opposite – those usually occupied by the Liberal and SDP peers – sat the diplomats' wives; or some of them, as space limitations only permitted a proportion to attend each year. Their dress ranged from the full evening dress with tiaras of the Western ambassadresses through the grandeur of some national dresses of African or Asian countries to the rather plain dress worn by what I took to be the ambassadress of a Socialist country.

Moving along the benches to where Labour peers usually sit, I recognized the peeresses. But here again, my neighbour told me, only a proportion was present as, with the exception of Duchesses who were above all that, they were obliged to ballot for a place. This would equally be the case for the husbands of women peers and peers' eldest sons. (I wondered when Robin might put his name in the hat, but, remembering him saying he didn't like elitism when I merely suggested he get himself a decent suit, I decided it would not be for quite a while.) I wondered how long the peeresses had spent at the hairdressers that morning having their tiaras settled into place; then, unashamed egalitarian that I am, I thought how the proceeds of their sale transferred into, say, the School Meal Service would ensure a substantial midday meal for every needy child in the country for the duration of their school lives. The rest of the seats were occupied by peers, and I marvelled at the fact that all those wishing to come had fitted in. Charles Barry when designing the Chamber had made his calculations based on there being enough room for 300.

The hubbub of conversation lessened with the arrival in the Chamber of two members of the Royal Family not in the procession. We rose to our feet for the Duchesses of Kent and Gloucester who had special places near the Throne among the ambassadors' wives. And then at 11.30 precisely the Royal Procession made its entry into the Chamber.

Before this moment the Queen had travelled in the Irish State Coach from Buckingham Palace with an escort of the Household Cavalry and following a procession of state carriages carrying the crown, the maces and other regalia associated with the occasion. Alighting at the Sovereign's Entrance she had mounted Barry's imposing Royal staircase; by that time the Union Jack normally flying from the Victoria Tower would have been replaced by the Royal Standard. At the top of the Royal staircase Her Majesty would have passed through the Norman Porch into the Robing Room. Once she had been attired in her robes and Imperial Crown, the procession had moved into the Royal Gallery and on to the Chamber. First came the courtiers and then, immediately preceding the Queen came the Lord Privy Seal, the Lord President of the Council, the Lord Chancellor, Black Rod, Garter King of Arms, the Earl Marshal and the Lord Great Chamberlain. Last came the peers bearing the Sword of State and the Cap of Maintenance.

When the Queen made her entrance the dresses and jewels of the peeresses and ambassadors' wives suddenly looked almost drab, so great is the splendour and glitter of her robes. The lovely but so very young-looking Princess of Wales took her place with Prince Charles on one side of the Throne, and finally the remaining members of the procession – Ladies in Waiting and other members of the Royal Household – entered and positioned themselves round the Throne. This, I recognized, was the moment for which Barry and Pugin had devoted all their artistic imagination and talent.

'My Lords, pray be seated,' came the voice from the Throne.

I confess I did not know why we all sat in total silence for the next few minutes. I thought the Queen might have lost the Speech or forgotten her specs. But if this were the case I was surprised that she looked so serene, as indeed did all the Officers of State attending her. (I blame such moments of abysmal ignorance on my mother. She insisted on taking me away from school at the age of sixteen, not realizing that while all I had learned up to then would be of little use in later life, I would have gained enormously by the years of learning which should have followed.)

Anyhow, the long and short of it was that I did not know about the time-honoured ceremony whereby Black Rod is despatched by the Queen to deliver the summons to the Commons to come to hear the Speech from the Throne. The procedure requires Black Rod to walk through the lobbies and knock loudly three times on the closed door of the Commons Chamber with his black ebony stick. 'The Queen commands this honourable House to attend Her Majesty immediately in the House of Peers.' At this summons the Prime Minister attended by the Speaker and Sergeant-at-Arms emerge and, followed by the Leader of the Opposition and a hundred or so MPs, walk through the two lobbies to stand at the Bar of the House of Lords. It is a tradition that they make a noisy arrival, talking in loud voices, in marked contrast to the silence in the Lords Chamber, and it was this din which first alerted me to the meaning of that part of the ceremony.

Listening to the Queen making her speech – her spectacles do not quite harmonize with the Imperial Crown – I couldn't help wondering how much of it she agreed with. There was a later occasion in June 1987 when the Speech from the Throne contained a reference to further privatization, and I thought the royal lips were distinctly unwilling to close over that word. I have always thought of the Queen as a Conservative of the old paternalist tradition, so she might well have found part of her parliamentary programme difficult to swallow.

Whatever Her Majesty's innermost feelings were, the whole speech was over very quickly. I suppose it took about seven minutes and ended on a note with which everyone could agree. 'My Lords, and Members of the House of Commons. I pray that the blessing of the Almighty God may rest upon your counsels.' Then the procession all happened again in reverse, and so ended one more State Opening of Parliament, the only moment in the year when Their Lordships – seated and resplendent in their robes – feel one up on the MPs standing in a huddle at the Bar, excluded from the Chamber.

Immediately following the Opening, at the beginning of each new parliamentary session, three days are set aside to debate the Queen's Speech. The first day is devoted to Defence and Foreign Affairs, the second to Home Affairs and the third to Employment, Trade and Industry. These debates provide an opportunity for peers to speak on any subject they like. If there is some reference in the Queen's Speech to an issue they wish to discuss, then they may open their remarks by saying – for example – 'My Lords, in view of the commitment to maintain our existing support to NATO which was included in the Speech from the Throne, I have the following comments to make ...' On the other hand, if the speech made no reference to a particular subject, speakers may use the omission as an introduction to their remarks. I remember using this device on a later occasion when I wished to speak about family issues: '... Remembering the claim of the Government before the election of being the party who championed the rights of the family,' I said, 'we were justified in anticipating that there might be something in the gracious Speech to assist this country's least favoured families. Now we know we waited in vain. There was no mention of either the family – or indeed the child – throughout the gracious Speech ...' I then went on to offer a few ideas of my own.

So the Debate on the Address provides peers with an excellent opportunity to have it both ways, and on 10 November, the day in 1981 reserved for Foreign Affairs, I decided to take the opportunity of speaking about Ireland. 'My Lords, I wish to say a few words about Ireland for not only was there reference in the Queen's Speech to close relations being maintained between the Governments of the United Kingdom and the Republic of Ireland, but also last week an important meeting took place between the British Prime Minister and the Irish Taoiseach ...' I went on to say I was 'happy that the initiative to create a new framework in which to build closer relations between the two islands has now been truly consolidated ... [This] must be right when there is so much at stake in the way of lives, property and happiness in Northern Ireland. The two sovereign countries immediately concerned should create a structure in which to replace the confrontations and misunderstandings of the past with consultation and renewed understanding ... therefore welcome the setting up of the Anglo-Irish Intergovernmental Council ... hope its work will be conducted in the open ... discussions carried out in secret about Northern Ireland's future cause real panic and consternation to the people.' In order to stress the importance of strengthening links between the Republic and Britain, I ended on a note of concern about the continuation of direct rule: '... direct rule is a system imposed by the wishes of the majority community. It has, as its major justification, the requirement that it should be effective in containing the security situation and administering the Province in wisdom, justice and humanity ... But with the insuperable obstacles being put in the way of direct rule we wonder how long it can continue to provide effective government. It is for that reason that I most earnestly hope that the work of the new Anglo-Irish Council will be constructive and positive and that the Loyalists will in effect try to safeguard their rightful place in Ireland by giving the new initiative a chance, by giving the politicians a chance to take over from the gunmen; for otherwise I fear that time is beginning to run out ...'

The speech seemed to go down quite well. The rumble of 'hear, hears' was reasonably loud and on leaving the chamber I was congratulated by several peers. No one could doubt my sincerity and I suppose this gave what I said a validity. Attracting some attention is more or less all one can expect from a speech of this kind for there is no way of evaluating its effect in tangible terms. It is like putting a message in a bottle and throwing it far out to sea in the hope it will be washed onto some receptive shore.

The subjects chosen by the two speakers who followed me seemed to indicate that they too might have similar expectations for their speeches. For example, the Baroness Airey of Abingdon, who spoke immediately after me, opened her speech by saying, 'My Lords, I venture to speak this evening on the subject of Poland ... some of Your Lordships may have had friends, comrades in arms, during the war, and you might feel pity for the plight of the country at the present time ...' She went on to describe her husband, Airey Neave's, escape from a prison in Russia where, as she said, we had an Ambassador, Sir Stafford Cripps. She described the gallantry and courage of the people who helped him on his way. Her speech was very short – only four minutes – and focused on the importance of giving moral support to the negotiations then going on between the Polish Government, the Church and Solidarity and of producing practical help in the way of food and loans to the country in its time of great need. She ended, 'I hope that Her Majesty's Government can hold out the hand of friendship with encouragement and hope so that Poland might have a chance to work out her future for herself.'

She was in turn followed by the Lord Bishop of London whose concern was as deeply felt but of quite a different nature. He brought up the vexed question of the proposed patriation of the British North America Act of 1867 and the effect this would have on the aboriginal peoples of Canada. The Bishop showed himself to be extremely well briefed on this complex constitutional issue when he described the danger to the human rights of the Indians and Eskimos resident in Canada if the treaties they had made with the British sovereign, prior to the 1867 Act, were not respected. He made a strong case on their behalf, but I shall say no more about it at this stage as I will be describing later in the chapter my own direct involvement with the aboriginal people of Canada over this thorny matter.

The number of peers sitting on the Labour benches had been dramatically reduced when the SDP was set up during the previous year. Those who changed their allegiance moved to the benches designated to accommodate the new party directly behind those occupied by the Liberal Party. Many of them had been prominent members of the Labour Party and were sorely missed. Yet the feelings of bitterness and acrimony towards the 'turncoats' was not as keenly felt by the Labour group in the Lords as in the Commons or elsewhere in the Labour movement; although it certainly existed.

I had felt a mild twinge of interest in the party when it was starting up. This came mainly through a shared commitment to the European Community and a common abhorrence of the bullying tactics of the extreme left wing of the Labour Party. I had seen Shirley Williams, David Owen and Roy Jenkins providing the target for mindless heckling at the Party conference. And I had admired their courage in withstanding the onslaught for so many years.

Moreover, like so many who flocked to the new banner, I was a committed internationalist – still hooked on the old socialist belief in a world community with the only frontiers being those created by human divisions. Like most of them I was also moderate in my political views but radical about the need for electoral reform to bring about a more democratic system. So all in all, I must admit that I presented a likely-seeming recruit for the new party, and should not have been surprised that so many took it for granted that I would be joining. 'You'll be coming in, won't you, Jane?' or 'I suppose you'll be the next one.' Others recognized a very real problem; 'Of course I can see it's a bit difficult for you, now you've accepted a peerage from the Labour Party, to leave them and join another party ...' These were the sort of remarks continually levelled at me. To make it harder, my good friend Kevin joined the new party at the very early stages.

What was it that kept me with Labour? There were two main reasons. Walking away from the Party because I disagreed with some of the things going on would have meant admitting defeat; staying on and joining forces with likeminded people to oppose the extreme left seemed a better option. The other reason for staying with Labour came from a concern that SDP policies might increasingly mirror those of the Conservatives. I feared that their priorities might move towards economic policies favouring the well-off and away from the fair redistribution of wealth and services to all. I know that Socialist parties are often blamed, with some justification, for being strong on social policies and weak on economic planning. But then for so many of us the rock upon which all our political thinking rests is the achievement of a more equal society. For my part not only do I consider this to be morally right but I believe that countries who have attained a greater degree of equality seem to get on better than we do. I know how difficult it is to bring this about because of the natural cycles which prevail whereby on the one side privilege, wealth, intelligence, etc. are inherited whilst on the other bad luck, poverty, ignorance and ill health are passed on from one generation to the next. I believe that the Labour Party – in spite of all its faults – genuinely works towards interrupting these natural cycles to bring about a fairer balance. So that was why in early 1981 I made my decision to stand firm, and in a letter to *The Times* at that time I responded to an article of Geoffrey Smith's headed 'What makes a Labour moderate stay on?' I wrote: 'The party for which Labour supporters have been voting in successive elections as the one representing their convictions still exists. It has not disappeared, nor have those supporters been abandoned by it. ... In spite of conflicts and defections it remains a party able to represent men and women with views based on realism and tolerance ...' I really believed what I wrote.

In the end people stopped asking me if I was going to join the SDP – or, even worse, taking it for granted that I had already done so. But not before I sometimes got heated: 'People have had their teeth kicked in for asking that question,' I said once.

'And there are one hell of a lot of people walking round London with no teeth,' was the good-humoured reply.

But when all is said and done, I still think Roy Hattersley's description of the new party was the most apt. 'The SDP is like a team arriving on the playing field,' he said, 'all wearing clean shorts.' But alas it took only a few years of the rough and tumble of internal strife to remove the pristine look of the new party.

By the end of 1981 – my first year – I was feeling much more at home in my new setting. I could even find my way around without the hesitation which, in the early days, brought a policeman hurrying along to make sure I was indeed a new peer with no sense of direction rather than a suspicious stranger. Becoming acquainted with the Westminster Palace staff made me feel part of a family again. I had sorely missed the extended family provided by an embassy group and welcomed the sense of belonging to a small community which came with getting to know not only my colleagues but also the policemen at the Peers' Entrance, the tailcoated attendants in the Lobby, Mr

Jones the librarian, Mr Scott and his good-natured group in the mail office, Iris who ran the bar in the Peers' Guest Room, Mary the Irish girl in the Bishops' Bar, and many others. I noticed these staff members treated some of the more elderly peers with a kindhearted, nanny-like approach. They were well aware of our various idiosyncrasies, and the Lobby attendants could accurately predict the length of speeches: 'Lord x, he'll be up for fifteen minutes – sure to be,' one would gloomily predict as a debate droned implacably on through the evening. Or Iris at the Guest Room bar, 'Lord Y? Yes, he takes a double malt whisky around this time of the day.'

They also kept themselves informed about the outside activities of their so-called charges, taking a pride in any achievements. One morning as I arrived at the House, I was hailed by the policeman at the Peers' entrance: 'Well My Lady, what about that gold medal?' When I got up to the Peers' Lobby it was the same thing. The tall ex-naval warrant officer turned House of Lords attendant looked at me with a flicker of surprise mixed with approval and said, 'Ah, My Lady – the water baby.' The banter came as a result of my ignominious performance the previous evening in the Lords versus Commons Annual Swim in aid of the Women Caring Trust. This was a London-based charity who supported work for mothers and children in Northern Ireland, and as I had previously been one of its trustees I felt I should carry on my allegiance by taking part in the swim.

The only problem was my not being able to swim very well, however conscientiously I had practised every early morning for the preceding week or so at the Kensington New Pools. This training took place under the eagle eye of my friend Tilli Edelman. Holding my head high out of the water to keep my hair dry, I struggled backwards and forwards completing six or eight lengths each morning, all the time lamenting that swimming had not been included in my school curriculum. The pool at school was out of doors and filled with dark green stagnant water, and our swimming was confined to one or two glacial dips a year.

The Women Caring Trust Swim took place on 15 November at Dolphin Square. As this was the day before Kate's birthday and a Sunday, she came along too. Unlike me, she is an excellent swimmer but, knowing her mother's deficiencies, she viewed the evening with hilarity as well as some trepidation. The members of each team – all men – had been kitted out with matching trunks and bathrobes:

red for the House of Lords and green for the Commons. As the only woman competitor I had been despatched to Simpsons in Piccadilly to buy a plain one-piece black costume, and wore this under a red House of Lords bathing robe. I thought I presented a reasonably workmanlike look until Kate whispered, 'Don't you think you'd better take your pearls off, Mum?' My sense of inadequacy increased when I realized that the MPs were more than adequate swimmers — all of them having done daily quotas of lengths — and the members of the Lords team were all young, athletic, hereditary peers. Names such as Montgomery, Alexander, Elton, Brabazon of Tara. A group photograph was taken with me feeling small and out of place flanked by the tall young men. And then to raise extra funds there was an auction of the swimmers by a Sotheby's professional. The most likely winners naturally attracted the highest bids. In an effort to protect my sensitivities and safeguard me from more embarrassment I was thrown in with another of the swimmers; a job lot.

Kate was at the start to see us off and as I stood waiting with the pool stretched in front of me, it seemed enormous. Over-eager, I dived in before the gun went off and had to climb out again. Kate looked sombre but the false start had the opposite effect on me and when the race finally started I was overcome with such hopeless giggles that I could only just keep afloat, let alone make much headway. Thus incapacitated I struggled forward with my breast stroke whilst watching the rows of feet churning up the water in front of me. When I eventually reached the other end, Kate helped me out and I heard the voice of the commentator Jeffrey Archer saying, 'Now we haven't seen who was last, have we?'

I can't say I felt very proud of my performance. The photographs in the next morning's papers showed Peter Bottomley, the winner, and me wet and laughing, while the reports omitted reference to my lamentable swim, but I was mortified by the *Evening Standard* which said, 'Lady Ewart-Biggs, in blue and two strands of pearls, slid gracefully into the water ...'

'But I took them off and gave them to you,' I said to Kate crossly.

'Don't worry, Mum,' she replied in her most robust way. 'If you're in the public eye you've not got to mind the crap they talk. Imagine what it would be like if you were *really* important.'

As time went on I naturally became interested in finding out more about my colleagues in the House. I recognized that Their Lordships represented a wide section of the community, indeed were probably a more accurate cross-section than the members of the Commons, and I also recognized that there were a great number of specialists among them. But, until I read Janet Morgan's excellent book *The House of Lords and the Labour Party*, published in 1975, I had not thought of classing them in types. The groups presented by the author are most apt and I have drawn extensively from her observations. In the first place she suggests one group should be entitled 'The Apprentices'. The peers who have been in the House for less than three years and who, in spite of feeling a bit frightened, find it a warm and tolerant place. They are impressionable and receptive to advice from veterans as to how they should conduct themselves and which way to vote. Their approach is to be openly friendly to everyone without pushing themselves forward. Older peers speculate on how these newcomers will turn out: '– promises to be good front bench material.' And when a self-assertive import from the Commons arrives, the veterans comment on how 'this House tames them all in the end.'

The second group is described by Janet Morgan as 'The Innocents'. These are Apprentices who never blossom into front-benchers but make distinct contributions from the back benches. In the first instance, they provide an audience for the prima donnas who create the impetus to make the whole House function. Moreover they are people who really enjoy the House, attach little importance to the Whips and indulge what is basically a dilettante interest. 'The whole point of this House,' they say, 'is to represent the rational voice,' or 'You hear a lot of frightfully good stuff in here!' Nevertheless there is little doubt that Innocents make their presence felt. They intervene, for instance, on minor subjects about which they know a lot; perhaps countryside issues, speeding regulations or service conditions. It is as if they treat the Lords like a more ample correspondence page in *The Times*. I remember the whole House on its feet anxious to speak when a question was put down by what Janet Morgan would term an Innocent on the emotive subject of Gibraltar.

And on another occasion there was a question about the control of weeds which attracted a number of peers not known for their regular attendance. The exchange was both informative and entertaining. The question was: 'To ask HMG whether they will sponsor a study of the use of insects to reduce and control bracken, ragwort and other persistent but unwelcome weeds'. Baroness Trumpington, the Parliamentary Under-Secretary of State for Agriculture, Fisheries & Food, replied that her department had already decided to do so. Jean Trumpington, previously Mayor of Cambridge, is as large in heart as in frame, and a great favourite of the House. When she took on her job with the Ministry there was a move to pass the hat round for a huge pair of green wellington boots for her. However, having answered very specialized questions about weed control, she gave a more lighthearted reply to Lord Ferrier when he asked whether she was aware of the possibility of controlling the spread of ragwort by grazing sheep on an infected field in the month of May? 'My Lords, quite a lot of things happen in the month of May,' she said to Their Lordships' delight.

The group which follows The Innocents are undoubtedly 'The Adventurers'. They provide an obvious driving force. Many of them confess surprise at finding themselves in the Lords at all. Barbara Wootton, the distinguished academic and author, and in 1958 one of the first women created a life peer, found it 'hard to resist blitzing an all-male institution'. Adventurers talk of their role in the House in terms of function, 'A sort of ombudsmanship – a platform for the things you're interested in'. They see the Lords not as a forum for advancing a political programme but as an extension of a personal platform, an additional area for promoting their own causes, and they think nothing of voting against their own parties. In the courteous and dignified environment, peopled by members of a high average age and some tendency to somnolence, the existence of this group is essential to bring innovation and change. My favourite in the category is a Conservative, Lady Faithfull. Previously a Director of Social Services, she has used her place in the Lords to represent the interests of disadvantaged families, children and young people even if this has attracted the disapproval of her Chief Whip and Party. Sometimes during debate she reminisces about her work in the field. During the Criminal Justice Bill, she described an instance when a child found to be glue-sniffing had been brought before a panel as used in the Scottish children's hearing system. 'The chairman of the panel was a postman and one of the nicest men I have ever met. He leant forward and said to the child, "Why did you do it?" The child said, "I were unhappy." The panel members said, "Yes, but tell us why you did it?" "I were unhappy," said the child. The panel members said, "Why

73

were you unhappy?" The child sniffed and looked frightfully awkward. Then he looked across at the two heads of the home who were sitting at the end of the table. He said, "Well, look at 'em". We looked at them, and thought we might have been unhappy too!'

It is generally thought that the crossbenchers divide more or less equally on most votes. These scantily camouflaged Conservative or Labour peers could be categorized as 'Legalists' or 'Proceduralists' who are dispassionate and who apply a microscope to intricate points. They believe the Lords has a steadying effect on the Commons. Others have argued that there would be far less need for this painstaking work in amending bills going through the Lords if the staff of parliamentary draftsmen were increased. The draftsmen counter by pointing out that the problems stem from departments where policies are drawn up and who are obliged to present them to Parliament in a rush, and then the proposals have to be altered as a result of undertakings in the House. The Legalists are temperamentally inclined to ensure that Bills are technically correct and concentrate on that rather than the rights and wrongs of the underlying principles. Their moderate attitude nicely counterbalances the enthusiasms of the Adventurers. Some of them strike one as being essentially private men, each bringing his own legal experience and sometimes eccentricities to bear on the collective body.

Lord Denning is a prime example. Master of the Rolls for twenty years and famed for championing the cause of the common man when a judge, he participates actively in debates. But when the remarkable eighty-nine-year-old intercedes at committee stage of a bill, no one can be sure on which side of an argument he will eventually come down. In his distinctive accent he cites a series of cases brought before him when a judge in days gone by, and then at the end of a preamble which has given no clue as to his intentions to his audience – many of them by that time at the edge of their seats – he ends, '... and, My Lords, that's why I can ... not support this amendment', or on other occasions, '... why I can ... support this amendment.'

The last two categories of peers go under the heading of 'Politician' or 'Elder Statesman'. The former represent the Lords with the most explicit image of the House as a parliamentary workshop. They give different reasons for their political proclivities: 'Got sucked in ... Don't vastly enjoy it ... Bloody hard work in opposition'. One told me, 'I thought I'd take my seat when my father died, that's all, and then got sort of hooked on it.' Or another, 'I came as a Labour supporter. I wouldn't have done it otherwise and I've been a constant attender from the very beginning.' The sort of remarks overheard in the Peers' Lobby or corridors show them to be as much students of form as their Commons counterparts: 'Did you see, they've brought old x back to the front bench to make it look respectable', or 'Should be interesting this afternoon. If they're sensible they won't press an amendment'. The Politicians regret that Lords reform has been dropped and want to see a professional House, more closely resembling the Commons. They all welcome the influx of life peers which gives a better party balance and more bite to the place. It is true they have rather an inferiority complex *vis-à-vis* the House of Commons – a waspish admiration. It may be this emotion which provokes them to keep things moving; ensuring that the Lords act as an effective legislative chamber and that peers are organized and cajoled to attend, speak and vote. It is without doubt the Politicians who see to it that government business is smoothed through and that the opposition is tenacious. I can think of several peers who fulfil this role. On the Labour side Ted Graham, a life peer, previously in the Commons, is a cheerful, bluff, popular colleague who does a lot of 'fixing'. He is the one who waylays comrade peers when they have it in mind to slip away around six o'clock. 'One more vote expected, Jane, in about half an hour. It'll be an all-important one to win,' he says with his enormous smile; which broadens even more when he suddenly remembers one of his appalling puns. He is popular with everyone on both sides of the House and enjoys getting things organized.

Finally, the 'Elder Statesmen' are those who eventually burst from a Politician's chrysalis. From both sides of the House they move discreetly from the front benches to seats at the end of the Chamber furthest from the Throne. All have spent decades in political activity. They rise to support party leaders on a procedural point, recommend a business arrangement, advise, warn and admonish. They show instinctive loyalty and affection for the House. This is not a characteristic of newer members who are less blind to the self-congratulatory complacency to be found in the Lords. And speaking of this, it has often occurred to me that if all expression of exaggerated congratulations – directed toward self or others – were dropped, we might get home at least an hour earlier each evening. There are innumerable examples but I particularly remember the profusion of compliments handed out during the passage of the second reading of the Animals (Scientific Procedures) Bill, an entirely admirable non-controversial piece of legislation designed to safeguard from cruelty animals used in laboratories for scientific and medical experimentation. The compliments started early, directed by the independently minded ex-Labour Minister Lord Houghton – a well-known exponent of animal welfare – towards the good-looking young hereditary peer, Lord Glenarthur, who was the Home Office Minister introducing the Bill.

This was followed by the much venerated Earl of Selkirk paying the customary respects to a maiden speaker when he followed the Viscount Allenby of Megiddo. 'My Lords, it is my privilege to congratulate the noble Viscount, Lord Allenby, most warmly on an interesting and extremely well expressed speech. I am certain that everyone in the House heard without difficulty every word that he said. I wish that could be said of every noble Lord!' Lord Walston from the SDP benches took up the chorus: '... I should like to pay my tribute to the noble Viscount, Lord Allenby, for his very delightful, knowledgeable and wise speech. I will not say that it was refreshing to hear from him because that would sound as if I needed refreshment after listening to the speeches of those noble Lords who preceded him, and that is not so. It was a very happy speech indeed.'

Other speakers followed, until finally Lord Mishcon summed up for the Opposition. He uses the English language to the best avail and as usual did not miss an opportunity to praise. 'I entirely agree with my noble friend ... Lord Walston, when he says what a pleasant debate this has been,' he said. 'It has been pleasant for a number of reasons. First, because there has been unanimity throughout Your Lordships' House in regard to the courage with which this Bill has been brought forward ... It has been pleasant, too, because we have been congratulating each other. Rightly was the noble Lord, Lord Glenarthur, paid the compliment of having introduced this Bill with great clarity. Compliments were also deservedly paid to the noble Earl, Lord Halsbury, who in the course of a most informed speech tried to compare the painfulness of stings from wasps, bees and hornets. Such is the regard in which the noble Earl is held in this House that I want him to know that possibly the most painful sting of all is when we come to disagree with him in debate and find that he is an antagonist and not an ally ...'

Lord Glenarthur, the Minister replying, had the last innings and did not wish to be outdone: 'My Lords, we have had interesting and lively debate. It has attracted expert scientists, on the one hand, expert campaigners on behalf of animals, on the other. Throughout the debate much varied experience and wisdom has come from so many of Your Lordships . . .'

And so it went on, presumably to everyone's enormous satisfaction.

I have digressed from my description of Elder Statesmen, who fill such an important place in the Lords. Lord Home is the undisputed chieftain. He sits at the end of the front bench for Privy Councillors – a place reserved for ex-prime ministers – but used to give way to Macmillan when necessary. He always looks calm and benign. When he speaks everyone listens, in particular when the subject is Foreign Affairs. He might well be viewed as being the sort of patron saint of the village he took his title from. The telephone number he gave the Foreign Office at weekends when Foreign Secretary was Coldstream 1. Elder Statesmen quite often take up causes out of the genuine concern felt by paternalists. They involve themselves with, say, housing associations providing accommodation for the elderly, or the disabled or a voluntary agency looking after prisoners' families. The Elder Statesmen speak of the co-operation, respect and friendliness of the Lords and are publicists for the whole House to the outside world.

I have wondered to which group I belong. On arrival in the Lords I was of course an Apprentice of the purest blend. But I believe I have gradually broken out of that mould and might now describe myself as a mixture of Adventurer and Politician. With my background of diplomatic life it would be impossible to develop into a full blown politician, yet it helps me to see things from an independent viewpoint. I certainly believe in using the Lords to advance my party's policies whilst at the same time seeing it as an extension of my personal platform, a readily accessible soapbox for the furtherance of causes in which I believe.

Causes are plentiful, either those for which I have long campaigned or new ones. I might become the standard bearer for a new cause quite unexpectedly. For example, in the early part of 1987 a telephone call came early one morning. 'I wonder if you could get something going from the House of Lords, Jane?' came the voice of an old and dear friend from the Foreign Office. 'It's to do with the visit of the Soviet Foreign Minister Mr Shevardnadze which starts tomorrow.

The Office will be discussing a whole range of subjects with him but we plan to bring up one humanitarian issue – the imprisonment in a Labour Camp of a young Russian poet called Irina Ratushinskaya. She wrote some poetry which the authorities there consider to contain anti-Soviet propaganda and, as her health is bad, and the conditions in the camp are appalling, her life might become endangered. She's only thirty and has a big following over here. People don't see her poetry as political but, on the contrary, as of a completely peaceful nature.'

'But what on earth can I do about it?' I said.

The plan then unfolded: 'It might be very helpful if you could write a letter to the Soviet Minister expressing concern – from a humanitarian viewpoint – for Irina's health and ask some of your colleagues to countersign it with you. If it arrived at the Russian Embassy at the same time as our representations, it might add weight to our request.' Naturally I agreed to do my best, but added, 'I find it really hard to believe that the Russians could be impressed by the House of Lords – or indeed anything any of us might say or think.'

The answer was emphatic. 'They may not think much of the institution, but they have a great respect for many people in it. If you could get some ex-prime ministers to sign the letter, like Lord Home and Harold Macmillan. And Lord Grimond – anyone else you can think of and' – coming just a bit too late – 'your own signature will naturally be very important too.'

When a draft of the letter arrived from the Foreign Office, all hopes of continuing with my planned afternoon disappeared. I had a list of telephone calls to make, some research for a speech to devil out, stamps to buy, a letter to write to Kate who was then away learning Italian in Florence, and so on and so forth. They were mainly jobs which could have been done by a secretary (I've often thought I could conquer the world if I had a full-time secretary) or a wife – and I certainly could do with one of them too! Instead, I found myself engaged in the unusual pastime of waylaying ex-prime ministers in the corridors. Positioning myself in appropriate places to intercept my quarry, I felt like a reasonably highly placed prostitute.

'Could I have a word with you after the vote?' I asked Lord Home as we crossed each other *en route* to opposite lobbies.

'Of course. Shall we meet in the Princes' Chamber?' said the very engaging and much respected Elder Statesman.

With Henry VIII and his six wives peering down at us from their portraits on the walls, I explained what I wanted and showed him the letter. Displaying the characteristic sense of calm which always inspires so much confidence in him, he agreed. 'Yes, it might just do some good. But you won't be publicizing our intervention, will you?'

By the end of the afternoon the list of signatures was impressive. I folded up the precious letter, carefully addressed the envelope to Mr Shevardnadze, c/o the Russian Embassy and sent it off, 'special delivery' from the little post office in the Central Lobby. Walking back to my desk and the jobs I was belatedly to embark on, I wondered who would actually open the letter, what the response from the embassy staff might be and the rather baffled discussion they might have as how to advise their Minister about such an unexpected intervention.

As it transpired, there was a happy outcome (for Irina) but it will never be known whether our letter played any part. I remember my sense of overwhelming joy and satisfaction when a few weeks later I read of the first moves made by the Soviet authorities in her favour. The *Observer* reported that she had been permitted a visit by her husband and also, for the first time, had received medical attention. Eventually she was released. We may or may not have affected this, but there was no doubt that the House of Lords was the correct setting from which to launch such an appeal. Equally certain was the fact that the operation provided one answer to those who ask, 'But what do they *do* all the time?'

On a subsequent occasion I used my place in the Lords to oppose the return of capital punishment. I had always been unequivocally against hanging and could never understand after the 1965 abolition legislation why we kept reverting to the question. Before the debate on restoration in the House of Commons after the 1979 general election, I had written a letter to the *Guardian* putting forward my arguments. This is roughly what I said. '... the issue of capital punishment can be seen from a practical and moral viewpoint. Is hanging a deterrent to killing, and is it morally defensible that the community should be empowered to decide on whether one of its members should live or die? Statistics convince me that the threat of execution does not deter the potential murderer. This leaves the moral standpoint. In my view it should be the responsibility of a civilized society to contain the destructive elements within it without resorting to similar methods; whilst striving to eradicate the root causes of crime and violence. We must judge the criminal, condemn him, isolate him – but not emulate him. On another aspect, and one which touches me close, it is felt that certain categories of murder justify the supreme penalty more than others. Murder through terrorist action is deemed one. Again, from both practical and moral viewpoints, this is to me indefensible. Society cannot degrade its own behaviour to match that of a terrorist. It must, within the limitations imposed by a democratic state, wage continual war against the terrorist and strive to protect the community from his action. I am convinced that the execution of a terrorist – thus making him a martyr – would infinitely enrich his cause. Many would rally with renewed vigour to fill his place. His supporters, sharing his contempt for human life, would in retaliation make further reprisals ...'

By the time the hanging debate was reinstated after the 1983 election my views had not changed but my platform for presenting them had become a great deal more powerful than the correspondence columns of national newspapers and university debating unions. I accepted an invitation from the National Council for Civil Liberties to take part in a discussion which they had organized prior to the House of Commons debate. The event was scheduled to take place in the Grand Committee Room – which had been wrecked by an IRA bomb in 1974 and later restored. It is situated at the end of Westminster Hall. Among others, Roy Jenkins (ex-Home Secretary) was invited, as had been the press and media. I knew this would provide an influential platform and, as I was anxious about the outcome of the Commons debate, I accepted it with alacrity. I was concerned for the following reasons: first because of the influence of Mrs Thatcher's presence in the 'aye' lobby might have on others, and second that the arguments put forward to restore the supreme penalty for certain categories of murder, such as terrorism, might prevail.

After speaking at the NCCL meeting, I went to listen to the Commons debate. It was the first time I had heard the new Health Minister, Edwina Currie, speak and was appalled by the crudeness of what she said. I remember the occasion when at a Conservative Party conference she had stood up, waving a pair of handcuffs in the air both to illustrate her belief in the basic and primeval principle of 'an eye for an eye; a tooth for a tooth', and to satisfy her insatiable need for publicity. I stayed to listen to a few more speakers and felt relieved to hear the issue taken out of the emotional plane, made up of the need for revenge and the quest for punishment, into the higher realm of rational argument.

I had been invited to a dinner that evening at the French Embassy, with some MPs among the guests. They were required to go to the vote on the death penalty debate at ten o'clock, so there was time over dinner for my last campaigning. Then at about ten minutes to ten came the incongruous – and to my mind distinctly sick – sight of the elegant figures immaculate in their black ties, white evening shirts and dinner jackets leaving the sophistication of the embassy to immerse themselves with the most fundamental question of all, the decision whether society should be empowered to take the life of one of its members or not. Half an hour later they filed back to resume the life of cigars, liqueurs and chandeliers.

Enough of them had pronounced against restoration to defeat the hanging lobby once again. I was deeply relieved, but got quite a shock the next morning when one of the Irish newspapers came out with the most remarkable headlines: 'Biggs opposes a return to capital punishment'. I had not thought my views deserved such prominence.

As the time went on, I realized how much I needed to find the means of acquiring information about what was actually going on in the life of the country. How, from my position sitting in the House of Lords, could I possibly know what difficulties ordinary families were facing, how young people were affected by social and economic changes, how children coped with their mothers being out at work, and so on? How could I make speeches without accurate and up-to-date information? I realized that I should confine myself to one subject area. I knew that I was most interested in social policies, but they cover a vast field and I was unable at that time to pinpoint one particular issue on which to concentrate. In the end I decided it would be best, as a start, to become involved with all the questions brought to me by voluntary organizations or pressure groups. Then, in time, I might acquire enough knowledge and experience to specialize.

It was this decision which led me – soon after coming to the Lords

– to respond to Mr Maneyfingers's letter. It was about the Bill going through Parliament regarding the patriation from the British to the Canadian Parliament of what in fact represented their 'constitution', namely the British North America Act of 1867. I did not initially realize he had also written to everyone else but felt impelled by his expressed concern for the effect this might have on the indigenous peoples of Canada – Indians and Eskimos – to reply. The issue was an esoteric one and something with which I certainly would not have become involved had I not just made the decision to become well informed on a variety of subjects.

So I wrote back to Mr Maneyfingers and said I would be delighted to meet him. The appointed day arrived and, wishing to go into the Chamber while waiting for him, I asked one of the attendants in the Peers' Lobby to let me know when my visitor arrived. I listened to the debate whilst keeping an eye open for the signal. But, when it came, I was totally unprepared for the manner in which it was given. The attendant duly made his appearance at the Bar of the House and, having caught my eye, he solemnly raised one hand high in the air and waggled all the fingers in a sort of visual representation of my visitor's name. I hurried out to the Lobby and had no trouble in recognizing my guests, for there, sitting on the bench in one corner, was a colourful group.

I sat down with them and Mr Maneyfingers presented the members of the group. It was from then on that things turned awkward because my Indian and Eskimo visitors had taken it for granted that my response to their appeal could only mean I was an expert in consti-tutional and human rights issues. As soon as they discovered my abysmal ignorance – which was almost immediately – and consequen-tial inability to champion their cause, they found it difficult to disguise their disappointment. It was not long before they took their leave – making sure their exit was as conspicuous as their arrival.

Feeling rather deflated I went to the Earl Marshal Room to get on with some work. Trixie Gardner came in and sat down at the desk opposite me. She was the first Australian ever to be given a life peerage. I told her about Mr Maneyfingers. She laughed, 'Better stick to what you know about.' 'But that's the whole point, Trixie.' I interrupted. 'I'm searching for a particular area in which to become involved, but am not sure yet what it should be.' It was easy for her. First she was a dentist, which gave her expertise in medicine;

then she was on the Westminster City Council, so she knew about local government; and finally she was identified as an expert on women's interests. So she was deeply immersed in three subjects. But what could I specialize in? Her only advice was 'Keep clear of constitutional matters. That's for lawyers.'

Trixie was a Conservative and had become one in a strange way. When she and her husband arrived in London from Australia, she wrote to each of the local political parties in their constituency asking them round to explain what they stood for. Only the Conservative answered and visited them. So she became one, although this did not stop her expressing some independent views in debate later on.

Trixie's account of how she became a Conservative had the effect of concentrating my mind yet again on why I was a Socialist. I have already described how my deep-rooted opposition to inequality and poverty played a part in this. But what brought on the inequality and who were the poor? Social change and economic adjustment usually affect the most vulnerable members of society. So for Britain in the 1980s the new 'poor', or the occupants of the 'bottom of the heap', were largely single parent families (from rising divorces), the unemployed (coming from economic recession), and the elderly (people were living longer). These were the people who were falling through the safety net provided by the Welfare State, a set of safeguards which had not been designed to deal with such a vast number of human casualties. It had therefore become necessary to provide alternative provision to satisfy the needs of these groups. This was unlikely to be forthcoming from a government led by Margaret Thatcher, who had moved so decisively towards the establishment of a more polarized society on the American lines. So the rescue operation to prop up the new poor would have to come from the voluntary and charitable agencies. Indeed, the pioneers of the Welfare State had themselves argued that the State should do that which the State alone could do, namely ensure an appropriate allocation of financial resources; and having done that it should leave as much as possible to the initiative and enterprise of individual citizens, many of whom are able and willing to serve the public.

I decided that instead of wasting the time of Mr Maneyfingers and others, I must take part in representing the interests of this large constituency, the 'new poor'. And the group within that constituency with whom I most closely identified were the single parent families.

Although I had been fortunate to escape the financial hardships endured by so many lone mothers, I knew the difficulties of bringing up children alone and the emotional stress of combining the roles of mother and father. Furthermore, there would be nothing new about such an involvement, for members of the House of Lords, deprived of real constituents, often take up the causes of affinity groups reflecting their own personal experiences or circumstances. Indeed, having heard Lord Teviot, a Conservative, speak with authority on the Transport Bill, I discovered that he had once been a bus driver. And the reason the Countess of Mar had immersed herself into the debate over the Telecommunication Bill was because she had earlier worked as a postwoman in the Highlands of Scotland. Lady Sharples had not long acquired a public house in the West Country before she was on her feet influencing Government policies on the licensing laws. Lord Kagan, with courage, spoke of conditions in prison and the importance of the rehabilitation of prisoners; and he spoke from personal experience of being in prison. Then there is the group of six peers who are affectionately known as the wheelchair brigade. Physically disabled for varying reasons, they manoeuvre their compact electric chairs at high speed along the corridors, into the lobbies, chamber, bars, etc. – woe betide anyone who gets in their way – and represent the interests of the country's disabled with efficiency and passion.

With such an impressive list of precedents it seemed in order for me to use the platform provided by the House of Lords to speak on behalf of my own affinity group of single parents. I immediately made contact with the relevant voluntary organizations – notably the National Council for One-Parent Families and Gingerbread – to set up a working relationship with them. This was my first major involvement in what has generally become known as 'alternative Britain'.

CHAPTER FIVE

Finding a 'Constituency'

KATE AND I WERE listening to the car radio on our way to a performance of *Macbeth* at Stratford-on-Avon. The date was 3 April 1982, and both Houses of Parliament were debating the Falklands crisis following the Argentinian invasion of the islands. As we drove along, I listened with mounting amazement to the note of bellicosity and wounded national pride in the majority of speakers. I could hardly believe the emotive language used: 'The Government must now prove by deeds ... to ensure that foul and brutal aggression does not succeed in our world ...' Another speaker went even further: '... the very thought that our people, 1,800 people of British blood and bone, could be left in the hands of such criminals is enough to make any normal Englishman's blood boil – and the blood of Scotsmen and Welshmen boil too ...'

At lunch time, Kate and I stopped for a picnic down a grassy lane just beyond Oxford, but the voices from the Commons carried on relentlessly. Just before two o'clock the Secretary of State for Defence wound up: '... From next Monday, the Royal Navy will put to sea in wartime order and with wartime stock and weapons. That force will include the carriers HMS *Invincible* and HMS *Hermes*, the assault ship HMS *Fearless* and a number of destroyers and frigates armed with anti-surface and anti-air missiles together with afloat support. A strong force of Royal Marine commandos and a large number of Sea Harriers and anti-submarine and troop-carrying helicopters will also be embarked ...' The Foreign Secretary, Lord Carrington, had ended his speech in the Lords: 'I know the House will join with me in making clear to all concerned our resolve to uphold the wishes of the islanders in the face of Argentina's cynical disregard of them. The Falkland Islands are British. The Falkland Islanders wish to be British. Our duty is clear.' The end of our sandwiches coincided with Britain being at war. I was dumbfounded. The very size of the decision taken by the Government – with all-party support in Parliament –

was too much to absorb all at once.

I should have been taking part in the debate myself but, as was happening more and more often, my parliamentary and maternal obligations had clashed, with the decision being taken to go to Stratford-on-Avon with Kate and her school friend, as planned. But listening to the outraged male voices from Westminster, I wondered if I would have found the courage to voice doubts in such a welter of certitude. Even under normal circumstances I am reticent about discussing military and defence matters, as, with an overwhelming repugnance for violence and conflict, I tend to speak from my emotions instead of using objective arguments. I realize that God – for his own purposes – succeeds in reconciling the need for both war and peace, but my own bias is so heavily weighted on the side of negotiation, compromise and conciliation that I cannot achieve his balance. (Indeed had I not quoted from the 9th century Indian poet, Panchatantra, for the inscription on Christopher's memorial tablet: 'Not by a radiant jewel, not by the sun nor by fire, but by conciliation alone is dispelled the darkness born of enmity'.)

So driving through the lovely, peaceful countryside, I feared I might have funked speaking out against the military option in favour of continued negotiation and diplomatic pressure. I recognized that any practical arguments based on the technical difficulties, the risk to life, the expenditure of funds so badly needed for home policies, the eventual failure to find a long-term political solution, etc., would have borne no weight against those arguing from wounded national pride. Moreover, I realized dissenters would be regarded as traitors once the task force had sailed and the lives of our servicemen put at risk. Yet it was a long time before I ceased to regret my cowardice in failing to speak up against the futility of war. Fenner Brockway characteristically pressed for further negotiation and the search for peaceful solution through the UN, and his speech in the Lords was powerful. '... I suggest that today the greatest need is to secure maximum democratic support in the world for our point of view. There are three spheres in which we can act for that purpose. The first is the United Nations Security Council.... I want to suggest that we should place the whole emphasis on the right of the people of the Falklands to self-determination; that we are not concerned in maintaining the old political imperialist authority of the past; that we should be quite ready to leave the Falklands tomorrow, if that were the desire of the people themselves. I am quite sure that, if that point is emphasized in the Security Council of the United Nations – self-determination, not the retention of colonial power – we can win the support of the Third World nations for that point of view.... I should like to suggest that Her Majesty's Government might propose to President Reagan ... that he should use his influence among American nations to press upon the Argentine to withdraw their troops. I believe that, if that were done, great influence could be exerted upon the other American nations.... We want to make it abundantly clear that we are there because it is the desire of the people of the Falklands, and I suggest to Her Majesty's Government that we would be prepared to take that issue to the Hague tribunal.... I believe that in this issue we are right. What we have to do is to convince the world that we are right, and I believe that the three proposals I have made will assist in that purpose.'

The Foreign Office came in for a lot of flak for – allegedly – allowing the situation to erupt through failure to give due warning. This accusation was manifestly unjust. In reality the Foreign Office, wishing to get rid of a potentially explosive situation, had been for years pressing the politicians to come to a decision. But when the Foreign Office Minister proposed a solution to Parliament, the advice was rejected by both sides of the House of Commons out of chauvinism and a sense of nationalism.

After it was all over, the Archbishop of Canterbury, at the memorial service to the dead, voiced the feeling of so many when he said, 'War is man's greatest failure.'

During those early months of 1982 I realized that, although I had made a reasonable start and had spoken in a number of debates, I had not yet taken part in the passage of a bill right from the start to the end. In fact I had not even made the move from the ranks of the Innocents to those of Apprentices. So I was pleased when Pat Llewelyn-Davies, Labour Chief Whip, came up to me one day as I was working at my usual desk in the Earl Marshal Room (I was acquiring the reputation of being a dreadful swot).

'I wanted to ask you something, Jane,' she said. 'We have a lot of bills coming up this session and I wondered whether you would like to join the working group for one of them and help pilot it through all its stages.'

We discussed the different possibilities and decided that I should participate in the Local Government (Miscellaneous Provisions) Bill. This was legislation to give local authorities extended rights of control. Our front bench spokesperson was Lady Birk, a good-looking and elegant figure who had served as an Environmental Minister in the previous Labour Government, and was to be supported by a group of backbenchers. Once appointed, the members of the working group held regular meetings to be briefed by advisers from the interested organizations such as the Associations of County Councils or Metropolitan Authorities. Where there were changes they wanted making to the Bill, they suggested amendments to be moved at committee stage.

The first reading of a bill is a formality and involves no discussion. The Government Chief Whip from the despatch box declared, 'I beg to move that the Local Government (Miscellaneous Provisions) Bill be now read a First Time'. The Question was then put by the Lord Chancellor: 'That this Bill be now read a First Time'. The second reading, which takes place in not less than fourteen days, gives the Minister the opportunity to explain the Bill and there follows a wide-ranging debate on its content and principles.

At our group's first meeting, held in one of the small stuffy interview rooms on the principal floor, well in advance of the second reading, we discussed the Bill's provisions and each made ourselves responsible for certain issues. It was rather like an auction: 'All right, I'll take on pop festivals and sex shops,' one said, with someone else bidding, 'And I'll do graffiti and fast food shops.' This meant that each of us would be putting forward the case for local authorities to be given powers to control these practices within their area. Many of the problems, arising from changing social trends, had only recently come into being, and the purpose of the Bill was to bring the previous Act up to date by giving local authorities revised powers to control them. For example, one intention was to allow local authorities to initiate health safeguards, and another was to protect local communities from annoyance. The advent of fast-food shops was after all comparatively recent and new restrictions regarding closing hours and the proliferation of litter had become necessary. Moreover, the emergence of sex shops had scandalized local communities, particularly if one made a sudden appearance right next to a church or school.

I started work on my second reading speech and decided to concentrate on four subjects. First, the safety aspect of self-operated laundrettes. Second, the whole question of pop festivals and how to prevent them causing nuisance to local communities. Third, regulations necessary to control the establishment of sex shops and, lastly, powers enabling local authorities to prevent spray painting on public buildings.

I started my research, and decided one way of becoming informed was through personal inspection. I visited our local laundrette. I knew it well as, before buying a washing machine, I had been a regular customer. 'Have you had any accidents here involving children using your washing machines?' I asked the manageress.

'Not since I've been here, dear,' she said.

'But have you heard of any incidents of children catching an arm in the blow dryers or being injured in some way or other?'

She said, yes, she had heard of a few but thought accidents could only occur through lack of supervision or through the machines being defective. She warmed to the subject when I told her the reason for my questions and we went on to have a long, animated discussion.

I then turned my mind to graffiti and decided to investigate the streets of London. I walked round Chelsea with my eyes pointed upwards and for the first time noticed unsightly bill posting and graffiti applied with spray guns. Some of it was racist and highly offensive. However, my resolve to urge for restrictions weakened when I fell upon a very appealing slogan sprayed onto a wall somewhere off the King's Road. Obviously the work of a disillusioned damsel, it read, 'You have to kiss a hell of a lot of frogs before you find your prince'.

My speech was well on its way, but I had still not gone into the whole murky world of sex shops. Nor did I quite know how to set about it. Then I remembered recently passing a rather mysterious shop front with heavily curtained windows on my way with the children to the swimming pool at the refined Hurlingham Club. It was called Josephine, printed in large letters over the door. Although there was no sign whatsoever of what its wares might be, I somehow sensed it was a sex shop.

So one day when my courage was high I set off, scarf tied round my head, feeling and looking ludicrously middle-aged and middle-classed. I parked my car at a discreet distance and cautiously entered

Josephine's. The smallish, badly lit room was empty except for the man in charge. He was completely absorbed watching a football match from a very small television set perched on the counter. I peered round the walls at the glass-fronted show cupboards containing sets of skimpy underwear, some pornographic books and a weird-looking implement or two. On a door leading to an inner room a sign read, 'Video – 50p'. It all looked low key and sort of pathetic. I wondered from whence the huge profits, about which we had heard, could come. Then, just as I was thinking I might slide out unobtrusively, the man at the counter dragged his attention from the television and turned to me and asked, 'Can I help you?' The question panicked me. What could I say I wanted? After a moment's hesitation, looking and feeling ridiculous, I blurted out, 'Well, I was really just wondering how business was?'

'Like most places, I suppose,' said the astonished man. 'Good on some days, not so good on others.'

Feeling I really must pull myself together, I said, more coherently, 'The real reason for my coming is because there is a Bill going through Parliament about...' I searched for the right word to describe his trade politely... 'establishments such as yours.' I'm speaking in the debate and wanted to find out more about what goes on. Could you tell me a bit about it?'

Looking much more interested, he turned the television off and started talking. After listening for a bit, I interrupted, glancing at the 50p sign on the door opposite. 'But I've heard that fortunes are sometimes made – where do your profits come from?'

He was outraged. 'You must be meaning them clip joints up in Soho. We're not like that. We're perfectly straight dealers and provide for local needs. After all, there are quite a lot of people who want to try to make their marriages go better and they find a bit of help here.'

'But who are the ones who actually come here?' I asked. The room was still empty.

'Well, there's the elderly gentleman who drops in every day at about 5 o'clock just before we close. And then...' he had just noticed my silk scarf and unequivocally conventional look '... then the other day there was a lady on her way back from Ascot races. She dropped in here to do a bit of shopping; she was wearing a big hat and looked very smart.'

The day of the second reading debate came round. My speech was ready. As I sat listening to the first speaker, any idea I might have had that only a few would concentrate on sex shops was dissipated. Some of them – speaking at length – seemed almost to savour the subject. However, their points were not the same as those I had planned to make as a result of my visit to Josephine's. They spoke in general terms of the break-down in moral values. Some deplored how sex shops had opened in small towns and villages, provoking justifiable local indignation.

Lady Saltoun, a crossbench peeress in her own right, rose to her feet. In her speech she correctly pointed out the degradation imposed on women by sex shops. Peers listened approvingly.

My turn came. I set off at the high speed my nervousness so often prescribed. Soon I managed to rein myself in. At the start, when I was describing my visit to the laundrette, I received admiring looks and there were murmurs of 'Hear, hear' from various parts of the House. Obviously this was considered a suitably feminine subject, appropriate for the attention of a baroness. I then moved on to pop festivals. Here I spoke with less authority as most of what I said came second-hand from what my son Robin – a keen participator – had told me. However, the principle I advocated of accepting such manifestations of modern youth culture whilst protecting people from annoyance was certainly listened to. I followed this with a brief commentary on the disfiguring and distasteful aspect of racial slogans being daubed on the walls of public buildings, but funked telling the joke about having to kiss a hell of a lot of frogs in case they missed the point and didn't laugh.

Finally I got to the bit of my speech about sex shops and my visit to Josephine's. This definitely provoked a different reaction. Heads which had been nodding in either mild approval or gentle somnolence suddenly jerked upright, eyes swivelled round to me with a look of disapproval. 'I suppose that, as this is such a highly moral issue, we should perhaps ask ourselves why we dislike sex shops so much; why do they appear so offensive to us and why do they instil in so many of us a sense of outrage and disgust? I expect that we would all answer that question slightly differently. For my part, I judge them from the following viewpoints: first, I do not like the way they look; secondly, I am totally opposed to the fact that fortunes are made out of a trade concerning the degradation of women; thirdly,

I abhor the fact that the sensitivities of so many are being hurt by the presence of such shops in their localities; and fourthly, I am appalled when I think of the coarsening and brutalizing effect the exhibition of the kind of wares they trade must have on young people who no doubt frequent them. After all, a twelve-year-old can easily be taken for eighteen nowadays, and I should think that quite a few children pass undetected through these shops not least because they are curious.

'I suppose that if my first requirement were met and sex shops could be transformed from sleazy, down-at-heel premises filled with shifty, unhappy-looking people, into highly decorative and brightly painted places full of open-faced, laughing people, then my further objections might slightly diminish. But I am afraid we cannot necessarily count on that happening, so for those of us who find it difficult to wish to ban any institution for which there appears to be a place in society, all we can do is try to see that this Bill contains the necessary provisions to diminish the ill-effects that such institutions can have on the rest of the community.'

I feared I might have forfeited the respected place I had so far held in Their Lordships' estimation. The lack of any 'Hear, hear' brought it home to me that as far as my noble colleagues saw things, a sex shop was definitely not the place for a baroness.

Once the second reading debate was over and the content and underlying principles of the Bill thoroughly explored, then came the committee stage. Several days had been set aside for this and, unlike the Commons where Standing Committees are usually set up to consider amendments, the Lords conduct their committee stages on the floor of the Chamber with the participation of any peers wishing to do so. Our Labour working group headed by Alma Birk met regularly with specialists to advise on the amendments they thought necessary.

At the committee stage the detailed scrutiny of a bill is undertaken, and this provokes animated and interesting discussion. The major function of the Lords is after all as a revising chamber and this is certainly reflected by the knowledgeable and specialized interventions made during committee. Amendments, which have been tabled during the preceding days, are therefore the subject of a mini-debate. First the mover explains the objective of the amendment. For example, when introducing mine about spray gunning, I said, 'I beg to move

Amendment No. 110A. The purpose of this amendment is to provide that the control by local authorities of fly posting should be extended to include spray painting of slogans and expressions on walls and buildings... the two forms of defacement go together. If fly posting is found offensive then so, surely, must be the scrawling on walls of slogans – often of a racist nature....' Several other speakers intervened and the Minister then responded. He gave reasons for rejecting my amendment and it was then for me to decide whether to divide the House on the issue or not. I decided against bringing such a relatively minor question to the vote and withdrew the amendment, whereupon the committee moved on to discuss the next one.

At report stage, about ten days later, the House receives the Bill as reported out of committee and has a further chance to consider amendments. Finally, third reading is for the passing of a bill and a brief debate, although, unlike the Commons, it may also contain amendments.

The bill is then sent to the Commons where, if unamended, it will be presented for Royal Assent. If however amendments have been made by the Lords, the Commons consider them and either accept them or reject them. Agreement between the two Houses is usually achieved, but if the Lords insist on retaining an amendment which has been rejected in the Commons, then the Bill cannot go onto the statute book during that parliamentary session.

Involvement in this Bill not only made me better informed and brought me new-found confidence, but also had the effect of opening up new areas of interest for me. In tennis terms I moved from the tramlines of the legislative process to the centre of the court. I no longer felt obliged to restrict myself to speaking on familiar subjects, like the EEC and Northern Ireland, but could allow genuine personal interests to intervene. For instance, I was, for obvious reasons, absorbed by family issues. I felt keenly about injustices to women. Having never myself suffered from sex discrimination I had not become a feminist in the true sense of the word, yet as time went on I realized more and more that we live in a man's world and that if a woman is lucky enough to achieve a place in a decision-making body, she should make full use of it to represent women's interests whenever and wherever necessary. I was also fascinated by policies relating to children and young people. Reminded daily of their existence as I watched my own family growing up around me, I became more and more concerned about how outside factors such as unemployment, family breakdown and so on were affecting our young.

It was this which spurred me on to my next initiative. On 12 May 1982 – still under a year since I joined – I introduced my own debate. I should explain that it is the custom in the Upper House to spend Wednesday afternoons debating subjects of general concern. Being a non-elected body we are disqualified from debating financial matters, so we have more time. To make use of this, each of the parties chooses a subject for discussion and these are then taken in turn on consecutive Wednesday afternoons. Usually the subjects chosen provide scope for a five hour debate, with thirty or forty speakers taking part. But, on other occasions, two subjects of less wide ranging nature are chosen and only two and a half hours are given to each.

This time I had brought up the theme for the second debate of the afternoon, and this was accepted as one of the Party's official debates. The motion was: 'To call attention to the difficulties currently encountered by those responsible for the upbringing and care of children at home, at school and at leisure.' I hoped the contribution from peers – many very experienced in children's issues – might point to ways of dealing with some of the problems. I had put a lot of reasearch into my speech. The panic brought on at the start by not having enough material usually means one ends up swamped under it and agonizing over what to choose. Luckily my major adviser was Brian Jackson, who had championed the interests of children for a long time. Director of the National Educational Research and Development Trust in Cambridge and son-in-law of my friend and political mentor Tilli Edelman, Brian had campaigned long and hard for the appointment of a Minister for Children as be believed this to be the only way for policies concerning children to be better co-ordinated.

We met for lunch and I outlined the aims of 'my' debate. It was not long before his ideas were flowing. 'I think you should start,' he said, 'by stressing the point that at present the child is never seen as a whole. It is chopped up into a whole lot of small pieces and each piece is looked after and dealt with by a different Ministry, department, agency or whatever. Children represent one quarter of society, but as they have no vote no one is directly accountable to them. And what's more, I have never felt that the British are particularly good to our children. There are so many pointers; the upper classes send their children away to boarding school at the age of seven; we were until very recently the only country in Western Europe that allowed corporal punishment in schools; we don't let children into restaurants except on sufferance, and so on.' I agreed with him. Why *are* we so hard on our children?

It is only by talking things through that my ideas develop and take on significance: the stimulation brought on by exchange and discussion is essential. It was the same then, and Brian and I soon worked out how I could best describe the situation of a child against the three backgrounds of home, school and leisure, and outline the pressures which modern-day circumstances impose on each. Taking the home first, I would show how many children were feeling the adverse effects of their fathers being out of work with little money coming in, and then describe how the home lives of others were undermined by the break-up of their parents' marriages and all the emotional upset that went with it; finally, I would point to the funda- mental deprivation provided by cramped, damp and inadequate hous- ing. Moving on to the other two great areas of experience in a child's life, the world of school and the facilities provided for leisure, I would describe the children's feeling of imprisonment within the present examination system, coupled with the scepticism over whether the teaching or the pressure of exams would gain them a job at the end of it all. And finally what did the child gain from his leisure time, and were the facilities for recreation geared to the increasing demands resulting from the lack of jobs? The conclusion which flowed from weighing up the elements embracing a child's life was that the most undermined was the home, the family unit, bearing as it does the brunt of so many of the social changes through which we live. There- fore, with one area under pressure, the other two should take up the strain, with the child's school on the one hand and the community and youth services on the other taking up some of the burden weighing on the family unit.

As we stood outside the restaurant after our lunch, Brian made some final, hurried suggestions. Why not include a few of his pet theories at the end of my speech as recommendations to the Govern- ment? There was a long list of them, including pleas to switch resources behind poor children to 'smash the cycle of deprivation', to reappraise the British education system, to seek new ways of dealing with young offenders, to give additional support to single parent families, and finally to think again of the infrastructure and machinery for dealing with all these problems.

Tilli and Kevin came to listen to the debate. I rose at 5.21 and launched into the carefully prepared text all of which was written down, but scarcely legible as I had made so many hand-written alterations. This was what produced the crisis. I felt I had gained the attention of the House for the main part of it, but unfortunately just as I was approaching the end I turned two pages of the notes together, lost my place and my confidence. After a few seconds – seeming like several hours – scrabbling among the sheets of paper I gave up and recited from memory the final recommendations worked out on the pavement after lunch with Brian. I could sense Kevin bracing himself during those agonising seconds. I spoke for seventeen minutes – my longest so far.

Lord Beaumont, fluent and serious, followed from the Liberal benches and then came four or five other speakers, including one of the bishops giving his maiden speech. Baroness David, who is really beautiful and our education spokesperson, wound up for the opposition with the Government Minister doing the same from the other despatch box. As I had moved the motion, I had the right of the last word, but, as these short debates are restricted to two and a half hours exactly, there was only one minute left. Quite relieved that this was the case, I merely thanked all the speakers for making such valuable contributions and touched very briefly on what they had said. Then, just as I was about to sit down, the thought of Kate and her homework flashed into my mind and made me end on a more personal note than I had intended. 'My Lords, in the course of this debate there have been several references to the latchkey child. This is a keen reminder to me that it is nearly four hours since my own child let herself into an empty house, so I shall now beg leave to withdraw the motion.'

'Well done, it was a marvellous speech,' Tilli said kindly to me as I joined them in the Peers' Lobby. 'Did you see the Bishop of London smiling when you said that bit about Kate being a latchkey child?'

An opportunity came for me to use the platform of the Lords to represent women's interests, or rather the interests of a certain group of women, when the Matrimonial and Family Proceedings Bill passed through the House towards the end of 1983. Among other things, it brought together my previous diplomatic life with my present political existence. One of the provisions of the Bill was about maintenance. Its aim – putting it bluntly – was to eliminate the species of women known popularly as 'alimony drones'. This was a label given by the tabloids to women without dependent children who refused to work and instead subsisted on the meal ticket for life provided by their divorced husbands. There had been one or two highly publicized cases of women living luxuriously with their new boyfriends on maintenance money, whilst their impoverished ex-husbands survived in garrets with their second wives on bread and water.

I took part in this debate after an approach made to me by Jane Reid, chairman of the Diplomatic Service Wives Association, which could be described as a rather genteel trade union trying to improve conditions for Foreign Office families by lobbying, for example, for increases in the number of holiday fares for school children to join their parents posted abroad, and so on.

Jane Reid and other DSWA members came to see me in the House to discuss the Bill over tea. (Tea is much appreciated there; mainly because of its remarkable toasted tea cakes. These are positively saturated with melted butter – liable, I would have thought, to fur up many a noble artery.) The women explained to me the great injustice suffered by Diplomatic Service wives after divorce, for not only do they lose out more than home-based wives from being cut off from the job market when abroad and therefore less able to keep up their abilities or expertise, but on top of that they receive no part of the occupational pensions their ex-husbands receive on retirement. And this was particulary unfair in view of the many years they would have spent helping their husbands to earn it.

Jane went on to explain their fears about the clause relating to maintenance. It was ridiculous, they said, to think that women emerge from marriage on an equal footing to their husbands. For so many of them, reasonable career prospects have been sacrificed because of responsibilities towards their children. And then there were the additional setbacks to their long-term career prospects because of helping and supporting their husbands in building up their careers. How well I remembered that while all was going well it seemed the most normal thing for a diplomat and his wife to consider it a joint career, involving both their efforts. But with either divorce or widowhood, then the position of a diplomatic wife would be more seriously affected than any other profession. If divorced, she suffered the additional injustice of missing out on her former husband's pension, which on remarriage went entirely to him and his second wife.

An amendment tabled at report stage provided a perfect opportunity to present their case. By that time I had discovered that in the USA special arrangements were made to remove the injustices to American Diplomatic wives, and this example strengthened my argument.

There was support from other speakers and Lord Hailsham, the Lord Chancellor, also expressed sympathy. But what pleased me a lot was to read the next edition of the DSWA magazine, in which Jane Reid had quoted from my speech.

Soon after this Jane rang me up and said, 'We are wondering if you would like to do something else with us?' Every year the DSWA gives a tea party at the Norman Shaw building opposite Westminster Pier and lots of Foreign Office wives, both past and present, go to it. They enjoy just seeing each other and having a gossip. Jane said they wanted to include a speaker and my name had been suggested.

I still have the rough notes I made for that talk and they remind me how anxious I was about it. 'I've never ever seen you in such a state about a talk,' Kevin had said, 'but surely it should be relatively easy. You'll be speaking to the kind of people you know. After all you were one of them yourself once.'

'That's the whole trouble,' I said miserably. 'It gives me a split personality. So much of me feels as if I still am one of them. But the unequivocal proof that I'm not will come from the fact that I'll be standing up there in front of them giving a speech.' It wasn't only that, though. I wanted my talk to be the best I had ever made. Putting myself into their shoes, I could well imagine how they would be more critical of what I said than if I had been a total stranger.

In the end it was alright. I just told them the story of what had happened to me since being one of them. I described the crises brought on by sudden death, and the struggle to carry on from day to day. And then I told them how little by little a new life developed. While they had continued being the wives of diplomats, I told them, one of the things I had been doing was to go round the country giving a highly popular talk entitled: 'The wife of a diplomat'. And I ended by telling them a bit about what went on in the House of Lords. They listened intently. It was if they wanted to stay close to me through all the stages I described. At the end they smiled, applauded and gathered round me. And then suddenly, the division between us melted away. Yes, I remained one of them – I always would – but at the same time I had become an independent person with a profession of my own. My unhappiness at feeling excluded from their magic circle disappeared.

One Friday morning, when, as usual, Liz Travis and I were working in my miniscule office at home, I opened a letter with a Belgian stamp. It was from somewhere called the Management Centre Europe in Brussels and invited me to chair a three-day Women in Business conference in London in May. 'I don't think I could possibly give up that amount of time,' was my reaction. 'Perhaps we had better write back saying no.'

I handed the letter to Liz, who read it more carefully. 'I don't see why you should give them your time for nothing. After all, it's a commercial enterprise, not a charitable organization.'

'But they haven't offered a fee,' I said rather pathetically; proving beyond a doubt that I come from the generation and family background that doesn't know how to talk about money and finds the whole subject embarrassing.

'We could ask for one,' Liz said firmly. 'I'll get on to them and see what can be done.'

'But I still wonder why they want me. I know I've made a few speeches in the Lords about women's interests but I can hardly be considered a leading member of the Women's Movement.'

'You have spoken at several events lately, though. There was the Women in Management conference in Manchester. Some of the women came – do you remember? – to find a "role model" and you didn't know what that meant.' Thinking back, I remembered being saddened that there should be women with so little confidence that they feel obliged to emulate the behaviour and style of another woman rather than develop one of their own.

'And then there was the Women of our Time luncheon at the Mansion House,' Liz went on. 'And the Nancy Astor annual event given by the 300 Group'. You do seem to have been very involved with women's groups lately – I suppose that's why they have asked you.' I remembered how high-powered the women attending these events had been and the coincidence that both times my co-speaker had been Jeffrey Archer. Each time he had told the same story about his mother, not realizing, I suppose, that the same women tend to congregate at such events. The story, told in the accent of the region from which the Archer family come, was meant to be to the glorification of women. It described how his mother, having taken her O-levels in her seventies, then moved on to do her A-levels, and the story came to a climax with a vivid rendering of Mrs Archer giving her son the news that she planned to go to university. Even at the first time of telling it was received rather sombrely by the high-powered audience.

Finally the matter of the Brussels invitation was satisfactorily resolved. Liz did a magnificent job persuading the organizers of the Management Centre that I was worth paying, and I found myself immersed in a different side of feminism.

The conference was held at the Portman Hotel near Baker Street and was highly luxurious. I arrived in good time on the first morning and took my place on the platform, rather intimidated by the long lines of women sitting in the auditorium below. I felt cut off from them both by the distance and the difference between us. They were the professionals, and I the amateur. I realized from the list of participants that they came from many different countries but yet I felt there was a common thread uniting them.

The clock told me it was time to start the conference off. I didn't much like rising to my feet; but then I never do. There is the moment of truth for every speaker when he or she has no choice but to stand up, leaving everyone else seated. Once upright, with the words flowing, everything becomes easier. My opening remarks reflected (and still do) my view of a woman's position in our present-day society; how, whilst they benefit from the movement forward, they are faced with new problems arising out of that progress. I went on to say that the conference would focus on the changing role of women in a changing corporate environment. How they should best challenge old assumptions without upsetting the traditional corporate culture and how careers for women in industry could best be promoted in the prevailing economic climate. I continued with a theme I have often presented in which I believe entirely, namely that it is impossible to view the circumstances surrounding men and women separately; they have to be seen together. When considering the choices facing women, it is essential at the same time to look at the choices confronting men. Slavish adherence to the old concept of the stereotype woman and the stereotype man narrow the choices for both, I went on to say. It had become ludicrous to think that in bygone years many men were expected and impelled to spend all their time out of the home, returning in the evening too tired to enjoy their home or children, whilst, at the same time married women were not allowed to make a contribution to the life of the community wider than the one they had traditionally made from within the home.

I stressed how wrong it was to assume that, while a man's position and role in society were more or less inflexible, the woman must adjust their role according to what society requires of her. In Victorian times, society's view was that she was needed in the home and expected to bear large numbers of children and to run the house. During the two world wars, women were brought back into the labour force to swell numbers in the munition factories. It not only suddenly became possible to provide nurseries, but it also became the acceptable theory that young children benefited from long periods spent apart from their mothers. The present day has seen the position once again reversed, with the moral argument being put forward that the cohesion of the family depends on the woman's presence at home.

I ended by making the point that the major difference affecting modern-day men and women in management fields is the extra burden carried by women if they are parents. Still considered as the partner dominantly responsible for the upbringing of children and housekeeping, she is faced with a dual role. And the proof that women more than men are forced to choose between marriage and a career comes from statistics which show that far fewer professional women than men are married. These statistics also show that married women managers are more than twice as likely to be divorced or separated. This seems to prove that the burden of carrying the dual role is too heavy and that there should be a redistribution of responsibilities between partners. I suggested that the two major barriers faced by female members of the Institute of Directors came from male prejudice and not being part of the 'old boy network', and that myths still persist that women are not 'management material'. This is part of the Catch 22 problem, wherein women are found to be either 'too feminine' and therefore not really managers, or 'non-conformist' and therefore not really women.

The delegates gave my speech a cautious welcome and then the conference started in earnest. Over the next three days we listened to fifteen speakers. They spoke on a variety of subjects with intriguing titles such as: 'Powerbase – how to build it, how to keep it', 'The Promotable Woman', 'How to manage your boss', 'The male model of management with its strengths and weaknesses', 'What does success mean to you?', 'New skills for tomorrow's leaders', and so on.

At the end I knew more about the problems of women in management and the solutions offered than I could ever have imagined possible. However, it was not quite the end, for a few weeks later I received the report on the conference. This was presented both in terms of what had been said and the benefit to the delegates: a clear assessment of the value of the conference. I was most pleased that the letter of thanks included an evaluation of the chairwoman. This was the first time since I left school that an assessment had been made of my performance. 'Your rating was the highest ever received by a Chairman in MCE history: 16.04 out of a possible 20!'

Some months later I met a woman who – unlike those attending the conference – had worked out exactly how to draw the maximum benefit from being both a 'traditional' and a 'professional' woman. As a highpowered TV executive, she drew a huge salary but did not have a bank account; married with three children but could not drive; her husband collected her from work each day by car and, her pockets full of banknotes, she was borne home to kiss goodnight her children neatly tucked up by the au pair. She had certainly achieved the best of both worlds.

I love speaking to women's groups. There is something exhilarating about their enthusiasm, as if when women are doing their thing together it brings on a resolve as well as an inner release. It felt like that when I went to the Business & Professional Women's Club in Llandudno for their International Night. The long train journey, getting on for five hours, at least gave me an opportunity to make some notes for my speech. I was met by the husband of one of the members, who took me to the hotel where the dinner was being held and where I had taken a room for the night. He didn't sound at all Welsh, and Llandudno looked different from what I had expected: it was more like a gracious Victorian resort than a typical Welsh town.

The order of events is always more or less the same on such occassions. First, the photographs and the glasses of sherry – but the glasses have to be put down while the photograph is taken. Invariably the picture shows me a head taller than the rest with the eager, smiling faces gazing intently at the camera. Then the receiving line, at which point I always regret that my appearance does not live up to theirs. The long queue of ladies files past, each shaking hands and wishing the President a happy evening. When they take my hand they look a bit nervous. I assume this is due to an unusual reverence for the Upper House, but they should see us typing our own letters and licking stamps. After the handshaking, we file into the dining-room – the President in the lead – to the accompaniment of slow hand-clapping. We stand for grace before the meal. I often notice the waitresses, who are usually very young, perhaps brought in specially for the occasion; the hand offering the fish sometimes shakes and I always want to offer comfort, but do not know how.

The conversation at dinner is absorbing. Local matters are discussed, and the Methodist minister presents views which are practical, constructive and caring. The Methodists always seem to me to represent the socialist element of the formal church. The President at Llandudno comes from Yorkshire but is married to a Welshman; 'He's not here this evening – hurt his knee. But he doesn't like parties, anyway.' She is full of enthusiasm and energy, and enjoying every minute.

The speeches start – each one with the elaborate preamble, 'Madam President, Mr Mayor, Lady Ewart-Briggs' (that offending 'r' so often creeps in), 'Honoured Guests, Ladies and Gentlemen'. The script of their speeches is written on white cards. This time the Mayor hadn't written his down. It was about preserving the architectural heritage of the town and rang very true. The President's speech was about peace, and how the Business and Professional Women's Club could contribute towards this.

I had not been able to finish my pudding – for which I am not usually forgiven – and after that the dinner breaks for fifteen minutes. I go to my hotel room to rethink what I had planned to say. I have always found it difficult to know what to say until I get the feel of my audience. There have been times when I have kept queues waiting in the ladies' cloakroom while I re-write part of my speech in one of the cubicles. I had, on this occasion, been asked to speak about the House of Lords and, having given the talk quite often,

I knew at least what jokes would make them laugh. Finally, the evening came to an end with a lot of the laughter and *bonhomie* that adds so much to my enjoyment of visiting these women's groups – although I confess another factor is that they always make me feel some kind of a star.

CHAPTER SIX

Home Affairs

HOME AFFAIRS SOUNDS so benign and cosy, in direct contradiction to some of the subjects such as guns, gambling, prisons which are covered by this Department. So often in other countries the title 'Minister of the Interior' has a sinister ring, in contrast to his British opposite number, the Home Secretary.

Lord Elwyn-Jones, former Labour Lord Chancellor, and Lord Mishcon, one of Britain's leading solicitors, head our Home and Legal Affairs group in the House of Lords. One day they intercepted me in the Peers' Lobby to ask me to join their team and speak from the front bench.

'But I don't know much about legal affairs,' I said nervously.

Smiling, Elwyn said, 'I suppose that between us Victor and I probably know enough. But you always inject genuine concern into your speeches, and we feel you would handle some Home Affairs debates very well from the front bench.'

The first time I spoke from the despatch box was on 30 November, 1983. I was petrified and opened my speech by saying as much. However, the bill was an interesting one in which to make one's debut. A Private Members' Bill moved by Lord Campbell of Alloway, it was about amusement machines. He had brought the matter before the House because there was no effective system of licensing and controlling the use of fruit machines. He described the situation in his opening speech. 'The concern is two-fold. First it is concern for those under the age of sixteen, who stand like zombies before these new-found gods. Some of them are tempted to petty crime and others to casual sex to find the ready cash with which to feed their addiction... The second aspect is concern for the community which in this regard is truly ill-served because planning law is only about change of use. Already the Minister, on appeal, has overturned some thirty cases where the local authority has refused planning permission for amusement arcades. Indeed there is one applicant who has won appeals in respect of all amusement centres in London against strong local opposition. In several cases there was already an amusement arcade in the same street which had already been a source of trouble... I conclude by saying that if this measure of concern should be shared by Your Lordships tonight either as regards the protection of the interests of the young or the protection of the interest of the community... then surely if only as a matter of principle the Bill is worthy of further consideration in Your Lordships House.'

To prepare for this debate, Kevin and I had visited some amusement arcades a few days before. The one in Brixton seemed calm enough. There was no rowdiness but we noticed quite a number of children obviously under sixteen. They were totally absorbed, playing the machines with skill and practice. It was evident that, given enough time, these young players could get through an enormous amount of money. 'But look at the women,' Kevin whispered to me, 'it's like a drug to them. They're hooked. There goes all the housekeeping money.'

A telephone call to Gamblers Anonymous brought me some astounding information: one out of five of its members are aged between twelve and sixteen, for whom playing machines had become an addictive habit leading to compulsive gambling. On the very morning of the debate I spoke to a young mother whose son had developed an addiction. She and I had been both invited to speak about the Bill on television. We met in the waiting room beforehand and what I heard brought home the reality in human terms. She was crying as she told me the unhappy sequence of events. 'We didn't realize for a long time what was going on. He began staying away from school but we didn't know why. Then things started disappearing. Things from the house, money from my bag. Then one day the police arrived at the door and said they had caught Billie pinching a radio from a shop. They had him at the station. Then it all came out; he was absolutely hooked on the machines.' Her voice became shrill with unhappiness and emotion. 'Why do they let the kids into those horrible places? It's because they want their money and they don't mind about anything else. Oh, do please do something,' she turned her eyes to mine, 'something to stop kids being allowed into those evil places. Our Billie may never be cured. His whole life could be ruined.'

I tried to inject this mother's anxiety into my speech, and I think many of the peers who were present recognized the human tragedy and revised their attitude to the seemingly innocent pastime. In spite of the serious intent of Lord Campbell of Alloway's Bill, it never found its way to the statute-book, because, although time can usually be found in the House of Lords for Private Members' Bills, the same cannot be said for the Commons where there is more business to get through. However, one hopes this does not necessarily mean that all the ideas and proposals put forward in the Lords debate are lost. It is quite possible that the material will be used when at some future date the Government decide it necessary to introduce their own bill on the subject.

I soon discovered how very wide ranging are the Home Office responsibilities. Being a sort of dogsbody to the Home Affairs team I am expected to take on the shorter bills and unstarred questions, whilst Elwyn and Victor handle the complex legal bills. I know something is up from the look in the eye of Tom Ponsonby, our Chief Whip, when sometimes I bump into him in the corridor. 'I wonder if you could possibly take on the debate about pseudo-religious cults,' he says tentatively. 'It's in ten days' time and Victor says you would do it *beautifully*.' So over the months and years I find myself speaking on an astonishing variety of subjects: crossbows, billiards, gambling, Sunday trading, telephone bingo, pub opening hours, laboratory animals and many other topics which had not previously occupied a very prominent place in my life.

But with these new responsibilities came a perk. Something which could be described as a much coveted privilege in the House of Lords: a *desk*. It happened very suddenly when one afternoon I was sitting as always in the Earl Marshal room with one of my colleagues; I had been giving her a French lesson. Although competent in so many areas, she would be the first to admit her deficiency in this language, which she needed to strengthen her candidature for the 1983 European Parliament elections. 'Perhaps you could impress them by just dropping a remark in French at the end of the selection process?' I suggested, trying to be helpful. 'After all, it's quite probable the committee won't know much themselves. As you end your speech you could say in French something like, "I'm sorry, I had fully intended to speak some French to you, but now there's no time left." And that would be perfectly true!'

We had just embarked on steering her vocal chords round the

phonetically impossible sound of 'Veuillez m'excuser...' when one
of the attendants came in with a note from Wendy Nicol saying
she needed to see me urgently. Wendy, previously active in Cambridge
politics and Deputy Mayor, became one of my closest friends. She
could never do enough to help people, and was both intelligent and
kind. So I left my noble colleague practising her pronunciation and
went to look for Wendy.

I found her in the Chamber sitting on the front bench, 'Do you
want a desk?' she whispered urgently.

'Of course, but I had rather given up hope. Is there one going?'

'Yes, and as you're a spokesperson now, you have a right to it.
But Tom Ponsonby says you haven't asked for one so he's going
to give it to Muriel Turner [speaker on Trades Union affairs]. But
you *have* been here longer so really you should have it.' I was reminded
of the day when, walking along the passage with Wendy and her
husband, she said to nobody in particular, 'You know I'm not the
maternal sort...' 'You can say that again,' Ian interrupted feelingly.
'But,' she went on, 'I always want to look after Jane.'

In due course Tom took me to Room 7 and pointed at a small
desk placed not very advantageously just inside the door and closely
encircled by those of six Labour colleagues. On each desk lay a long
wooden slat bearing the name of the peer elegantly printed, a telephone, a lamp and an old-fashioned Pugin brass inkstand. I felt as
if I had been elevated to the ranks of the angels. (It must have been
like that, but even better, for a very pleasant but silent Tory backbencher who was promoted to Government junior Whip for reasons
which were uncertain, but may have had some connection with the
fact that although he had not offered a word in the debate, he had
voted more often than any other peer in the long and tedious Local
Government Bill abolishing the GLC. When congratulated on his promotion, he said, 'Well, I must admit, I've not been so surprised since
I got a double remove at my prep school.')

The atmosphere of our room is highly charged: desks piled high
with papers, loud voices on the telephones arranging foreign trips
or enquiring about complex legislative details, advisers or colleagues
coming and going, all bring a feeling of rather disorganized industry.
Lord Ennals, previously Labour's DHSS Minister, fails to make his
telephone work, while I open a pile of mail and Andrew McIntosh,
previously GLC leader, tries to write a speech for an Education debate.

It all makes me wonder what it must be like for a US Senator, spoiled with his own suite of offices and team of helpers.

Over the last few years I have got to know my six room companions pretty well. Fortunately we are not often all in the office at the same time, but there are occasions when the air is thick with cigar smoke (less so now because Wendy put her foot down about smoking) and the noise deafening. So it's not an ideal place for serious work and concentrated thought – the Writing Room on the first floor is better for that – but it's wonderful to have somewhere to go; a hook to hang one's coat on; a telephone extension of one's own; and to be part of a group. It all adds to the feeling of belonging somewhere.

I was sitting there one day talking to Kate on the telephone when Frank Longford appeared at the doorway. Among many other distinctions he has been Leader of the House of Lords and heads the remarkable Pakenham family. I knew from the press that he had just celebrated his eightieth birthday. 'Congratulations, Frank,' I said. 'How does it feel?'

'It's rather as if I have read all my obituaries and come to life again.' Then he asked: 'Would you take on the New Bridge, Jane?' Seeing my bewildered look he explained that the New Bridge was a small voluntary agency he had founded thirty years earlier, concerned with prison visiting and the rehabilitation of ex-offenders. At that point, sensing another time-consuming responsibility coming my way, I went onto the defensive and offered umpteen reasons why I was the wrong person to ask. 'Now that you're doing Home Affairs, it would be wonderful if you could get involved with penal issues and prisons,' he persisted. 'Don't decide now. At least have a talk with the chap who runs it. He's a retired naval Commander called Paterson and very nice.'

As I heard myself say yes, alright, I would see him, I knew it was the same as accepting outright and it meant another burden hanging round my neck. In the event, my acceptance – which inevitably followed – introduced me to an absorbing new subject. The whole question of what to do about crime and how best to protect the community from its effects is of such fundamental importance that those who become interested in the subject get obsessed with it. They no longer see it in simplistic terms whereby as long as those who offend pay for their crime society is revenged. They believe that this crude rationalization gets one nowhere and that what matters is to uncover the root cause of crime, and by using remedial and therapeutic methods turn people away from criminality whilst at the same time protecting innocent members of society.

When I visited Holloway prison for women for the first time, I was shocked. Charles Paterson and I were shown round by the Assistant Governor. The atmosphere in the canteen wasn't so bad because women were working there; doing a job as they might have been anywhere else, they could keep some self-respect by seeing themselves as workers rather than prisoners. We went to another wing where we met a group of women waiting in the passageway to be paid their small weekly wages for work done in the prison. From then on I started feeling steadily worse. We went to the mother and baby ward. Although well cared for, there is something quite awful about seeing tiny babies in a prison ward. Moreover, there is strong evidence that it has the most traumatic effect on the future of both the mother and baby. It provides a hopeless background for the mother to become a good parent on release.

We went on to the CI unit, where the mentally ill women are confined. Most of them are on remand. Previous to our visit, there had been a lot of press reports about this unit. The reporters called it the Muppet House and gave heart-rending accounts of the deeply disturbed girls and women confined there, often put into solitary confinement because they are so disruptive and to prevent self-multilation. Suicide attempts are tragically high. Indeed, while we were speaking to the officer in charge of the wing in her office there were constant interruptions. First a warder came to report that one of the inmates had flooded her cell; there was water everywhere. Next, another alarmed prison officer put her head around the door and said a cell was being torn to pieces by its occupant. It's unbelievable how strong mad fingers can be; some of the flooring was ripped up, the bed smashed. The officer herself had been attacked on entering the cell.

We left the wing with the cries of some of the crazed women ringing in our ears. 'But why are these women in prison at all?' I asked the Assistant Governor. 'They should be in hospital.'

'I agree,' she said, 'but there are not enough secure beds in hospital so when they are picked up for doing something mad but criminal – like setting fire to a telephone kiosk, behaving in a rowdy way, or attacking people – there is nowhere else for them to go but here. Of course we do our best for them and there is a medical staff who work with the discipline staff, but prison is thoroughly bad for their mental state. What they need is therapy and medical treatment, but a prison is not the place to provide that.'

It took a long time for the image of those women to leave my mind. I had looked through the grilles into some of the cells. Girls were huddled up on their mattresses – the worst cases in strip cells – with the blankets pulled over their heads. Stubs from thin rolled cigarettes lay on the floor. In one case a girl's arm – she was obviously so very young – had fallen outside the covers and I could see the lines of scars left by injections along the inside of it. 'Do their parents visit them?' I asked the Assistant Governor.

'No, not many. Most of the girls are probably only here because of what their parents did – or didn't do – for them.'

I decided to introduce a debate in the Lords about women in custody. I intended to point out that through there being so few women in prison – the most recent figure, for June 1983, was 1,380 – the danger was to find it not worth looking into the whole question. I argued in my speech that the effect of a custodial sentence was different for a woman than for a man, and sentencing policies should therefore distinguish between men and women. For instance, the effect on children should be borne in mind. Not only the babies in prison but also those bigger children separated from their mothers – in care or staying with relatives – who would suffer the trauma of separation. I suggested that visiting hours should be changed for a woman to keep in closer touch with her children and help her to be a good mother on release. With the small number of female prisons in the country many women are confined in places far from home. They should therefore be offered extended facilities such as more uncensored letters, more home leave, the use of telephones, etc. This should contribute to their keeping in close contact with relatives and children and enable them to occupy a constructive place within their families on release.

I came to the end of my speech with the memory of the young drug addict of Holloway's CI unit in my mind. 'I believe everything should be done to move policies and attitudes away from regarding women's imprisonment as punishment, which is essentially negative in character and has little to do with reform or treatment, and towards a more imaginative, humane and practical view of the penal system which, as a priority, has a remedial side to it.' I was well supported in the debate and I think the subject was recognized as important.

Soon after this I went to see a New Bridge client in Bristol prison. Sitting in the train going through the autumn countryside, I was reminded of one of Christopher's bosses in the Foreign Office who disliked seeing people behind bars. There had been the occasion in the early 1960s during the Belgian Congo disruptions after independence when a very gentle cultivated man called Basil Boothby was the head of the department dealing with that part of Africa. Christopher was the Number 2 and had spent half the night on the telephone because Patrice Lumumba, a leading dissident, had escaped from prison. Christopher went into the office next morning, exhausted, and told his boss.

'Oh good,' said Basil, 'I am so glad. I hate people being locked up.'

On the way to Bristol I started thinking of the New Bridge and how humane and practical its outlook was that offenders should be given help and guidance towards re-establishing themselves within the community on their release, rather than punishing them further by allowing the stigma to disqualify them from getting a job or house. Unfortunatly, this perfectly reasonable attitude was in direct conflict with the prevailing punitive and revengeful climate of opinion towards crime. This contrasts with the 1960s when so much thought had been devoted to devising more thoughtful ways of dealing with criminality. Many experiments were made, but of those, Grendon Prison – which I visited a few months later – with its group therapy, was the only one left.

The cause of the reformers is not helped when the Prime Minister votes in favour of each parliamentary initiative to bring back hanging. It does not help that a strong streak of fundamentalism runs through so many MPs and supporters of the party in power; nor when the tabloids report crime with glee, playing up their readers' baser instincts. But there are others – in high places – who see the thing differently. I heard Princess Anne make a good point when presenting the Butler Trust awards for the prison service. Standing there in Lambeth Palace she referred to the 'forgotten service', regretting the fact that prisons are not regarded in the same light as our schools and hospitals. She went on to say, 'When offenders are put into prison, most people forget about them or would like to forget about them. However, it is expected that these offenders will emerge as changed people.' Then, raising her eyes enquiringly towards her large audience, she added, 'And how, one might ask?'

My train drew into the beautiful Brunel station at Bristol. It was visiting day at the prison, and raining quite hard. The queue of relatives outside the prison gate looked so sad. There were very young mothers with their babies, older relatives, a man on crutches and a girl with the brilliant colours of a punk. The prison staff behind the counter in the reception area were kindly enough; they took the various provisions – apples, cartons of milk, biscuits and so on – examined them carefully and then dropped them into special blue bags with handles on each side. The visitors were required to fill in their names and addresses on scraps of paper; one old lady couldn't quite manage and, joking, the prison officer did it for her.

Unnecessarily I handed in my visiting permit, which was made out to Mrs J. Ewart-Biggs. The prison officer looked at it. 'What's special?' he asked. This was a stern reminder of what it is like not to have a title. I explained, 'I've come to see James X – but I'm in a bit of a hurry as I have to get back to Parliament this afternoon.'

Looking mystified he said, 'Let's say we'll do our best – but we're short of staff today. Blame this Government.'

After a few winks and me saying, 'You'd better change it for another one, then,' and him saying, 'Oh, they're all the same,' I went and waited with the rest, sitting on benches along the side of the long entrance room.

'Visitor for James X,' called one of the dark-blue uniformed officers who soon came into the room. I followed him next door into a big room filled with square tables, at each of which there were four chairs. Two of these tables were occupied; one by a very pale young man with long dark hair falling down each side of this thin face, and at the other – by the window – sat a man in his forties with his eyes glued to the door. It was obvious that he was keenly awaiting his visit. When I came in he got to his feet and shook hands with me. He had an Edwardian look. His moustache was clipped short and greying, his hair was neatly combed. He had long, fine hands and wore a crisp blue and white striped shirt with the collar turned over his grey sweater. He was very thin with high cheek bones and melancholy blue eyes. His voice was quiet; 'I hope you had a good journey,' he said politely.

I sat down and we talked about the prison. 'They're all much the same, I imagine,' he said. 'This one is having a bit built on.' Except for the New Bridge volunteer I was only the second visitor he had had in the last five years. He came from Liverpool and had little in common with his three brothers because he was an inventor and a music lover. One sister had died while he was in prison and the other had lost touch with him. He referred to the murder for which he had been convicted as 'the incident'. He discovered later that his common-law wife had been mixed up with it and he explained that the two attempts on his life were in order to steal his inventions. He had tried to get off on the grounds that he acted in self-defence. He showed me the plans of a wooden toy he had designed. He worked each day in the carpentry shop and attended a music course in the evening. He had worked for his o-levels in prison and passed some. He kept himself to himself.

The room was filling up. At the table next to us a young couple sat very close, engrossed in each other. They were kissing passionately – it was as near to a conjugal visit as you could get. But outside the open window the fence topped with barbed wire served as a stark reminder of where we were. 'What's worst for you?' I asked and, as if in acceptance of the wire, he said 'The loss of liberty, I suppose.'

At another table a huge man, muscled and with a shorn head, sat surrounded by a group of people; his wife perhaps and two relatives. I asked James X, 'How much longer?'

'A year I suppose,' the soft voice said, 'and then somewhere else to do a course. Then the whole saga of parole will start.'

'What about after you get out?'

'I want to start my own business.' Out came the plans again. 'But it will be difficult to find somewhere to live. I was hoping you might help me.'

'I'll ask the New Bridge. They do try and get sponsors and help with accommodation.'

My eyes then caught sight of the clock; any hope of catching the 2.35 back to London disappeared. He noticed my look and said, 'I know you have a lot of commitments.' We got up and shook hands. I wondered what had actually happened – whether he had really committed a murder.

The taxi which had been ordered for me was waiting outside the gates. 'They said it was for a gentleman and it's most certainly not,' said the driver looking at me. I told him the problem about catching the train. 'I'll get you there,' he assured me. On the way, darting down side streets and jumping traffic lights, he gave me some of his views about prisons and the penal system. 'One thing I just don't understand,' he said, 'and don't get me wrong. I'm not criticizing anyone, but how can we afford to imprison people for not paying fines? And how can the magistrates who are usually middle-class ladies or professional people, have any idea about why poor people can't pay big fines?' He warmed to his subject as he screeched down a one-way street, 'I went to court with a friend the other day and there was this woman who was caught for not having a TV licence. So she got fined. Then her husband left her and she was out of work so of course she couldn't pay it. The magistrate gave her twenty-eight days in prison. 'But who's going to look after my two children during that time now that my husband has left me?' 'The answer to that,' my taxi driver said in a shocked voice, 'was, "I would have thought that was your problem."''

Home Office bills have sometimes brought humour to our debates, however. The Sunday Sports Bill introduced in December 1987 by Lord Wyatt of Weeford, Chairman of the Tote, was an example. The intention of this Bill, among other things, was to legalize Sunday racing and betting on and off course. The attendance in the Chamber during its passage provided a different aspect of the House and the speeches by the opposing sides were highly entertaining.

I was speaking from the front bench on the Bill and on my way to the Chamber bumped into Tom Ponsonby. 'Can you smell the turf?' he said, sniffing the air. I saw what he meant when I took my place. Some of the benches opposite were occupied by a new species. The Jockey Club was present in force. It wasn't only the broken noses – although there were quite a few of those; it was the smooth tweed suits and shiny brown shoes. One could almost see the imprint of the binocular straps across the tweed-covered shoulders. And where were their shooting sticks? Perhaps they had left them hanging on their pegs at the Peers' Entrance. And then I noticed the bishops' benches. They were well filled. I began to feel we could no longer be called the Lords Spiritual and Temporal; more like the Lords

Spiritual and Equestrian.

The Bill raised contentious issues. Among them was that Sunday racing might adversely affect the traditional Sunday; another that Sunday opening of betting shops in the high streets might open the way for Sunday trading to become law. It was little surprise, then, that early in the debate, Lord Tonypandy – best known as George Thomas, ex-Speaker of the Commons – made his famous Welsh Chapel speech which he brings out in slightly adapted form for most debates which touch on Sundays.

He started off by having a crack at his old protagonist Lord Wyatt: 'My Lords, I always listen with great pleasure to my noble friend Lord Wyatt. We spent many years together in another place and I have admired both his facility in writing and his ability in speaking. He would never try to hide the main thrust of the argument he had in mind. When the noble Lord is mellifluous he is dangerous... That is the time when all of us need to weigh the words that he has addressed to the House. As I look at the serried ranks from the Jockey Club who are with us tonight – outnumbering the bishops, it is true – it is clear that there is a large attendance in the House for this Bill than there was for the earlier debate on the international agreement between the Communists and the United States. So clearly, Your Lordships' House is aware that big issues are at stake. This is not a piffling Bill at all. It is only small in size. Never mind the length, note the quality. This Bill has major consequences for our country... The truth is that working people in Britain are not crying out for betting shops on Sundays. Working people in Britain like the British Sunday... To increase the opportunity for gambling would be unworthy of our Lordships' House. Who are the people who want it? Apart from the highly respectable and distinguished members of the Jockey Club whom it is not often my pleasure to address, I know also the bookmakers call for it... They want Sunday betting and not for any high moral reason. Let us not pretend. They want it because they think they will make more money... The quiet Sunday is an essential strand in the fabric that represents our heritage in this land. The Bill drives a coach and four through the protection of Sundays. If betting shops are open we know that everything else will follow... The House is aware that I feel strongly about Sundays. To me, it is a precious day. I am not alone. None of us can say that we speak for the majority in the land. However, I know that at the very heart of our nation there is a tenderness towards Sundays which noble Lords will underestimate at peril to our national interests. By God's mercy, I hope that this House tonight will still be a guardian of our Sunday...'

This was powerful stuff, but Baroness Strange, another guardian of the Sabbath, was not to be outdone. In a short speech, she said: 'My Lords, many of our Lordships have spoken much better than I shall and have made the point which I wish to make much better than I can make it. I shall quote from the higher authority. I shall quote from the higher Lord who created us and this world in six days and rested on the seventh. With all its joys and pleasures and everything else. It was created in six days on the seventh He rested. Verse 15 in Chapter 31 of the Book of Exodus states: "Six days may work be done, but in the seventh is the sabbath of rest, holy to the Lord". Let us follow divine precepts and have one day which is different, one day devoted to rest and recreation.'

The tall figure of Lord Manton, Chairman of the Jockey Club, was the next to rise. He spoke for all his members present. First he pointed out that the Jockey Club had won by a short head over the bishops – nine to eight – and then, not surprisingly, presented a strong case in support of the Bill. After he had finished, I made a brief intervention; first I stressed some points made by previous speakers. Describing myself as a non-racing, non-betting person but regarding Sundays as opportunities for happiness and not hopelessness, I said: 'I am not a strict Sabbatarian and therefore believe Sundays may contain fulfilling occupations if people so desire and others are not inconvenienced. I therefore believe in racing on Sunday. For lonely people Sundays can be the saddest of days. I therefore have nothing against making race meetings available to them... However, I cannot see why it is necessary to allow betting shops to open in our high streets when it is perfectly possible for punters to place bets on-course at Sunday races... My noble friend Lord Tonypandy made a powerful speech this evening because he cares deeply about the matter in question. He pointed out, in unequivocal terms, who would most benefit from the Bill in financial terms; and this would be to the disadvantage of those wishing to retain a traditional Sunday.' I ended on a possibly apocryphal note. 'The noble Lord, Lord Manton, in supporting the Bill said it was wanted by everyone. I think I heard him say that even the horses wanted it. Although I am not sure how even the Chairman of the Jockey Club could have found that out...'

Even if this was an exaggeration, it got a laugh. Soon after that, following the Minister's reply giving the Bill the Government's blessing (the Treasury's haul from the Tote's takings is not inconsiderable), at 9.13 p.m. the vote was taken. The Bishops and Co. lost to the Jockey Club and Co. 78 to 61. But the fact that 139 peers forewent their dinner to attend and vote showed the priority in which the subject was placed. Had it been about Social Security or people having nowhere to live, the attendance might have been in single figures.

The Shops Bill, about Sunday trading, was the most contentious legislation I have taken from the despatch box. Introduced in the Lords it was taken through all its stages there only to be thrown out at second reading on arrival in the Commons. But from my point of view it provided a memorable picture of Harold Macmillan who was one of my favourite 'Elder Statesmen'.

The intention of the Bill was straightforward enough. On the one hand, it allowed shops to trade twenty-four hours a day, seven days a week should they so desire it, but on the other it removed safeguards shop workers enjoyed under the previous Shops Act of 1950. There was general agreement on the need for new legislation to regularize the existing retailing practices whereby many shops – especially small Asian grocery shops and large do-it-yourself establishments – broke the law by opening on Sunday. But people were not happy at the idea of complete deregulation with shops staying open the whole of Sunday. It was because of this concern that the Bishop of Birmingham had proposed a compromise.

The second reading of the Bill presented me with a great challenge as I was required to wind up for the Opposition, Victor Mishcon having led from our benches. It was just after ten o'clock in the evening on the 2 December 1985 that I rose to speak after the speeches of over twenty peers. It was an awesome occasion for me. The House was packed and the interest in the subject intense. It is strange that although not a church-going nation, we all get very stirred up when there is any question of changing the character of Sunday. Many of the speeches had reflected this concern, and the bishops – there were ten of them there – spoke out strongly against the complete deregulation of shopping hours proposed by the Bill.

Feeling nervous, I had sat on the bench listening carefully during the whole of the six-hour debate. I noticed the Earl of Halsbury

With Sir Colin Cole, Garter King of Arms, before my introduction to
the House of Lords, 1981.

On the Lords' back benches, making last-minute changes to a speech.

The Lords in session. On the bishops' bench (*top left, front row*) the Archbishop of Canterbury in his usual place, fourth from the end; on the Opposition benches, Manny Shinwell (*second row, extreme right*) and myself (*third row, fourth from the end*). Two *Hansard* reporters sit behind the Clerks, while a Government Minister is at the despatch box. Lord Hailsham is on the Woolsack.

In Belfast presenting the Christopher Ewart-Biggs Memorial Community Award to the Newtownabbey Women's Project. (*Left to right*) Shirley Rhodes, Sandra Gilmore, Brenda Courtney and Edel Teague.

Visiting a primary school prior to the Lords' debate on school meals.

The Duchess of Kent, Madame Laïdi (the Algerian ambassadress), Patti Boulaye and myself at the Hope for Children banquet held by the wives of the heads of African missions in London in aid of UNICEF.

Talking to Philip Rock of BP and Jimmy Boyle prior to his giving New Bridge's annual lecture.

Sunday lunch at Ellis Green:
Robin (*seated*), his cousin
William Randall and guests;
(*below*) Kate and Henrietta.

With Kevin in the Dolomites and (*below*)
Millie. (*Right*) On holiday in Avignon.

Peter Bottomley MP and I celebrate after the Lords v. Commons Swimming Match.

In Khartoum with Dirdire, Project Manager of the SOS Sahel afforestation scheme, and members of the local committee.

staring at me. One of the country's most eminent scientists, he is a good friend of mine. I knew the reason for his intense gaze was that he saw a strong resemblance between me and a model used by the pre-Raphaelite artist Burne-Jones; Tony had said he wanted to try his hand at a picture of me. At eight o'clock I went out to get a sandwich in the Bishops' Bar. In my absence Victor Mischon noted down for me any relevant points made by speakers. The debate dragged on, and my mind kept wandering. I wondered whether Kate and the friend she had staying had eaten the supper I had left them.

Finally the time came for me to speak. I tried to draw together the threads of the debate and found my notes useful. Once I got into the swing of it, I felt happier. My speech ended on a personal note with a plea that, as nearly all workers in the retail business are women, mothers should be safeguarded from working on Sundays to allow them to enjoy this day with their children.

What pleased me most was a congratulatory note from colleague Lord Ardwick (previously John Bevan of the *Guardian*) one of the attendants brought me after the debate was over. 'I trembled for you when you rose to speak,' it said. 'To wind up a complex debate of such length before a crowded House is an ordeal even for old Parliamentary hands. I soon stopped trembling. You had everything under perfect control. You might have been doing this kind of thing all your life. Heartiest congratulations. It was a real triumph!'

Harold Macmillan did not speak in the second reading debate and I do not think he had really planned to intercede at committee stage. I had been watching him after he took his usual seat at the end of the bench reserved for previous prime ministers or Cabinet Ministers. He always sat with his tall figure leaning slightly forward, hand on the silver topped black stick, his slanting eyes impassive and still. The Minister of State for Home Affairs, Lord Glenarthur, was arguing in support of a clause in the Bill which removed certain rights, such as meal breaks, and the amendment we were debating was intended to reinstate those rights, ensuring that workers might enjoy the same protection as they had under the 1950 Shops Act. The argument being that if they needed protection in 1950 when there was only 2% unemployment, they must need it even more in 1985 with 13% unemployment.

As the debate progressed I noticed Lord Stockton, as Harold Macmillan now was, becoming restless, moving around in his seat. It was clear he wanted to intervene, but he was immensely frail by that time and it was impossible for him to rise without assistance. Lord Boyd-Carpenter, who always occupied the seat beside him, usually gave him a helping hand. Lord Stockton's previous record made it unlikely that he wished to rise in support of the Government line and I thought Lord Boyd-Carpenter might be in a quandary: should he or should he not help his noble friend to his feet and thus enable him to embarrass the Government? In the event he of course helped the old veteran to his feet. Resting on his cane and with his head held high, Lord Stockton made his position clear at the outset: 'I must say frankly that I do not like this Bill at all... I do not like it out of a traditional feeling that we are sacrificing, by what I can only call a sort of Pakistani relief Act, a very old tradition – because that is the chief object of the Bill: to make a lot of small shops legal which are now illegal. We are sacrificing a very old tradition. We are making another move in the gradual secularization of our people and in abandoning the old principles which made our forebears great and kept them powerful. However, that is not the point now, we have done that.

'What I do not see is the argument which my noble friend Lord Glenarthur and others have introduced: that we ought somehow, on a quite different issue, a purely economic issue, to go to this new extreme which seems, greatly to my regret, to have inspired part of my Party. There are no longer the principles of Lord Shaftesbury, Mr Disraeli or Mr Churchill. The paternalist elements and traditions of the Tory Party that come from its very roots are now unpopular. We are making a great error. It is because the people as a whole trusted those whom they regarded as their natural leaders to help them, support them and protect them, that we have had the great authority in the past in our country. But this Bill is quite different. It is saying that because it is impossible to please or satisfy some opinions, and in order to please some strange new doctrine of liberalization, we should adopt all the worst elements of the liberal Victorian tradition, which has somehow infiltrated my old Party like some kind of disease. Are we to abandon a principle that has nothing to do with the main purpose of this Bill?...

'The Bill is meant to make it possible for people to trade freely on Sundays. It is not meant to make life more difficult for shop assistants. It is not meant to make the conditions of labour worse. I am not talking now about the kind of shops that probably will not open on Sunday anyway; great employers of large, well-managed institutions. But there are many small shops that will take advantage of this legislation. They will be just the kind of people who will try to exploit the weak and often transient population who are the kind of people likely to become shop assistants. I would have thought that given the present state of unemployment, especially north of the Trent, such people needed more protection than every before. As one noble Lord has pointed out, there was 2 per cent unemployment in 1950. In my old part of the world that I knew so well, it is now more like 13 or 14 per cent. Your Lordships should make sure that before this Bill leaves us it incorporates a clause or clauses that will reinstate, in whatever form the draftsman thinks is right, the whole system of preserving rights and of preventing the exploitation of a large class of people who are perhaps among the weakest in our great industrial and commercial system. I beg Your Lordships to do that. Whether or not we agree upon this Bill from a Sabbatarian point of view is not the issue. It should leave at least this domain with everyone determined that nothing should flow from it that may do some injury to any – and especially to the weakest class. I fear that I ought not to have intervened, but I listened to the whole debate and I was moved by it. I remember that when I led my Party in the House of Commons, I warned young Members that on no account should they attend committee stages of bills. I told them that if they did so, they would always want to vote for the amendments because the arguments put up by the Government would not convince them. I told them to stay in the Smoking Room and to come out and vote when the bell rang. I am afraid that I have not followed my own advice today.'

Looking rather shamefaced, the Earl of Stockton then sat down to affectionate laughter from his own side and acclaim from the Opposition benches. But the more profound effect of his intervention was to remind us all how much the Conservative Party had changed from the one he had led in the 1960s. How the paternalism and the continued movement towards a more equal society espoused by him had been replaced by a drive towards the creation of a polarized society. This was very much along the lines of the American system where the rich were meant to look after the poor and state provision was frowned on. Although Socialists regarded this return to Victorian values as ill-conceived and harsh, the affront felt by old-style Tories such as Macmillan was in a sense even greater.

Soon after this debate, I sat next to Lord Stockton at lunch when Lord and Lady Longford entertained Prince Michael of Kent and his glamorous wife. We all met in the Peers' Guest Room for a pre-lunch drink and when the royal couple arrived it created quite a stir. Princess Michael looked very pretty and seemed full of life and enthusiasm. At lunch I sat between the Prince and the elderly ex-prime minister. During the first course Prince Michael talked to me about Ireland. This was not unusual as, unfortunately for me, I still reminded people of Ireland, and probably always will. Often, wishing to end such a conversation, I say that as I was there for only three weeks it was not long enough to learn much about the country. However, on the arrival of the next course the Prince turned to speak with his hostess, Elizabeth Longford, on his other side. I turned to Lord Stockton and found him engaged in slightly acrimonious discussion with the waitress. 'No, no – what *is* that? No, I dont want it.'

'But, My Lord, it's your fish and I've boned it for you.'

This didn't make any difference. 'Take it away. Yes alright, I'll have an omelette.'

I felt sorry for the nice waitress who was doing her very best. 'I'll have it then, shall I?' I said, looking at the rejected plate in her hand. It must have been the first time for many years that I had had my fish boned.

At the end of the meal, the old gentleman got up and before shuffling off he learned towards me and with a conspiratorial look said, 'Another afternoon of being lobby fodder, I suppose.'

CHAPTER SEVEN

Foreign Affairs

ALTHOUGH I HAD so much enjoyed my sixteen years within the comforting embrace of the Diplomatic Service, I did not feel like hanging around the embassy drawing-rooms after I returned to London in 1976. I am pleased to receive the occasional invitation, but it is strange to see everything the other way round and find myself on the receiving end of lavish parties. I notice every detail, it was all so familiar. Not only do I recognize the regular Diplomatic party-goer, but also the faces of the professional *maîtres d'hotel* who do the rounds earning themselves a tidy packet. Seeing them always reminds me of a memorable incident which once rocked the Diplomatic Corps in Brussels. The British Ambassador, attending a cocktail party one evening given by his colleague accredited to the EEC, saw his own butler handing round the drinks. Outraged, the envoy returned to his residence, grasped the telephone, dialled the number of the other excellency and – in spite of the party still being in full swing – demanded the immediate repatriation of his butler.

There are occasions when I regret knowing all the secrets of the trade, for, once a person is aware of the esoteric rules concerning the placement of guests at table in order of precedence, they never again can take their seat carefree and happy. The glaring mistakes intrude. Quite often I am doubtful whether the place allotted to me is the correct one, although of course I keep my doubts to myself, unlike South American diplomats who register theirs by turning their plate upside down. It is not a question of rank but of sex discrimination. For instance, I notice that whereas a fellow (male) peer is correctly placed on the right hand of his hostess, I am not given the equivalent place of honour beside the host; instead the peer's wife is given it. It is not that I mind in the least where I sit; but what bugs me is knowing they have got it wrong.

One of my visits to the French Embassy, soon after joining the House of Lords, provoked longer-term repercussions than a mild preoccupation about precedence. Bobbie and Hélène de Margerie had been friends of ours when we were *en poste* in Paris. He was subsequently appointed French Ambassador to the Court of St James, a mission he carried out superbly. 'Come and have lunch tomorrow, Jane,' Bobbie's voice said on the telephone. 'We want to introduce you to General Mirambeau. He is involved with some important work in the Sahel which we thought might interest you.'

Driving through the beautiful avenue of trees lining Kensington Palace Gardens on my way to the Embassy, I made some rapid calculations as to the exact location of the Sahel, but came to no precise conclusion. When I arrived and was ushered into the drawing-room, the elderly gentleman met me and bowed over my hand. 'Madame la Baronne ... quelle joie de faire votre connaissance ...' then throughout lunch the General described to me in agonizing detail the plight suffered by the Sahelian countries following the severe drought of the early 1970s. He told about the initiative African governments took to alleviate the suffering when they set up a relief organization called SOS Sahel International based in Dakar, Senegal. This agency determined to attract funds from countries and individuals and redistribute it for emergency and development work to counter drought, famine and desertification in the worst affected countries of the Sahel. He described the suffering of the people, in particular the nomads, whose livestock having perished were left destitute and starving.

I listened attentively to the General's moving story. He then told me how he had set up an SOS Sahel committee in Paris to support the work going on in the African countries. His eyes met mine and I recognized a slightly different note in his voice: a note of interrogation. An alarm bell went off in my mind. Was I once again falling into a 'Mr Maneyfingers' trap? But anyhow it was too late. The voice went inexorably on. 'Madame, I would like to see other national committees set up in the European capitals to add weight to this humanitarian work. I have recognized compassion written all over your face and am convinced, Madame la Baronne, that you are the person most fitted to sow the seeds of SOS Sahel, Great Britain.'

Panic seized me. How could he have mistaken my polite interest for a desire to help? I could not possibly become involved in development aid. I knew nothing about it. Indeed had I only just identified the location of the Sahel as constituting the countries stretching across central Africa? Blurting out my misgivings, I thanked the General for the rare honour he was showing me but explained my reasons for saying no. Wriggling like an eel on the end of a line, I looked despairingly at Bobbie and Hélène, pleading with them to give me a way out. But it was to no avail; *'Mais c'est magnifique, mon Général, ce que vous faites,'* the Ambassador said approvingly; adding that if I needed help from the embassy in setting up the British committee I only had to ask. I drove back through the avenue of trees, my feeling of calm dissipated. The following days saw the General's campaign mounting. The postman deposited on my doormat weighty documentation describing SOS Sahel from all its aspects. The telephone rang continually bringing me the old gentleman's courteous but determined voice; 'Mais Madame la Baronne – je vous en prie . . .'

Eventually I gave in under the pressure. My new title: President of SOS Sahel, United Kingdom, was unwanted and claustrophobic and I had no idea how to start. What on earth did I know about setting up a charity? Anyway, who in Britain would give me money for work in the ex-French territories? Liz Travis, on her weekly visit to help with my correspondence, was disapproving when she heard what had happened: 'But you've got so much to do getting started in the House of Lords. Do you think it's wise to take on something out of the blue like this?' I could only agree with her.

We took many halting steps in the following years to get the new organization going, find experts to join the ranks, finally choose the afforestation project in the Nile Province, and raise the money to fund it.

Several years later, in February 1986, I went to the Sudan to combine an inspection of the tree nurseries on the project site with a visit to Robin and his friend Katherine who, after leaving Durham University, had both gone to teach English in El Fasher, Western Sudan. My flight on Sudan Airways delayed, I sat waiting in the airport lounge. Airports give people a special licence. Travellers feel neither constrained by their normal circumstances nor have they taken on the mantle of their next destination. They are in limbo, temporarily free. I love staring at the moving masses. The Asian families, usually with a succession of small children and a babe in arms, who always seem to be flying off somewhere. The businessmen easily identifiable by their thick black briefcases and the carefree look of those not paying for their own tickets. And then, at the departure gate, the anguished leave-takings. That day a fat, plain, spotty English girl saying goodbye to her Arab lover. Moving along in the queue, they kiss and fondle; brushing each other's faces one against the other. The boy passes through the barrier. It could only have been a transitory relationship; the young Arab needed a romance and the girl, unused to love, had grasped it hungrily.

Once on the aircraft I looked around. On one side of me was an old Greek obviously unaccustomed to flying, for when we had taken off, he crossed himself at regular intervals. But later he made original – and practical – advances by offering me a Greek/English dictionary to have a conversation. On my other side there was an elderly English couple who, when the plastic meal arrived, removed the silver foil cover from the dish, poked their plastic forks into the food and sampled very small mouthfuls with heads tilted back and lips moving rhythmically upwards and downwards. And in the background a film was showing – based on Elizabeth Longford's book about the Queen.

It was about four o'clock in the morning when we arrived, greeted by the brightly illuminated sign KHARTOUM AIRPORT; but the light behind the giant 'I' was extinguished leaving the rather puzzling message: A RPORT. Kevin, who had become chairman of our SOS Sahel committee in its early days, was there to meet me. Just arrived on a flight from Lesotho where he had been on business for his firm of consulting engineers, he was sitting on his suitcase intently reading a book. He had been much impressed by the First Secretary from the Embassy who was also there to meet me. 'Do you realize,' he said, 'that chap got a double first at Cambridge but yet he's had to spend two hours in the middle of the night waiting to meet you?' I agreed the young man's academic achievements had been misdirected, but reminded Kevin that peers didn't get many perks.

I was introduced next day to the afforestation scheme dreamt up so many years earlier in the beautiful drawing-room of the French Embassy in London. Kevin and I set off from Khartoum driving along the desert tracks in a Unicef Landrover with the smiling, white-teethed Mustapha at the wheel. After about three hours of bouncing and being thrown around we arrived at Shendi, the capital of the Nile Province. Stephen Bristow, the British forester, his Austrian wife, Andrea, and their two small sons lived in a brown stone Arab house in the dusty little town. As he was a forester and she a landscape designer, there were some beautiful plants and shrubs growing in their patio. Although we had discussed it often during meetings in the House of Lords Committee Room, Steve told us about all the different stages of bringing trees to the desert. First choosing species of trees most suitable for desert conditions, like leucaenas, mesquite, or balanites, the seeds were planted in small tubular plastic bags about six inches long filled with earth and punctured to allow excess water to drain out. The bags were ranged along the bottom of shallow trenches in the nursery and watered. Once germinated and the shoots grown to about a foot high, they were transferred to trenches outside to become acclimatized to the full glare of the sun. The little trees then ready for transplanting would be used for wood-lots or shelter belts to protect villages and farmers' fields from the moving sands.

The village women were very enthusiastic about the project, and worked hard toward its development. I met some of them in the village of Seyal Kabir. Graceful in their brightly coloured 'taub', they were making a shade for the nursery. As Shadia, the Woman Development Officer and I entered the big mud-walled room, silence fell. They gazed at me; then came a strange sounding word from their soft voices: 'Dzane, Dzane'. They were trying to pronounce my name. Once observed, they burst into peals of laughter covering their mouths with their hands.

There were a lot of children at the nursery. They went there most days on their way back from school to do some watering and any odd jobs. The building contractor was a tall, distinguished-looking Sudanese called Abdel Karim who had been a teacher and spoke English with panache. 'Just come from Blighty, have you?' he enquired amiably. And when Kevin asked him why he had given up being a teacher, his answer was unequivocal. 'It wasn't a going concern and I was cheesed off.' We talked to him for a little while and were amazed to hear him producing a quotation to cover every situation. As a funeral procession passed by we heard him reverently mutter, 'Ashes to ashes, dust to dust.' But he didn't always get it quite right. 'It's a cat's life,' he gloomily remarked on returning to his work in the nursery.

Meeting the workers on the project made me think of all the people in Britain who had given us money and encouragement. I had been so moved by many of the letters. An elderly lady of eighty-seven had written to me: 'I enclose a cheque for £5.00 which is half the

£10 the Government gave me as a Christian bonus. I am sending it to you because I admire you for your hard work in the Lords and your care for the poor of this country ...' Then there were the British schoolchildren who had raised money through sponsored runs and so on. Their letters were very moving. And once having recognized the child's implicit trust that his pound would be put to good use in helping the poor countries, I was determined that not a single pound would ever be wasted in administering the project, for it might have come from the generous old lady or the trusting child.

The part of the scheme which had attracted most attention and interest when fundraising was the educational puppet programme which went with it. The plan was to raise consciousness about the value of trees through the medium of puppets, and after putting on small shows to schoolchildren in the area, the first big showing was in Seyal Kabir. Two expatriate puppeteers, Ann Shrosbee and Bill Hamblett, had written the script which was then translated into Arabic and performed by Magdi and Hamad, young Sudanese trainee puppeteers. Ann's eleven-year-old son, Biggles, organized the lighting.

I still hold the vision of that show in my mind. The mini theatre was set up at about seven o'clock outside the village school, and the audience grew and grew. The men arrived first and, as is the order of things in a Moslem society, stood in the front, totally obscuring the view from the women and children. After the first ten minutes there was nothing for it, the show had to be stopped to re-establish order as the audience participation had been so intense. Crowd control was a new phenomenon for Seyal Kabir!

The story which had roused the villagers to such a pitch opens with a boy, Ali, on his way to the market to sell his goat. Tired, he lies down and in his sleep dreams that all the trees are being cut down. This sequence, illustrated through a shadow session, is so realistic that the audience went silent, except for one very old woman who let out a little sigh as each tree fell (she was the only one old enough to remember this actually happening in her childhood). Ali continues on his way and soon meets a traveller who sets him a riddle. Holding out his closed hand he says, 'What I am holding is more precious than seven camels, a water wheel, a house, a son or anything. Guess what it is?' In spite of many attempts, Ali fails to do so; whereupon the stranger reveals that he is holding seven seeds, which he then hands over to Ali. The rest of the play is taken up with Ali's adventures. He tries planting the seeds but, spurred on by raucous intervention from the audience, he makes a mistake each time. The first seed gets too much water, the second too little, the third is eaten by chickens and so on. Despairing, Ali kneels to say his prayers, whereupon a deathly silence envelopes the audience. Finally he returns to his grandmother who, remembering how her father planted trees, shows him the correct way, and against the background of the little stage emerges the cardboard silhouette of a beautiful tree. The whole audience goes wild with delight and the session closes with the narrator inviting all the participants to come together to plant trees.

We went back to the Bristows' house for the night and lay on the rope and wood beds thinking of the electrifying scene set in the dark desert background we had watched. What we found most encouraging were the signs that our project was becoming accepted and known by the people in the area. Requests were coming in from farmers all over the area for advice. They themselves had no knowledge of how to hold back the on-coming sand threatening their villages and fields, and wanted help to plant shelter belts. In some cases they had made pathetic attempts to hold back the advance by building low mud walls. Steve showed us a letter he had received written in painstaking scrawl and reflecting an anguished appeal. It had a nautical note as the writer related SOS to a message sent out at sea. It read:

Dear SOS,
Realizing your philanthropic purpose and goodwill gesture, we have touch your intensified effort which are of fruitful outcome. We are extremely grateful and you warmly welcome to gruesome sight and owning to you are humane we would like to catch your attension and capture your kindness. Please have seat to share us our ordeal. We are dwellers of El Rahamab Poor Society, consist of all walks of life, two-third peasant by trade. Simple life we lead not bad not good – so/so. Toiling for crust of bread. Hardship and gloomy life we labelled it as 'A great bonanza'. But this happiness has been disturbed and upset years ago as soon as the nature sneered and became foul and above all it turned to be ruggard. This is not the boundary of the gruesome sight but the thing which compound our trouble the heap of

the sand which surround and besiege our village. Unless you give us a hand we will perish and our fatherland will disappear for ever without your help we will be of scuppered hope and deprived happiness, to conclude this tragic scene will send 'SOS' and being sure you will not allow us to sink. Lastly every progress and happiness, ever sincerely ...

Since my visit the project has grown enormously. Nurseries have been set up in numerous villages and the seedlings in Seyal Kabir have grown into quite big trees. Everything looks quite different now. Ahmed Dirdiri, a Sudanese forester, has taken over from Steve and the local people feel the whole scheme really belongs to them. Moreover, using it as a model, other social forestry projects are now being set up elsewhere and we have the support of influential people in the development aid field. But I often think of things that happened in the early days when we were struggling to get things started. I remember two incidents in particular. The first happened very early on when the project was being run from my drawing-room. All sorts of people interested in trees telephoned or wrote to us, and had been immediately struck by how knowledgeable the British are about trees. But one day when I came home I found Kate in quite a state. 'Why do you get yourself mixed up with such funny things and people?' she said very crossly.

'What on earth do you mean, darling?'

'Someone terrifying came to the door asking for you today. He said he was from the Men of the Trees. And that's just the way he looked!' There was no way of getting her to believe that this was a highly regarded specialist organization representing the interest of trees.

I also well remember the time I spoke in a House of Lords debate about development aid. I was trying to persuade the Government to fund projects such as ours and described the way it worked. I reached the part about the types of trees we used. 'Fast growing species which do well in desert environment are the most suitable for these afforestation schemes,' I said and then, looking hard at Lord Trefgarne, the Minister replying, added, 'A good example, My Lords, is a tree called the Ipel Ipel which I am told grows as much as sixteen feet each year ...' I then came to a faltering stop. This hesitation was brought on for two reasons. First, I panicked as to whether I had got it right. Sixteen feet seemed rather a lot – perhaps it should have been sixteen inches. Then, to confirm my doubt, the Minister, looking at me hard, raised his arm to measure the distance. At the same time he slowly shook his head in disbelief. Later I was much relieved to confirm that I had been correct.

A few years after my original initiation into overseas affairs through SOS Sahel, I became involved with the developing countries through another channel. It was the autumn of 1984 and I picked out an interesting looking envelope from my usual pile of buff-coloured mail. It was an invitation to become the president of Unicef, Britain. This was one of the few invitations I accepted without hesitation. Considered a jewel among the United Nations agencies, Unicef's mandate was to protect the interests of the woman and child in whatever way possible, and through its programme of primary health care provision of clean water and education it was thought to be successful. It had been set up I knew in 1946 to bring help to the children of war-ravaged Europe and to reunite the families who had been broken up during the conflict years. Following this the United Nations International Children's Emergency Fund was established as a UN agency, but with the difference that it should be funded on a voluntary basis. By now 113 countries contributed to its funds; about 70% from governments and the remainder from the generous public. Each of these countries has a national committee. Here in Britain the Duchess of Kent is our Royal Patron, then there is the president, the chairman and Executive Committee to decide policy matters. The work of fundraising and advocacy is carried out by a team in London and regional groups throughout the country.

I wondered how best I could help and decided that my role might develop in four different ways. First, by inspecting the field work carried out in the Third World countries. Second, by visiting branches in the UK to encourage the volunteers in their fundraising, confident that the money was being put to good use in the field. Furthermore, I would be well placed to speak in House of Lords debates to urge the Government to be more generous. I could also carry out representational work like meeting VIPs, attending functions, or having my photograph taken accepting cheques. Once this happened outside the House of Lords. The cheque was from Northern Ireland and the photographer, Linda Jarvis, one of the dedicated Unicef workers. However, her devotion had brought her a broken wrist, sprained ankle and black eye through sponsored parachute jumps in aid of the Fund. Battered and bandaged she took the shots – but was still smiling brightly.

In 1985, a year before going to the tree nurseries, I went to Khartoum to visit the Unicef office. This was when Sudan was crippled by drought and famine and I was horrified by what I found. The relief workers were gripped by a sense of panic. It made me think of Albert Camus's *Le Peste*, where the overriding preoccupation, the central issue to the little town of Oran in Algeria, had been the plague. Everyone was trying to escape from it; the fear of it pervaded everything. In Khartoum it was the same thing; but instead of the plague, it was the drought. Everything was centred round it. Refugees driven out of the neighbouring countries poured into Sudan and the numbers of displaced people within the country grew and grew. Dr Samir Basta, an intelligent and charming Egyptian, was head of the Unicef office and his wife was an exquisite Frenchwoman: I had not anticipated meeting any of 'the beautiful people' in Khartoum's shabby, dusty setting. He took me to a meeting of the international aid, development and relief agencies. Trying to keep track of where help was needed, they used esoteric language like 'A pocket of nasty malnutrition at Atbara'. This meant that several thousand hungry and exhausted nomads, driven from their traditional mountain grazing area by lack of water and having lost all their livestock, were camping round a small Nile town. But with the typical generosity of the Sudanese, the townspeople had welcomed the interlopers and given them assistance. There was another 'nasty pocket' at Omdurman, on the outskirts of Khartoum itself, where 80,000 more hungry people had arrived from far away villages after days on foot or by truck. At each of the camps, relief workers tried to set up the minimum structure to preserve life. Three French women from Médecins Sans Frontière handed out EEC food aid; the Islamic African Relief Agency had set up a relief centre and a volunteer Sudanese doctor worked tirelessly at a medical tent. The day Unicef arrived to drill a borehole for water the people went mad. 'Moya, moya,' they cried as the water spurted up into the air.

I soon realized the enormity of the task facing the relief workers. Much as they rushed from one area to another trying to keep pace with the crisis, all they could do was plug the holes. The sense of panic at the size of the impending catastrophe was hardly surprising.

But I was lucky to see another picture of Sudan while I was there; one which demonstrated the way in which people struggling against overwhelming odds maintain a semblance of family life. I was flown in the small Unicef plane to Kordofan, well south of Khartoum, and taken round some of the villages. There were the women, tall and infinitely graceful, each carrying the 'zeer' of water on their heads, grateful for Unicef's hand pumps which had replaced the traditional and probably polluted wells far from their villages. And there were the excited women in the south Kordofan village of Kolba, gathered with their babies for the immunization session. I was photographed with the mothers at a session where the babies were being weighed to monitor their progress. The chattering women all jostled each other to get their own baby into the precarious weighing harness, suspended from the branch of a tree, for the photograph.

I joined another group of women who were busying themselves in a Unicef project to help them make a little money. Each had been given a small allotment of cultivated, irrigated land plus a miniscule grant to grow tomatoes, or keep chickens or do whatever they wanted. The women had composed a song to show their appreciation and were singing it at the top of their lungs – to the amazement of the children, who thought their parents had gone mad.

There is still so much I remember about that visit – but also things I have tried to forget. I mean the memory of those places where the old wells had almost run dry; and the rains, even if they came, were still two or three months away. I saw the children drinking the remaining yellow, stagnant, polluted water, and agonized at the thought of when even that ran out. And there were the dark eyes of the child in the poster on the wall of the Unicef office in Khartoum following me down the stairs as I left for the airport. The caption read: 'What do you want to be when you grow up?' Came the answer, 'Alive' I wondered how many would be denied that wish in the coming months.

Soon after coming home, I went to Aberdeen to meet the Unicef workers there to tell them what I had seen. After an interview at the small friendly Grampian Television Centre, Freda Reed, Father Bell and Mrs Forrester showed me the Unicef shop. Freda's shop sells second-hand articles she has cajoled out of Aberdeen's well-to-do, oil-rich burghers. She was very proud of the fact that under the table she keeps a box for things falling below her high standard which she sends to other charities. We went next to the Town Hall for a party given by the Lord Provost, along with the members of the Junior Chamber of Commerce, in the hope of inspiring them to set up a Unicef branch. Exhausted, I was taken to the Huntly Hotel where a young porter carried my luggage – a carpet bag – to my room. As we entered, the telephone rang and it was my daughter Henrietta at the end of the line. While I talked to her, the young porter, already thinking a carpet bag was not quite the thing for a baroness, started unpacking for me and became more and more astonished as he laid the contents on the bed. First a bottle of whisky – present from Grampian TV; then my purchases from Freda's wee shoppe – an iron, some china, a baby's christening robe and so on. Finally, shaking his head despairingly, thinking the Sassenachs – and Sassenach ladies in particular – were even stranger than he had been led to believe, he left the room.

These were some of the things I thought worth doing to help Unicef. But what happened to me at the Japanese event in the Guildhall went far beyond the bounds of duty.

'I wonder if you could possibly attend the Japanese Cultural Evening in the Guildhall to celebrate Unicef's fortieth birthday?' Robert Smith, Unicef's director, asked me one morning early in 1986. 'There will be a film, a kimono show, some music and supper. It is organized by a foundation that promotes Japanese culture, and they will be handing you a cheque for Unicef. Perhaps you could say a few words of thanks.'

Henrietta agreed to come with me and we arrived, a little breathless and slightly late, at the packed Guildhall on a Sunday evening in February. We sat down with Robert in the front row and after a longish wait the film started. It was mainly about a girl having her long, long black hair cut shorter, little by little, and I felt the Foundation's attempts to clarify Japanese culture to a British audience might have just the reverse effect. Next a group of earsplitting musicians played, and then came the kimono show.

'They want you to go on the stage at the end of the show to receive the cheque,' Robert whispered in my ear. Fully prepared with my few words of thanks ready in my mind, I waited for the sign.

A smiling Japanese girl came to where I was sitting and invited me to follow her. She took me to the back of the stage where three other Japanese women surrounded me and drew me onto the stage.

Panic set in when my three handmaidens produced a huge box of clothes and to my horror proceeded to go through the stages of dressing me up in a kimono. Imprisoned by being in public view of an audience of 900 or so, I could do nothing but submit. After what seemed like an age of embarrassment (out of the corner of my eye I could see Henrietta giggling in the front row) I thought the torment was over, but an additional horror presented itself. I saw one of my captors pick up a huge brown-haired wig, stuck full of combs and hairpins and, standing on her toes, attempt to lodge it on to my immensely Anglo-Saxon blonde-streaked head. Shaking with fear and humiliation I implored her with my eyes, and sensing the intensity of my misery she gave up. The final torture came when they took me by each hand and led me round the stage, from time to time twiddling me round. Head and shoulders taller than them, I minced along, grateful only that they had at least left me my own hair and shoes. Finally I was allowed to receive the cheque and say my few words of thanks.

'You were great, Mum,' said Henrietta when, the ordeal over, I was restored to my seat. 'Your whole personality – even the way you look – seemed to change while they were leading you round. Your eyes changed shape. You started taking tiny little steps, and I've never seen you look so positively self-effacing.' Small wonder, I thought. I told Robert I'd get my own back on him one day.

I remember another occasion – for a different reason. President Arias of Costa Rica came to England later that year and his wife requested a meeting with our Unicef committee. Robert and I arrived at Claridges and the beautiful, gentle young woman welcomed us. Her soft voice told us a heartbreaking story. 'In Costa Rica,' she said, 'we are very proud of our children and after many years we had driven away all those killing diseases like smallpox, measles, diphtheria. The immunization programme which Unicef helped us with was going well. But now we have a crisis. Because of the war in Nicaragua the refugees are pouring over the border. Many of the children are ill and little by little they are bringing the diseases back to our own children.' She went on to say how the hospitals could not carry the weight of the refugees. 'They are weak and malnourished; many of the Nicaraguan children arrive infested with lice. It is contagious.'

The following year President Arias was given the Nobel Peace Prize and I was reminded once again of the hotel scene and the soft voice – with no rancour in it – asking us to come to the help of children who were suffering so unfairly from a war of someone else's making.

I have spoken several times about Unicef in Lords debates, but the honour of being invited to give the address in the Westminster Abbey service celebrating the United Nations' fortieth anniversary in 1985 was for me the most memorable occasion, the more so as the Prime Minister was to read the lesson. Trying in my address to illustrate how the UN had done so much to provide the foundations on which to build a world made up of one people, I told the story of Unicef's roving ambassador, actress Liv Ullmann, with the street children of Mali. She described going to see the street children and how, come the evening, her small companions suddenly disappeared, returning later with the pathetic little bits of sacking or cloth which they had hidden during the day and which represented their beds. Having spread these carefully on the ground and then lain down themselves, each child instinctively made a gesture which is one that children the world over make when they go to bed – they raised their arms towards her to be kissed goodnight. Liv Ullmann then realized, she told us, that she was not only the mother of her own children but also mother to children all over the world. '... We are members one of another.'

CHAPTER EIGHT

A Working Peer

THE DAY STARTS with the arrival on my doormat of *Hansard*, delivered by special messenger. It comprises a verbatim report of the previous day's proceedings in the House of Lords up to between ten and ten-thirty in the evening. Hansard is in reality the name of the department of the Parliament Office where the record of the proceedings of the House, including all speeches, is prepared each day. *Hansard* is its colloquial name, strictly it is the Official Report.

The despatch rider's motorcycle makes itself heard outside my house in Radnor Walk as early as seven-thirty or eight, and, although I don't often have time to read it immediately, I always have a quick look if I have spoken in a debate myself. But as I hear the roar of the bike I am often reminded of a story Robin told me about a friend of his who was doing a stint as despatch rider for *Hansard*. One morning the young man in his biker's gear and at full speed arrived at the house of a London peer and was slightly surprised to find the noble Lord himself at the door. He got off his bike and handed the folded *Hansard* in its buff wrapper straight to its recipient. But the young man's face fell – and it certainly did no good at all to his job satisfaction – when the old gentleman with one motion took the *Hansard*, so diligently prepared and swiftly transported, and transferred it immediately to the dustbin beside him.

The efficiency and speed of the system producing the daily report is inferior to none. The reporters are capable of 180–200 words shorthand per minute and in the main are university graduates. They work in ten-minute shifts.

Where the House of Commons shorthand writers have to sit in the Gallery, their counterparts in the Lords are considered fortunate to be on the floor of the Chamber where they can sense the mood of the House, interpret the nuances and better comprehend what speakers are saying. I often become engrossed watching them. They arrive at the table behind the Clerks with a few minutes to spare, moving very quietly and unobtrusively to sit down and put their handful of biros or pencils in front of them. They then put their earphones on and, seeming to be taking in the atmosphere of the House, they wait until the hand of the clock points to the starting time, when as in a relay race they touch the arm of their colleagues whose pencil stops, while their own starts its seemingly unhurried journey across the paper and their face takes on a look of concentration. Some reporters use the stenotyping machines and arrive putting the compact palantype machines on the table before them, open the lid, ensure the spool of paper is running freely and wait with their headphones on. Having completed the ten minutes – after 9 p.m. it is reduced to five – the reporter will return to the office and dictate his notes to the typist, who must finish within thirty minutes. The timing must be scrupulously observed as the slightest delay will mean failure to meet the deadline for producing the report. Once Lord Denning was, unknowingly, the reason for delaying the process. He always occupies the seat on the crossbenches directly behind the *Hansard* table and sometimes, when stirred, he thumps the back of the shorthand writer's chair. This must in itself be disconcerting but, on this occasion, had a more far-reaching effect for, when she had finished her turn, the poor young woman found her departure blocked by the old gentleman who was still in full cry. For five minutes she crouched beneath the shadow of the gesticulating figure unable to make a getaway, bringing the whole highly geared process of producing *Hansard* to a full stop.

Back in the office, the reporter takes his notes and typescript to the reporters' room and with the help of a tape recording and, if necessary, the notes the peer has used, he corrects the typescript. Although, as is clear, every effort is made to avoid errors, a few occasionally slip in. There are some memorable examples; as when the mumbled rendering of 'read the *Guardian*' was transcribed as 'weed the garden', and 'the prevention of terrorism' was rendered benign as 'the prevention of tourism'. I also cherish the thought of a bill being ready for the 'Royal Ascent' and sympathize entirely with the reporter who did battle with '*primus inter pares*', settling in the end for 'the Prime Minister of Paris'. The *Hansard* office has also kept a record of gems uttered by Their Lordships. Lady Seear, to their delight, was recorded one day as saying, 'women are a real source of manpower', and, the backbench Labour peer Lord Stallard, 'social workers ... spend inestimable hours doing good'. My friend Lord Mishcon has had the honour of being remembered for saying: 'I hope I shall not be misunderstood if I say that if only the parts of the Bill were as comely and attractive as the parts of the Minister, we should be happier'.

Once the reporter has checked his typescripts it is passed to the editorial staff who go through it again, after which a photocopy is made for retention and the original copy is sent at half-hourly intervals to the printer, where it is broken down into small lots so that as many people as possible can work on it. The last collection by the printer for publishing in the current day's edition is made at 10.30 p.m. with the remainder – on the days the House sits very late – left for inclusion in the following day's report.

If I have left home before the arrival of *Hansard*, it is usually either to catch an early train or, perhaps, to take part in an early morning television programme, as when BBC *Breakfast Time* invited me to review the newspapers because of their interest in my debate about Freedom of Information, a proposal to make people's personal files – medical, education, housing, etc. – accessible to them if they so wished.

It was a typically active day. A car was sent to pick me up at 6 a.m. to allow time for me to go through all the morning papers at the studios. Lime Grove bears a slightly limp look so early in the morning, but the welcome at the reception desk is warm enough. The friendly girl who showed me the way had tired eyes from being there all night. 'I'll just pop you into this waiting room,' she said. I joined a variety of people waiting to be interviewed on the programme and I overheard bits of their conversations. A man with Parkinson's disease was sitting on one side of the room – his head and shoulders jerking and twitching – and the researcher was going through the points to be covered. On the TV screen in the corner, Kenneth Baker, Education Minister, with supreme confidence was extolling the terms of the pay settlement he had agreed with the teachers. On the other side of the room another man was in deep discussion with a researcher and it seemed he had written a book about what makes men attractive to women: good hands and a sense of humour was his recipe. At the end of the room, there were croissants and coffee keeping warm on a hotplate. Girls holding clipboards put their heads round the door from time to time and a West Indian cleaning lady ambled in with her broom and dusters.

After a while Kenneth Baker came in, having come off the screen where he was replaced by a dissenting Ian Wrigglesworth of the SDP. The Education Secretary – suave, smooth and healthy – accepted a cup of coffee and smiling at me said: 'You should complain to the BBC about bias – the place is packed out with Tory MPs.' (This was at the time of Norman Tebbit's onslaught on the Corporation, blaming them for anti-Government bias.)

My work started in earnest. I sat down in another room with all the morning papers and started to go through them. I was required to pick five or six items of news, one of which was a report in the *Telegraph* about my 'Access to Personal Files' motion, and to review each one of them in the programme. My final choices were a story about homelessness in the *Mirror*, a *Daily Mail* article about famine in Ethiopia and lastly, and on less sombre note, a story about Princess Diana, and Posy Simmonds' weekly cartoon. The researcher ringed each news item with black pencil and the relevant pages were to be shown on the screen during the programme.

In the make-up room, my poor early morning face was prepared for the viewers while, in the next chair, a Tory MP was undergoing the reverse treatment with his being taken off. Finally I was taken to the studio where I waited my turn standing at the edge of the stage. I counted eleven cameramen. While the weatherman was enunciating his gloomy forecast, I slipped into the seat on the sofa beside the interviewer. While I was trying to settle into a natural looking position with my skirt pulled down and feet crossed, I suddenly remembered when Selina Scott endeared herself to me forever. Looking at the words on the autocue from which she was to make my introduction, she said thoughtfully: 'You must get so sick of always being introduced as Lady Ewart-Biggs, widow of the British Ambassador to Dublin assassinated by the IRA. I shall just say, "This is Lady Ewart-Biggs, a member of the House of Lords",' she said, smiling.

The review of the papers went all right, though I always find the first item the hardest. Out of nervousness comes a danger of waffling. But the knowledge that we only had six or seven minutes acted as a spur, and I explained as concisely as I could why it would be fairer and more practical for people to see their own files, why should they be treated as children, and why should there be so much secrecy?

We then went helter-skelter through the other items and finished with Posy's lovely cartoon filling the screen and giving everyone, I hoped, a good start to the day.

Back I went to the waiting-room for my final cup of coffee. A girl in trainers looked round the door holding her head: 'I've lost two MPs,' she gloomily remarked, and disappeared. I was then led back through the tortuous passages, little staircase, over the flat roof and to reception. It was about eight o'clock by then and on the way home in the car I asked the driver if he always drove for the BBC. 'Yes,' he said, 'I'm a regular driver for *Breakfast Time*. Start at 3 a.m. – twelve-hour day – five days a week. They'd make it six if they could.'

At home again, I settled down with my speech for that evening. I knew it was too long, about a quarter of an hour's worth, and I wanted to speak for not more than twelve minutes. I tried to condense some of the material, make a few adjustments, cross a few things out and hoped that the adrenalin produced by rising to my feet in the Chamber that evening would do the rest.

My diary reminded me of an appointment with a young reporter from the *Eastern Daily Press* in the Peers' Lobby at eleven-thirty. I met him in his student days once when I spoke on Ireland and now, having embarked on a career of journalism, he wanted to do a profile of me for his paper. I arrived a few minutes late but then most of my life runs a few minutes late, if not more. I found him waiting with a slightly worried look on his face and we went to the Peers' Guest Room overlooking the river for some coffee. I never much enjoy being interviewed because I feel embarrassed talking about myself and this naturally causes a problem as the success of the whole operation depends on my giving an uninhibited account of myself. In a very British way I tend to water down my views, activities and achievements. However, there are some things I love talking about: politics, my children, human dilemmas are a few of them. So soon I forgot he was writing an article and we chatted away happily. I offered him a drink and he accepted. (Whilst not wishing to sound like a scrooge, I would like to point out that there are days when a working peer such as myself sees a substantial proportion of his/her precious attendance allowance slipping down the throats of visitors. Peers are generally considered to be rich – a hangover from the past – and inevitably most demands are put on the active ones who are often life peers and poor.)

The interview over, I say goodbye to the young reporter; hoping rather belatedly that I have not committed too many indiscretions for I know the risk that once the process of communication gets going my selective powers desert me.

There was time, before lunch, to open my mail. The letters addressed to me at the Lords are waiting on my desk and I add them to those I have brought unopened from Radnor Walk. One of my room-mates, Neil Carmichael, a Scotsman and former MP, is already there and, rather guiltily, smoking a cigar. Wendy Nicol has still not quite succeeded in talking him out of it. I glance at the newspapers lying on an unused desk. On the front pages there is the usual bad news about the Labour Party. 'We really are in a bad way,' I said to Neil. 'Why can't the Party do better?'

Joking in his nice Glaswegian way, he says, 'It's all your fault, Jane. You're not trying hard enough. That speech of yours the other night. It wasn't good enough.'

'Oh, dear,' I said in mock despair, 'haven't you got anything amusing to tell me?'

'Well,' he replied, 'have you heard the story about Jock Stallard [another Labour peer]? He came up to me the other day and said, "Now, Neil, I've been round here a wee bit longer than you" – he was introduced two weeks earlier than I was – "and I've noticed a few things you're not doing right. I feel I should mention them to you. First, you're walking too fast and what's more I distinctly saw you walk straight past the lavatory the other day without going in."'

The stock of jokes like this about the advanced age and frailty of peers is endless – but no one there seems to mind.

I had about twenty-five letters, most of them in boring brown envelopes. I picked out the more interesting ones with the name and address handwritten. After I had opened them and put them in three categories – one for action, one for reading and the last for the wastepaper basket – I went to lunch. On the way along the passage I saw suddenly flash on the anunciator screen the alarming message, 'Doctor required in Prince's Chamber': another reminder of the frailty of so many of my colleagues. I agonized who it might be.

The House of Lords does not have a very wide choice of places to go for refreshment. We can go to the Strangers' Cafeteria on the House of Commons side or the other cafeteria off the Westminster

Hall, but in the Lords itself there is the Peers' Dining-Room where we can entertain guests or, if we are eating alone, we go to the Bishops' Bar or Long Table. The Bishops' Bar is made up of two rooms formerly the bishops' robing apartments, one for serving drinks and the other for sandwiches and snacks. The walls are made up of oak-panelled doors, which used to be twenty-six cupboards where the bishops kept their robes. I am not sure when they were evicted, but the exact date the Commons commandeered the Pugin Room, next to the Peers' Guest Room, and used it as their bar, is still engraved on our minds. It was in 1906 and we refer to the dastardly act as if it took place yesterday.

Although my lunch usually consists of a hurried sandwich, or sausage, and a glass of red wine in the Bishops' Bar, I decided on that day to go to the Long Table. The Long Table is at the far end of the Peers' Dining Room and every day a rich variety of people congregates round it. Alongside it there are two other tables, one for the Law Lords and the other for the Clerks. While having lunch, afternoon tea or supper at the Long Table, I have learned a lot about the character of the House of Lords as an institution and a great deal about its inmates. And the Long Table acts as a leveller. Peers sit down wherever there is a place free and beside whomever is already there. This has a very civilizing effect on everyone.

An extraordinary variety of subjects come up during a meal. Peers talk about their children and grandchildren but usually in such a way as if everyone knows who they are: which may in fact often be the case, so many of the hereditary peers are related to each other. (During debate if a speaker wishes to refer to another peer who is a relation he will call him 'My Noble Kinsman'. The first time I heard Lady Masham refer to her husband, the Earl of Swinton, in this way I got quite a shock, but soon it became a familiar term.) Politics are often discussed at the Long Table but only in general terms and rarely does conversation descend to the level of party politics. There is no shortage of advice – either asked for or given – as experts in almost any field are seated there. If advice is needed over a horse race, a cure for some malady, or the names of those in line for high-ranking appointments and so on and so forth, the answers are always forthcoming. No one ever talks down to anyone else. Whoever we may be – social worker, trade unionist, general practitioner, teacher or duke – we treat each other as equals. There is a mutual respect between us all whatever we each represent. Lady Serota, Health Minister in a previous Labour Government, once told me she found the House of Lords the most egalitarian group to which she had ever belonged. Divisions brought on by ambition hardly happen at all for, generally speaking there are very few peers still fired with political ambitions and social aspirations among Peers of the Realm seem a bit out of place.

Arriving a little late that day, I found the table nearly full. I sat down between David Strabolgi, an hereditary peer and a Labour spokesman on the Arts, and Roger Skelmersdale who was at that time the DHSS Minister in the Lords. Opposite me sat my old friend Denis Greenhill and Lord Alport, an independently minded Tory backbencher. The menu showed there was either a two-course lunch for £3.30 or a three-course one for £4.25. Unable to decide what to have I noticed Lord Alport's plate looking tempting and asked him what it was. 'I'm not sure,' he said apologetically. 'It was my second choice. I wanted the grouse but it was off, as usual.' I decided on fried fillets of plaice which were always good. Some of my neighbours had reached the pudding stage and the sight of rice pudding, bread and butter pudding, plum crumble, etc. brought back memories of delicious childhood meals.

'How are the children?' Denis Greenhill asked me.

'They're fine, but Kate still has problems with her wretched asthma,' I said.

Immediately advice came from the other side of the table as Lord Colwyn who is a dentist said: 'Have you tried acupuncture? I became so impressed by some of its results that I took a course. I know it has most certainly shown staggeringly good results for asthmatics.' He wrote down some details on the back of the menu and handed it to me.

Roger Skelmersdale was a bit on edge as there were two Parliamentary Questions down that afternoon for him to answer. 'You've taken a terrible battering over the National Health Service,' I said sympathetically. 'But you're very good at keeping your cool and not letting yourself get rattled.'

'There's no point,' he said philosophically but gloomily. Hospital waiting lists, children needing operations, nurses emigrating and so on were a worry to him too.

On his other side Donald Soper, the Methodist Labour peer, was discussing development aid with his neighbour whilst Willie Ross was arguing about some Scottish issues with his immediate group. Becoming a little heated, Willie said 'Good God, but ...' and then stopped, respecting the Methodist minister's sensibilities.

'No, no, Willie, go on – it's quite all right. Your theology is perfect,' Donald assured him.

I eavesdropped on a conversation further down the table. It concerned the vexed question of peers speaking in debates about matters in which they have a personal interest. Our 'Bible' – a thick volume entitled 'Companion to the Standing Orders and Guide to the Proceedings of the House of Lords' – pronounces on this question as follows: 'It is the long-standing custom of the House that Lords speak always on their personal honour. It follows from this that if a Lord decides that it is proper for him to take part in a debate on a subject in which he has a direct pecuniary interest, he should declare it. Subject to this, and to the guidance to Members or Employees of Public Boards, there is no reason why a Lord with an interest to declare should not take part in debate. It is, however, considered undesirable for a Lord to advocate, promote or oppose in the House any bill or subordinate legislation in or for which he is or has been acting or concerned for any pecuniary fee or reward'.

But a group at the Long Table were concerned that peers were sometimes being taken on as consultants by outside groups – business or otherwise – to ensure their interests were represented during the passage of a bill, in direct contradiction to the Standing Order which says: 'Lords may indicate that an outside body agrees with the substance of the views that they are expressing; but they speak for themselves and not on behalf of outside interests'. I had become so absorbed in this conversation, the theme of which is of great importance to the integrity of Parliament, that I had forgotten that I had a question down that afternoon and should go to prepare for the ordeal. As I left the Long Table, I passed Lord Moyne, still sitting there. 'How is SOS Sahel going?' he asked. He had been one of the first to give us some money.

'Very well, Brian. We're moving into our second afforestation project, this time in Northern Sudan.'

I went back to my desk to work out exactly what supplementary question I would put to the Minister following on his answer to mine about tobacco promotion. I am always thrown into a state of great anxiety by having a question down. Standing Orders say that 'Starred Questions are asked for information only, and not with a view to making a speech or to raising a debate ... Supplementary Questions may be asked provided they are short and confined to the subject of the original Question, but debate may not take place. The essential purpose of Starred Questions and supplementaries is to elicit information from the Government and so they should not incorporate statements of opinion.'

The question I had down on the Order Paper was, 'To ask Her Majesty's Government what is their view of the British Medical Association's proposal for a ban on all forms of tobacco promotion.' *Hansard* of that day reported that this was the first of the four daily questions coming after Prayers which had been read by the Lord Bishop of Norwich. The fact that the Marquess of Aberdeen and Temair took his seat that day was also reported. As he succeeded to the title – on the death of his brother – there was no ceremony of introduction. Instead he simply took the Oath of Allegiance and shook the hand of the Lord Chancellor on the Woolsack in the usual way. The Clerk then stood to announce my question. 'Baroness Ewart-Biggs,' he solemnly intoned, looking in my direction.

'My Lords I beg leave to ask the Question standing in my name on the Order Paper,' I said, rising to my feet.

The Earl of Caithness, the Minister replying, gave the answer carefully prepared by the civil servants. 'This Government, like their predecessors, have chosen to regulate tobacco promotion mainly by way of voluntary agreements. When the time comes to review the present agreements we shall take account of all the relevant circumstances, including the views of the medical profession.' He read this out of a large loose-leaf book which contained, on separate pages, answers to as many of the potential supplementary questions as the civil servants could foresee. Many is the time that Ministers desperately leaf through the great book trying to find the answer to match a particular question.

The short debate which followed was about whether voluntary agreements were sufficient. In the supplementary which I had laboriously learned by heart, I pointed out that the tobacco companies had failed in their voluntary agreement not to advertise on television before 9 a.m. – a limitation designed to protect children – and also that they had tried to circumvent the law by sponsoring sports events and so, I concluded, would the Minister not agree that in order to protect our children from a product which kills one in four of its consumers, we should now follow the example of Norway and Finland and ban the promotion of cigarettes?

Several peers intervened but Lord Shinwell had the last word, and being quite a libertarian expressed considerable doubt about the restrictions I had requested: 'Is the Minister aware that I have been smoking for so long as I can remember, since I was aged thirteen, and that I still indulge in an occasional whiff when it suits me ... after all there is nothing really seriously wrong with smoking; there is no corruption about it. If there was I assure my noble friend Lady Ewart-Biggs that I would have nothing to do with it. I cannot understand why she raises this question. I should have thought that she was the kind of person who occasionally indulges in a cigar.'

This certainly added a completely different note to the short debate and, as always when he spoke, attracted Their Lordships' appreciation. However, by the end of about nine or ten minutes and interventions by eleven peers, there was little doubt that the Government had been made aware of a growing concern about the rise in smoking among children and young people with the known cancer risks involved.

I left the Chamber after Question Time feeling very relieved. The question had attracted a lot of attention and I had succeeded in making my points reasonably clearly. I moved on to my next appointment, an interlude with the voluntary organizations which I had come to think of as 'alternative Britain'. This was to chair a Management Committee meeting of the New Bridge, Frank Longford's organization concerned with befriending prisoners and finding them jobs on release. I had booked one of the beautiful Pugin-decorated rooms on the Committee floor of the House and there, waiting for me, were the fifteen or so members of the group. I took my place in the chairman's seat and looked at the agenda. By that time I was very accustomed to occasions such as this. Besides the New Bridge I also chaired a group called Family Forum concerned with family policies, the Women's National Cancer Control Campaign, Neighbourhood Energy Action who set up home insulation projections, and attended the meetings of the Volunteer Centre, Unicef-UK and some others. I was intrigued both by the type of person who took part in this work and the jargon used. Everything is an issue – 'very important issues', 'a complex issue', 'major issue'. Then there are

'The marker which so-and-so is laying down here' ... 'tremendous thrust' ... 'come up with a package' ... I see this as a major plank'. The word 'aspect' pops up continually, and the unforgivable use of 'at the end of the day' and 'in the final analysis' recurs regularly. When a committee member starts by saying, 'I won't weary you with the fine details of the question' it means he will. 'Just to pick up on that, if I may ...' means repeating what has just been said. The constant use of esoteric initials; 'the evidence on CNEA is very mixed'. And there was the occasion when the management committee members of an organization concerned with environmental issues were faced with the question of whether or not the staff members' request for 'toil' should be granted. I thought it seemed highly desirable and wondered why the discussion continued for so long. Finally the truth emerged. It was a demand for Time Off in Lieu.

Those working for 'alternative Britain' are sometimes viewed with suspicion by those who don't. There was the time Cecil Parkinson, freshly restored to high office as Minister for the Environment, addressed an Age Concern Conference about energy efficiency and home insulation. He was alarmed as he knew little of this breed of person. His private secretary, to reassure him, had scribbled at the top of his brief: 'They're quite good eggs – not so much the sandal brigade'.

Sometimes 'alternative Britain' workers do entirely live up to their reputation for originality or even eccentricity: like the employees of a voluntary organization who married each other but, contrary to normal practice, it was the man who took the name of the woman.

The members of the New Bridge Management Committee represented a genuine cross-section of the social classes and personalities, all united by their interest in penal affairs and the prison system. There were several ladies of advancing years who had been visiting prisons for decades, alongside younger members who felt deeply about what went on in prisons from a humanitarian viewpoint. They wished to help fellow human beings through the hardship of being deprived of freedom, responsibility and power of decision, and to draw them back into active life on release. 'Befriending' a prisoner was like throwing a lifeline to a floundering, drowning person. They were called VAS (Voluntary Associates) and often travelled miles to visit their 'client' in a faraway prison, sometimes giving up the whole day to the operation. They also corresponded with their prisoner and could judge the level of his morale from his letters. Many of these letters were both moving and sad, such as one received in September 1987 which read as follows:

> My father left us when I was eight. Well he didn't leave; he was taken away by police and he was given 20 years ... My mother divorced him and remarried and that's where the trouble started. Me and him didn't get on at all and we started fighting a lot. I got into trouble with the police and went to court and they put me in care for criminal damage.
>
> I was put in a children's home ... I did well at school ... I left with six GCE and four O-levels. I then went on ... and got three City and Guilds: Maths, Carpentry and Building Engineering. When I was at Tec my mother died of leukaemia.
>
> I met a lovely girl after that ... We have two lovely kids ... and I thought we were happy.
>
> I got into trouble with the law again because I was unemployed and I thought it was my place to supply the family. So I broke into W.H. Smiths ... and that's why I'm here. Anyway, (my wife) wrote to me saying she doesn't want to know me ... I don't blame her, I will have to sort it out when I have done my time...
>
> Thanks for reading about my boring life and thank you for your help.
>
> P.S. I think I have learnt my lesson now because I have hurt my family and myself.

And another later from a twenty-one-year-old prisoner:

> Since I came to the UK in 1980 from India I have suffered racial harassment and I don't have any friends to talk to outside and I am on my own ... My parents have got enough problems of their own. If I tell them they will worry about me and I don't want that to happen because my father has been through two heart attacks. If you could visit – if you could help me I would be pleased to tell you more...

One member of our committee was an ex-prisoner himself and had married his VA on release. Together they ran one of New Bridge's branches. There could be no more tangible proof of the success of befriending.

The ethos behind our group's work may be illustrated by what Winston Churchill had said as Home Secretary in 1910:

> The mood and temper of the public with regard to the treatment of crime and criminals is one of the unfailing tests of civilization of any country. A calm dispassionate recognition of the rights of the accused and convicted criminal against the State; a constant heart-searching by all charged with the duty of punishment; a desire and eagerness to rehabilitate in the world of industry those who have paid their due in the hard coinage of punishment; tireless efforts towards the discovery of curative and regenerative processes; unfailing faith that there is a treasure, if you can only find it, in the heart of every man; these are the symbols which in the treatment of crime and criminals, mark and measure the stored-up strength of a nation and are a sign and proof of the living virtue in it.

Sitting next to me along the table was the Director of New Bridge. As a retired Royal Navy Commander he ran the small office of six or seven paid employees as if it were a ship. (Indeed he had once conducted a mock court martial in the office, leaving relations distinctly strained.) The meeting went on for two hours. In common with many other voluntary organizations the most stressful item on the agenda was finance. Our Home Office grant was pitifully small and we found it difficult to raise private funds as an organization dealing with prisoners is not regarded as appealing to potential funders .

'Could you report on your visit to Manchester and tell us how arrangements for the new branch there are getting on?' I asked the Director. In his meticulous naval tones Charles responded: 'Our first open meeting went well and revealed a big potential for volunteers. The catchment area for prisons is large so we'll need a lot of VAS. We must now visit the prison governors and get their co-operation, and then of course we'll need to fund-raise among the Manchester area industrialists to set up a small branch office there. This office will operate through its befriending and employment services in the North in the same way as the New Bridge does in the South. We could then cover the prisons up there in a much more economic and efficient way than we do now from our London office.'

I had always seen the New Bridge as developing in this way and, by setting up a national network, we could offer our unique service to every prison in the country. I was convinced that one way of bringing down the appallingly high reconviction rate of ex-offenders was to offer them a 'bridge' back to normal life with the job and house that went with it.

Alessandra, the pretty, dark-haired young girl who had the job of setting up an experimental befriending service for Youth Custody Centres, reported to the committee that the regular groups were doing well at the Rochester and Feltham YCC. She was receiving referrals from the Probation and Education departments there. She then described her visit to set up a new group at the Dover YCC. 'The young people sat round listening to what I said but not reacting much,' she told us, 'then at the end just as I was leaving one of them – he looked a tough customer and had tattoos all the way up both forearms – pushed a bit of paper into my hand before rushing off. It said, "Please – I'd like some visits – no one else will be coming – but I couldn't say so because the others would have thought I was wet". That's probably how most of them felt,' Alessandra went on, 'but they come from backgrounds where the only thing that counted was being tough. Getting in trouble with the law was one way of proving just how tough they were.'

We struggled on through our long agenda. Everyone made lengthy contributions to the discussion, and the division bell calling me away to vote in the Chamber on several occasions slowed down the proceedings as well. The final two items were first for the Committee to look at the New Bridge Christmas card and second to decide who should give the next annual lecture. We had set up a competition for the card and some of the paintings and drawings sent in by prisoners were both impressive and poignant. The winning entry showed three scenes. The first was of the prison gate with the prisoner being let out. He was then seen battling through the wind trying to cross a snow-covered bridge set in the centre of the card. Last was his dream, a beautiful, cosy-looking little house with a girl holding a baby illumined in the top window.

The annual lecture was New Bridge's prestige event and over the years many Home Secretaries had given it. After a great deal of discussion, the meeting decided to invite Jimmy Boyle to be the next year's guest speaker. An ex-prisoner from one of Scotland's toughest gaols, he had become a writer, sculptor and director of The Gateway Exchange, an agency offering help and support to all those in need, and could give a valuable insight into prisons and the penal system.

The meeting came to an end after about two and a half hours. As always, I felt exhausted, deflated and frustrated. Why could all that energy, good will and practical action not be channelled to better advantage? Why could there not be more tangible results, with something to show for all the concern and hard work? The reality is that the limitation of time and resources means that the success rate of agencies such as New Bridge cannot be measured. The incentive to continue can only come out of conviction as to the importance of the work. The huge number of men and women, all of them so different, engaged in alternative Britain have that certitude. They know what they want to do but the means to that end is often debated at inordinate length and in a heated fashion. Sheila Childs, the Vice-Chairman and a constant source of good sense and encouragement and friendliness, sensed how I felt and reassured me, 'Don't worry, Jane. We'll get it all sorted out in the end.'

I went downstairs to the principal floor and rejoined the traditional side of life. It was nearly time for my debate about providing accessibility of information to members of the public; it seemed a long time since I had spoken about it on *Breakfast Time*. I went to take my place in the Chamber to listen to the end of the previous debate and get a feel of the mood of the House. It is always important to do this as, in the absence of any rigid disciplinary framework, the way the debate is conducted is the responsibility of the peers present, and to be in touch with what they are feeling is crucial. I remember the time when one of my colleagues, Lord Hatch, caused an uproar by continuing to speak at Question Time, in spite of it being the wish of the House for him to stop. Lord Elwyn-Jones had intended to intervene but had refrained because, he explained later, the mood of the House was so antagonistic that he didn't think it was the right moment to make the important constitutional point he had in mind.

It is difficult to define what exactly makes up 'the mood'. A reaction against any expressed insensitivity is part of it. Peers are also very conscious of unkindness and intolerance in speeches. The House certainly warms to some speakers more than to others. Elwyn's charm never fails to conquer. And Nancy Seear, Liberal Leader, presenting an impressive profile with her hands behind her back and feet well apart, has the same effect. The House listens to Lord Henderson with the utmost respect for previously he was our own much admired Clerk of the Parliaments. And Lady Faithfull, representing from the Conservative benches the interests of children, young people and all those in need, always carries the House with her. Perhaps it is best to define the mood of the House by saying it is affected by whatever happens to either strengthen or weaken the great sense of pride all its members have in it.

The time was three minutes past six when I eventually rose to introduce my motion. I set out the arguments in favour of the principles behind the right of access to personal files and gave practical examples of why individuals would benefit from seeing their own records relating to health, education or housing matters. Afterwards I listened to the other speakers who each covered a different aspect of the subject. Lord McNair speaking for the Alliance focused on the importance for adopted children to know of their origins. Then Lord Denning, the eighty-nine-year-old Lord of Appeal, said he felt the question was too delicate for lawmaking and should be left to the discretion of the professionals and the individuals concerned. Lord Rea, a general practitioner on my benches, gave a cautious welcome to patients being given greater access to their medical files – as long as there were safeguards to avoid distress. Lord Jenkins of Putney, previously Labour's Minister for the Arts, then brought up the whole question of the regulations governing security.

Lord Silkin, Attorney-General for the 1974–9 Labour Government, in winding up for the Opposition, gave an example of how the inclusion in personal files of opinionated statements can affect very many people. His father had won a mathematical scholarship to Worcester College, Oxford, but to acquire the grant he needed a recommendation from his head teacher who stated that in his opinion 'this boy would not benefit from a university education'. This resulted in his not going to university and instead of carrying out the important task of being a mathematics teacher he eventually became Minister of Town & Country Planning.

By this time Bertie Denham, the Government Chief Whip, obviously thought the debate had gone on long enough. He had a way of making this clear by fixing a penetrating and unfaltering look on the speaker from his place of advantage on the front bench. Finally Lord Belstead,

Deputy Leader of the House, spoke from the Government front bench and gave reasons why it was unlikely that any legislation based on the Access to Personal Files Bill as drafted by the Campaign for Freedom of Information would be given Government support. Although, he made clear, he felt it was wrong to withhold information unnecessarily from the public.

So, as always, the Government had it both ways. But that evening I didn't mind. There were two reasons for this; first because I always enjoyed listening to Lord Belstead who looks rather like Christopher – tall, thin and apologetic-looking. And second because I was so tired I could only think of sinking back into the comfortable seat of the new – although eleven years old – deep gold Triumph Stag given to me by Kevin, and getting home to bed.

CHAPTER NINE

Money and Perks

'WILL THERE BE an honorarium?' Not all peers ask that question when invited to speak at an official function; but some do. For a peerage certainly does not bring a livelihood with it, and even peers can't live on air alone. The only money the House of Lords pays is for expenses. First there is the subsistence and incidental travel allowance of £21 per day which all peers can claim if they attend. A further £22 per day for secretarial costs, postage, etc. and finally, for those members living outside London, there is the night subsistence allowance of £57. In order to qualify for these allowances, we have to make an appearance in the Chamber during the afternoon or evening sitting. The doorman inside the Chamber ticks off the names and one of the Clerks has a list of peers' names before him and, looking round the Chamber, he will put a line through the names of those present. At the end of the month we all fill in a form claiming for the days we have attended and receive a cheque. The money is tax-free.

For someone like me who lives in London and is entitled to claim only £43 per day, this sum falls very far short of what is needed when measured against the cost of secretarial, research and postal expenses, etc. And there still remains the question of a livelihood. Some peers combine their parliamentary work with a job. There are lawyers, academics, doctors, scientists in the House. Others use their peerage as an indirect source of income, acting as consultants for a firm, business, association, trade union and so forth. Having declared his interest, a peer may then represent in debate the interests of the institution with which he is associated, or act as a contact or arrange useful introductions on its behalf to MPs, etc.

No one has ever asked me to be a consultant but I do sometimes earn a fee or honorarium. The Foyles lecture agency, still run by my friend Miss Whalley, provides me with opportunities to speak to a variety of groups all over the country. The talk they used to like best was 'The wife of a diplomat'; but now I am always asked to speak about the House of Lords. Indeed, the talk formed the basis for this book. Miss Whalley makes the arrangements and settles the terms, usually my expenses plus a fee of about £100. The one disadvantage is that the dates for these talks are settled months – sometimes a whole year ahead – and may eventually clash with an important debate in the Lords. My talks are always very flexible and the conversation at lunch usually shows me how to pitch each one. Their length has become adjustable and I have almost come to think of the lecture as a long roll of material which can be cut to any required length.

As well as giving me a small income, the talks take me out of London to see what people in the rest of the country are doing and thinking. I remember a visit to speak to the Isle of Wight County Federation of Women's Institutes. The last part of the journey was on the handsome new catamaran ferry. I thought it excellent, but at lunch the ladies produced every criticism under the sun about it: the ferry was bad for wheelchairs, bad in rough weather, too cramped. Their final condemnation, though, was that it was not good for a nice chat because it made the crossing too quickly.

Character differences between the people in the North of England and those in the South are always striking. On a visit to Purley in Surrey, the organizers said the United Reform Church Hall where their meeting would take place was five minutes from the station; an easy walk. And so it was. But a group in, say, Yorkshire would never have done that. They would have been at the station, peering along the platform with anxious faces. A southern audience cannot express their appreciation so easily and with as much warmth as people in the north – or so it seems.

Many ladies in my audiences are convinced Conservatives, but I know that as a lecturer I must show no political affiliation. Proof of how well I succeeded came to me once after a visit to Wales. Kate had driven me to Paddington Station and was then going to the chest clinic at Brompton Hospital. She had had an asthma attack during the night and I remember she was silent and depressed about it. At Newport station I was met and taken on a beautiful drive through the white frost and soft January sunshine. An indomitable 78-year-old was at the wheel and the Area Chairman of the Conservative Women's Association in the back seat. She had just retired from the army and had some decided views, so I knew I would have to be more careful than usual to avoid offending political sensitivities. The letter I received later from my kind chauffeuse proved, beyond my wildest dreams, how well I had succeeded. 'Dear Lady Ewart-Biggs, hope you had a nice journey back. We all enjoyed your visit. I'm enclosing a button that fell off your glove, you may want to sew it back on. Just to satisfy our curiosity, which of the parties do you favour? You left us all wondering. Hope you'll have a return visit some time. Kind regards...'

But occasionally I do allow myself the mildest reflection of my bias. In Lincolnshire I sat beside the local mayor during lunch before my talk, and during the conversation he made clear his admiration for the Prime Minister. 'I think she's wonderful. Don't you?' he said.

'Now Mr Mayor,' I said, smiling, 'that may be the only point about which you and I could disagree.'

'What, do you mean you don't like her?'

'Let us say, I don't much like her policies. In fact I spend most of my days opposing them.'

I give about a dozen of these talks a year and a couple of times, annually, I am fortunate to be invited by the Civil Service College at Sunningdale Park, Ascot, to speak on the House of Lords for their courses to civil servants, for which there is a fee of £84. I have even spoken to a course made up of members of the Foreign and Commonwealth Office which gave me infinite pleasure as it brought me together with my old life again.

Apart from additional small amounts of money coming from television, radio and freelance journalism, the proceeds from the lectures make the major contribution to my income. There are nevertheless many other occasions when I am asked to speak when the question of money is always deemed to be inappropriate, even embarrassing. If the date suggested is far enough away, I usually find myself accepting. Saying yes takes less time than saying no, for an acceptance needs no justification whereas a refusal has to be explained. But I usually grumble dreadfully when the day arrives and I set off on a wet, dark Sunday afternoon in February to, say, a small United Nations Association group gathered in a freezing church on the Norfolk coast. It is on these occasions I know I must come to a policy decision over the whole question of invitations. The one I favour is to say, 'Yes, I'll do it out of love' if I like them enough, and refer the others to my lecture agency. Schools and groups supporting people in need come within the category of 'doing it for love'. Who am I to begrudge giving up one afternoon or evening to help them, when they devote their whole lives to the work?

The trouble about sixth form students is that they intimidate me. Standing on the rostrum faced by row upon row of frank, open, young faces, you know they will rumble the faintest trace of blarney or fake and are far too honest to hide their contempt. If I am asked to talk at the current affairs session – offered by some schools as an option to going to church – I speak either about Northern Ireland or the Third World, and am sometimes rewarded by a flicker of interest passing over student faces when I tell them about SOS Sahel's tree nurseries. But I find it difficult to hit the right theme and note for a prize-giving speech when there are three distinct groups to satisfy: parents, teachers and students.

I went on just such an occasion to Worksop College in Nottingham-shire. The headmaster, young, likeable and a very concerned person, told me the school was established in 1892 by Nathanial Woodward, a philanthropist who had set up a trust to finance seven schools for the children of the less well-off parents. It was small – 400 boys and girls – but current fees had risen to £5,000 p.a. In an effort to prove that the founder's aim was still maintained, the headmaster kept pointing out young people from modest backgrounds. Once again the pity of it all came home to me. Why do we in Britain maintain such a divisive education system? Why cannot we achieve, as other Western European countries do, a state system to which parents are proud to send their children, rather than impoverish them-selves by using private schools? Of course every parent wants the best for their children in terms of a superior academic education, better discipline and social advancement. While private schools con-tinue to offer this, I suppose parents will go on struggling to send their children there, which in turn will exacerbate Britain's deep social divisions and promote the existence of two separate communities. This was strikingly reflected in a BBC programme describing an exchange, in the summer of 1987, between ten sixth-formers from Rugby, the £6,750 a year public school, and ten from Ruffwood, an admired comprehensive in Kirkby near Liverpool. Both groups thought they would like each other but during the fortnight there was no evidence of shared values or shared feelings. The Ruffwood young people thought it extraordinary for Rugby parents not to want their children at home, and a Rugby boy, horrified by the desolate council estate, said: 'If we lived here I think we would lose all our morale, and become left-wing people.'

I vividly remember the school concert on the evening before the Worksop speech day. The young people were obviously well taught: serious and conscientious, most of them played the often highbrow music with precision. And then suddenly came true talent as two sisters, one a soprano and the other a flautist, performed movingly, their very young faces filled with concentration and effort. It was like a sudden shaft of clear sunlight penetrating the depths of a darkened room.

Next morning after the service in the chapel was over – I have never remained dry-eyed after watching long lines of young faces filled with hope and listening to boys' choirs – came the prize-giving. I always find it difficult to think of something special to say while handing out each award. There is not much time but I learned from Dame Margot Fonteyn, who is Chancellor of Durham University, at least to call each winner by name: Henrietta told me how, on receiving her degree, the great prima ballerina had said, 'Congratulations, Henrietta'. Finally, after all the books, trophies and certificates were handed out, I gave my speech. On these occasions I keep it very short (I remember once asking my own children's advice about Speech Day speakers, and the only thing they agreed on was the need for brevity) – and usually cover only two themes. First about the world which awaited them and how it would offer them a wider choice than the post-war life I joined, in spite of the present decrease in jobs. The need to conform had disappeared and young people were lucky to feel free to follow their own interests and develop in the way they chose. I went on to describe all the openings awaiting young people in the Third World to bring the rich and poor countries closer together. I ended, on impulse, 'And in taking up your new lives, who knows, you may want to put something back into the kitty in return for all you have received by way of loving homes and a wonderful school.'

The Head of House – a tall, articulate young man – thanked me and handed over a book token. And that was the end. Heaven knows what they thought of what I said, even if they thought about it at all. Afterwards one of the younger masters who had been sitting at the back of the hall told me of a conversation he had overheard between two of the boys.

'She's really rather good looking, isn't she?' said one to the other.

'I'm not sure,' was the response. 'I'd like to see her from closer before I decide.' A sensible reply.

From time to time the two factors which had come together to transform my life return to occupy it. Ireland and widowhood; one brought on the other, and the two together indirectly led to my being in the House of Lords. I would willingly exclude myself from being linked to either but I have become so firmly associated with both the country and the condition that, try as I may, I cannot disentangle myself from this implacable stranglehold. I often feel that my name appears on all those card indexes kept by media, press, debating societies, etc. under not only Ireland and widowhood but also all related subjects, such as forgiveness, revenge, bitterness, hatred, faith, loneliness and so on; whereas all I desire is to be asked to speak or write about more light-hearted subjects like weekend cottages, winter sports, difficult teenagers or indeed things which make up the hard core of life's 'humour'; or, if a more serious theme is necessary, then have I not shown my devotion to women's interests, housing policies, penal affairs and the rest? The nearest I have ever come to achieving my ambition of changing my image was when I was once invited to appear on the *Wogan* televison programme. But just before the day, the invitation was cancelled. Apparently a voice from on high, the apologetic researcher told me, had telephoned down saying, 'This programme is getting too serious.' I suppose at the last minute they quailed at the thought of my dark and lugubrious shadow cast over the jollity. So there it is. I know perfectly well when the telephone rings or the postman arrives it will mean an invitation to re-immerse myself in an intense moral issue.

There was one occasion when Ireland reappeared; but through the back door. It all started with a telephone call from the president of the Oxford Union inviting me to come and debate the motion 'That this House believes that violence against civilians for political ends cannot be justified'. He told me Professor Paul Wilkinson from Aberdeen University was to move the motion with me supporting him, and Norma Kitson – an ex-member of the African National Congress – was to oppose it. He did not yet know who the fourth debater was to be. We talked for a while and agreed that Norma

Kitson's presence could only point the discussion towards the long, but largely peaceful, struggle of the ANC against apartheid in South Africa and exclude the activities of other terrorist organizations. Nevertheless, I hesitated for a moment, knowing that I do not excel in a students' debating forum. I lack the confidence and clarity of mind to present arguments convincingly and instead allow my emotions to act as the spur. It is as if the extreme shyness of my childhood takes over and turns my mind to stone. Moreover the subject is an emotive one for me, even if not associated with Ireland. I am close to the pacifist position whereby being myself unable to commit an act of violence I cannot envisage asking others to do so on my behalf. But yet should this unequivocal position be applied to oppressed groups trying to achieve justice from within a non-democratic state? After all, the ANC had for seventy-five years conducted their campaign, and where had it got the South African black population? Was there a point at which they could be justified in the use of violence? These conflicting thoughts rushed through my head even while I heard myself accepting; as I have said before, saying yes is quicker. I put the date in my diary and soon forgot about it. I live my life from one day to the next.

The first reminder – about six weeks later – came as a shock. It was Sunday evening at the end of a good day. Kevin and I had come back from taking Milly, our very sentimental cocker spaniel, for a walk along the Putney towpath and found the light on the answering machine blinking. The tape bore the unmistakable tones of a journalist. When I returned the call he said, 'I just wanted to confirm something with you. I see from a local Oxford paper that you will be debating with Gerry Adams at the Union next month. Is that true?'

At first, I couldn't think what he was talking about; then, the truth dawned on me. The Oxford Union had obviously issued the president of the Provisional Sinn Fein with an invitation to the debate after speaking to me. I felt very cross at having been deliberately led into such an unacceptable situation. But my indignation was nothing compared to that of the journalist. Seeing the look on my face, Kevin asked what was wrong. 'Of course, you mustn't go,' he said. 'Ring the Union up straight away and tell them so.' I did this, giving the reasons for my refusal, and hoped the whole tiresome thing would just go away.

This was too much to expect. Next morning the front page article in the *Guardian* (which had contacted me) bore the headline, 'IRA victim's widow angered by Oxford invitation to Adams'. There it was again; the horrible label I try so hard to escape. The telephone rang the whole morning: 'I'm from the *Mail* (or the *Express*, *Standard*, ITV, BBC, etc.) and it's about the story in the *Guardian*. Could you tell me what you feel about the Union's invitation to Gerry Adams?'

Time and time again I explained. Yes, I said, it had been insensitive of the president of the Union to put me into such a position and, no, I would not debate with Gerry Adams.

'Why not?' the callers asked. 'We live in a free country and he has the right to a platform.'

Again I tried to explain. 'I find it personally repugnant to share a platform with the leader of a political party which was responsible for my husband's murder and which advocates the use of violence for political ends.'

But they wouldn't leave it at that. 'Do you think it was wrong of the Union to issue him with an invitation at all?'

'I believe that a person who endorses political murder should not be invited to debate the theme of whether violence for political ends can ever be justified with people who are not themselves in the process of perpetuating violence. The two speak at different levels. As far as platforms go, Mr Adams as an MP can avail himself of the most prestigious one in the country but chooses not even to go near the House of Commons.'

I agreed to do radio and television interviews about it. I felt depressed by the constant barrage of questions on a subject I found so distasteful, but I also feel sorry for journalists who, forced by professional demands, are obliged to delve deeply into people's inner-most sensitivities in order not only to provide news but also to satisfy the lowest level of human curiosity.

I went to the Lords mainly to get away from it all. On my desk I found a note from my friend Billy Blease (Northern Irish Labour Peer and ex-trade unionist). 'Here are some press cuttings from the Irish papers. Your decision was very favourably received in the Province; especially the phone-in you did on BBC radio.' The headlines astonished me, so different was the tone from my mild reaction: 'Biggs fury at Adams invite' one of them read, and another, 'Ewart-Biggs defiant on snub'. Nevertheless, perhaps through their very inconsistency they did represent an appropriate ending to a small, meaningless affair which had been sensationalized only because, in England, Ireland is always news if an element of violence is included. I have often argued with my friends in the press or media that they do not give a correct balance to their reporting of Northern Ireland. They give wide coverage to violence and death while hardly touching on the widespread efforts made by ordinary people there, those who through their courage support and strengthen the everyday life of the community against overwhelming odds.

One of my colleagues, Hugh Morton, an Edinburgh lawyer, was at his desk in our shared office. 'You were quite right to withdraw from the debate,' he said sympathetically. 'People will support you over that!' I went to the Bishops' Bar because I needed a drink, and walking along the passage I knew, from the sympathetic looks, exactly who were *Guardian* readers. Their reaction also proved once again that the House of Lords always rally round if they feel one of their own has been unfairly treated. I pushed my way through the group at the bar and asked Marlene for a glass of red wine. She is everyone's friend and carries out her work in that rhythmic fashion used by really professional barstaff. The movement from the glass to the bottle to the ice to the money to the cash register and on to the next customer is one long uninterrupted flow.

'You must overhear some interesting things here,' I said to her as I stood surrounded by the male chatter.

'Enough to write a book,' she replied, shaking her head and smiling while pouring the next drink.

'But I *am* writing one,' I said. 'Couldn't you give me a few snippets?'

'Wouldn't dare. It's mainly gossip and we don't want to get ourselves had up for libel.'

I was due to speak at Hull that evening to the Literary and Philosophical Society (an engagement for which the coveted fee was included) and this provided an unexpectedly lighthearted ending to the Oxford Union affair. The president of the Society and his wife met me at Hull station but I noticed their welcome was tempered by an underlying nervousness. We moved off and then, to my utter amazement, I noticed that we were being followed by a uniformed policeman and an unmistakable plain-clothes officer. 'Sorry, My Lady, for bothering you', said the officer, 'but we're investigating a suspicious telephone call the Society received this afternoon. The caller enquired after your whereabouts and was most insistent. It was a woman with a strong Irish accent who said she was called Pauline. Wanted to know where you were staying and where you would be lecturing. She said she was enquiring on behalf of a Mr O'Sullivan, and knowing of your problem with the Oxford Union yesterday, we didn't want to disclose any information or take any risks. And what's more we're not too happy about your staying at the Willerby Manor Hotel. It's a difficult place to guard.'

I stopped myself from laughing to save the young man's feelings, but the pieces had fallen into place. Kevin, who was working in his Leeds office that day, had obviously decided to come over and join me for my lecture and had asked his secretary to make enquiries. Pauline's brogue combined with his own Irish name, coming after the Oxford fiasco, had resulted in throwing Hull's kindly constabulary and my hosts into a panic.

Yet there have been many other occasions when Ireland has reoccupied my life in the pleasantest of ways. Visits to the North and the South for presentations of the Literary and Community prize awards have been unfailing pleasures. The Memorial Trust set up for Christopher on his death aimed, each year, to select and reward authors or playwrights for works judged to bring about greater understanding between the British and Irish people. Seamus Heaney, the poet, described it as having 'a commemorative function and an ameliorating effect'. Also that it 'moved people in generally desirable directions'. A few years later, in 1984, a legacy made it possible for us to set up a further prize. This Community Prize was designed to reward those working at community level in Northern Ireland. Each year we choose a different area of activity. First it was youth work, and then the following year we looked at all the work being done to enrich the lives of children of primary school age.

The third year we decided the Prize should go to projects aimed at helping women living in difficult environments. It was for the presentation of this award that Robin and I found ourselves catching a very early shuttle to Belfast in March 1987. Each year one of my children comes with me to attend their father's memorial presentations and it was his turn. I had been over to the Province previously to visit some of the projects entered for the Prize, and I well remembered my visit to the Women's Information Drop-in Centre at Ormeau Road, Belfast. The spirit and enthusiasm of the two women in charge was high. They told me of their work in helping women contend with the strain, both financial and emotional, which wives and mothers in that socially deprived area of South Belfast endured. It was estimated that only about one in every forty heads of households was in regular full-time work. Philomena and Joyce wanted their Centre to provide a base for the local women, so many of whom suffered from despair, depression and a general feeling of isolation. They also hoped to encourage creative activity among the women and provide ideas for some kind of training to attract young girls, many of whom were getting into all kinds of trouble including joy-riding. One of their 'clients' was there; a very young, very pregnant, obviously single girl. I agonized at the thought of the life that baby faced. Could it possibly be a happy and healthy one?

The second project, the Ballybeen Women's Group, was set in an immense housing estate just outside Belfast which accommodates 2,500 Protestant families. Here the level of unemployment was as high as 76%. Like its Catholic counterpart, the project offered companionship, advice, and basic training to women. But, on top of that, it saw itself as a pressure group. Like everyone concerned with poverty in Northern Ireland the women had taken exception to the proposed changes in social security legislation and three Ballybeen women were among the group who travelled to Westminster to deliver a petition to Margaret Thatcher.

My visit to these two projects had left me even more aware of the overwhelming problems facing women in Northern Ireland and also provided a fascinating insight into the contrasting cultures of the two communities. The two women in Ormeau Road had spoken volubly, with passion and emotion, of their problems, describing them in philosophical terms. Whereas the women of Ballybeen, neatly dressed and speaking in the level, clipped tones of the Protestant, addressed specific issues; discussing practical ways of dealing with them.

These two were among the winning entries for the prize on the day Robin and I arrived, through Belfast's usual rain, to attend the presentation. The entries had been so numerous and of such merit, we had decided to forego an outright winner and divide the £2,000 prize into four awards. The room at the top of the tall building where the reception was being held was filling up. Along one side sat the groups of excited women and then there were the guests chosen from various sectors of Belfast life. The conversation, inevitably, centred on the current Northern Irish situation and 'the troubles'. Much as I love the people of the Province I recognize how introspective they are. I remember once listening to a long chapter of their problems, and interrupting: 'But don't you realize that problems exist across the water as well as here? Don't you know, unemployment in the North of England is as high as it is here now?' This caused surprise, but for the wrong reason: 'Oh but it's quite different for them,' I was told.

Then came the photographers, with Robin towering over the shortish Northern Irish women, and finally the presentation of the awards and the speeches. Looking across the gathering from the table at the top of the room, I felt so happy at the thought of the lifeline thrown out by the projects to help so many women. I am sometimes obsessed with the question of how people everywhere get through their days. For example, how do they feel when they wake up in the morning? Are they depressed and frightened, do they face the day with optimism and hope or – most likely – do they just automatically start going through the motions of living? I know that many of these women in Northern Ireland must wake in the morning wondering how to escape the entanglements of debt. Not just worrying about how to make ends meet, but how to stop the gas being turned off, how to have food on the table when the children come back from school. The majority of them are on social security; what happens when the giro cheque runs out before Thursday? People are really broke only when they need to go through all their pockets. And then there is the degradation of being dependent on social security. Paul Sweeney, from the Northern Ireland Voluntary Trust, had said as we drove past a high-rise council estate that very day: 'Every single person in that block is on social. Can that be right? Shouldn't we be looking for another way?'

Next morning Robin and I parted company: he returned to London, while I took the road to Dublin. Because of what happened to Christopher, everything takes on an aura of unreality when I am there. For instance, the mortuary where I saw him last seems to be everywhere, round each corner, at the end of every street. The people I hear in the streets are not just voices with Irish accents; they are an intricate part of what happened to Christopher.

But the National Gallery of Ireland, the setting for the tenth presentation of the Memorial Literary Prize, is real enough, and beautiful. After much thought from the panel of judges, the Southern Irish playwright Frank McGuiness had been chosen as winner for his stage play, *Observe the Sons of Ulster marching towards the Somme*. This outstanding play was described in the judges' citation as, 'not only to be a distinguished achievement in artistic terms but also to present Protestant culture in an extraordinarily revealing, imaginative and enlightened way.'

The winner arrived towards the middle of the party, just when I had almost given him up. Frank McGuiness, orange-haired and stocky, wearing an assortment of bright coloured clothes made an impressive entrance; he could only have been what he was, an Irish playwright. The ceremony then started. My speech of welcome was not quite good enough. I blamed my tiredness and headache but it might also have been something to do with being in Ireland. Before announcing the outright winner, a special tenth anniversary citation was given to Hubert Butler, not so much for the book *Escape from the Anthill* which he had entered for the prize, but more in recognition of his whole life and work, which had been dedicated to advancing pluralism, tolerance and the increasing of understanding which reflected the aim of the Memorial. The very old gentleman sat in his wheelchair, amazement and joy written over his face as the citation was read out. Next the announcement of the winner, unrevealed until then, brought on a cheer. After accepting the prize, the colourful, eccentric-looking playwright made a short but moving speech, in which he recalled how what I had said on Irish television after Christopher's death had had a profound effect on him: 'Her words made me proud to be an Irishman and also proud she was English.'

The room was packed. I didn't know who they all were, but recognized and much appreciated the fact that many of them were young, well dressed in an off-beat way. I went up to some of them: 'Hullo, how are you and it's good to see you here. But would you mind telling me who you are?' The answer, accompanied by huge smiles, was always the same: 'We're friends of Frank.' I remembered with affection how the playwright had asked me if he could bring two friends with him. He had been most precise.

Afterwards came the dinner for the judges in the Georgian splendour of the Provost's House. The assembled guests spoke – inevitably – of Irish politics. Kevin had come over from London for the presentation but, contrary to what his name suggests, he scarcely knew Ireland and after the initial shock brought on by this fact he became known as 'the sw3 O'Sullivan'. Frank was enjoying himself enormously. He told me his hopes for the play: a tour in the United States and a season at the National Theatre in London. His writing, he told me, was strongly influenced by one discipline: the deadline. 'I love it,' he said.

The dinner over, we drove out to West Meath and Tulleynalley Castle. I remembered so well when the children and I had stayed there with the Pakenhams immediately after Christopher's death and Robin had described the remarkable old house as 'the Crumbley Castle' in his diary. Thomas Pakenham made a present to me of V.S.Naipaul's novel *The Enigma of Arrival*, which was inscribed, 'For Jane – with love from Thomas. To mark the first ten years of our great endeavour'. It had been his idea initially to set up the Memorial Prize.

And then, next day, the Irish interlude came to an end. Ordinary things took over again, and on reaching home I found a Mother's Day present from Robin; some primulas and a note.

Not long after this visit came a crude reminder that in spite of all the efforts to promote understanding and peace in Ireland, violence still had the upper hand. I was sitting at my desk opening my mail one afternoon in November 1987 when I saw on the closed circuit television the announcement, 'A statement on the Enniskillen bombing is being made in the Commons and will then be repeated in the Lords'. This meant that the Secretary of State for Northern Ireland was telling MPs about the Provisional IRA's recent outrage on Remembrance Day, and the Minister responsible in the Lords would then repeat it to us.

I went into the Chamber to listen to Lord Lyell announcing the stark facts of the bomb exploding amongst all those people outside the church in Enniskillen who were paying their respects to the dead of two wars. Although there had been many previous occasions when a sombre House was given news of the latest terrorist atrocity, this time it seemed more horrific than ever before, and the words expressing the sense of horror and outrage felt by peers equally inadequate. By a sudden impulse I found myself on my feet – I had not planned to intervene – speaking urgently; slightly incoherently. First I expressed my condolences to the bereaved families, wishing them courage in the hard and painful times lying ahead of them. I went on, 'My Lords, the way to best commemorate the dead is by helping the living, so, following on such an atrocity, should we not once again evaluate all our methods of fighting terrorism to ensure they are the most effective? First, do we give Northern Ireland a high enough priority on our political agenda? Next, are we using the framework of the Anglo-Irish Agreement to coordinate the work of the security services, North and South, and wage the war against men of violence most effectively? Lastly, the people of Northern Ireland endure crisis after crisis. In order to show sympathy and support from this side of the Irish Sea, would it not be right to set up a fund to help the relatives of the victims?' I sat down feeling weak, powerless. I wanted so desperately for something to be done; something creative which, in a small way, would negate the grotesque act of violence and brutality.

Walking back to my office, I bumped into one of my colleagues whom I have never known particularly well. Looking at me with so much kindness and sympathy, he said: 'What you said in the Chamber must have cost you a lot. I just wanted you to know I realized that.'

If at all possible, I always accept invitations to speak at meetings of Cruse. I am firmly convinced that the practical help and counselling services given by the National Organization for the Widowed and their Children to those suddenly bereaved are immensely important. It was for that reason I found myself, in the middle of a busy week in November 1986, on my way to speak to the Salisbury Branch of Cruse. There was something immediately recognizable about the figure waiting for me at the station; how many times before had I been met by such a look both expectant and anxious, and seen it relax into a smile at my safe arrival?

'It's good of you to come. The car is just across the road; shall I get it for you?' I assured her I could just manage to struggle the short distance and we then climbed in.

'Do you bother about these?' she said, pulling on her safety belt.

I admitted that although making their use compulsory was the first thing I had voted on in the House of Lords, I still often forgot about them.

She went on with her friendly chatter. 'The Committee are longing to meet you before the talk – perhaps you'd like some sandwiches and a glass of wine?'

We stopped outside an impressive looking church. 'What is a United Reform Church?' I asked, genuinely wanting to know.

'Nobody better than the vicar to tell you about that,' she said rather elusively.

I was profusely welcomed by the president. 'We knew Christopher in Beirut,' she said, giving her voice that little dip people use when speaking of the dead.

Inside, the committee members were gathering. The well-known finger buffet was laid out: sausage rolls, very thick sandwiches, vol-au-vents, small sweet cakes, and, presiding from the centre of the table, the slim bottle of sweet German wine. 'May I introduce our Treasurer... our legal adviser...?'

'*Hon.* legal adviser,' interrupted the pleasant looking young man, smiling. He added to me, 'You may have bumped into my cousin Elizabeth Carnegy in the House of Lords.' Relieved to be able honestly to claim acquaintance as so often when asked I am unable to put a face to the name, I reflected for a moment on the impressive lady on the opposite benches who might sometimes in her speeches chide my party for its shortcomings.

Soon the small room was echoing with the unmistakable tones of the British upper classes. Two glasses, one after the other, crashed to the ground, victims of direct hits by swinging handbags. We moved into the hall next door and while the chairman was giving me an over-generous introduction, I looked at the faces in the audience. It was easy to recognize those who were there seeking help. The sorrow and suffering show in the eyes; they take on a blank look.

I spoke very personally, continually referring to the different stages of the long journey those who have suffered the trauma of bereavement have to endure. First the battle with all the negative emotions of bitterness, extreme grief, and so on. Then the struggle just to keep going and to get through to the end of each day. And then gradually the first faltering steps towards building a new life. I tried to illustrate ways in which people can help themselves, and then how the community in general and organizations like Cruse can give a helping hand during the journey through the long black tunnel.

In an effort to bring some relief into what can only be a sombre subject, I told them a story. It was a true one and, containing a high degree of black humour, was intended to illustrate how extreme grief can seriously affect a person's judgement and powers of rational thought. The story was about the trip the three children and I had made to France the Christmas immediately following Christopher's death. Hoping to escape from the greater-than-ever sense of loss brought on by the celebrations, we piled into the car and set off very early one morning to the ferry at Newhaven. Things soon started going wrong. Waiting at traffic lights on the outskirts of London I allowed my foot momentarily to stray from the brake pedal and the car gently came into contact with the one in front. An angry Italian remonstrated through my window demanding details of my insurance etc. My state of anxiety deepened as we set off again. But within minutes there was a further interruption. Flashing lights appeared from the darkness behind us and, after stopping the car, I found myself again under scrutiny, this time from a policeman. 'This is a built up area, Madam (pronounced sarcastically) and you're not allowed to overtake.'

'Oh, I'm so sorry, officer... how careless...' I blurted out excuses and apologies with the overwhelming desire to get on to catch the ferry.

'Well, I don't know, what with children in the car, it's not safe but...' He was cut short by the arrival beside him at the window of another figure. I hoped my eyes were misleading me, but no, it was the Italian from the previous mishap. Seeing my car parked, he had stopped to check on my insurance policy number. Listening to our exchange the policeman's eyes took on a look of incredulity. 'So you've already been in trouble this morning and it's not seven o'clock yet.' His doom-laden look hovered over the three children... 'What is it you're after, lady? If you go on at this rate, what'll you have? Three little coffins for Christmas. Is that what you want...?'

My nerves stretched to breaking point, I shouted back, 'Don't say that, don't say that... I'll go mad if you say that.' It was daylight when he let us go, catching the ferry no longer even a hope.

My audience listened to everything I had to say with total concentration. If I had said even *one* thing with which just one of them could identify and draw comfort, then my journey to Salisbury had been worth it.

On the train back to London I realized how tired I was and, looking back over the week, I reckoned I had over-immersed myself with alternative Britain. I had spoken to no less than six groups representing different interests and causes. First there had been the struggle to Liverpool Station the previous Friday to go to Saffron Walden to address a bunch of enthusiasts of the Brandt Report published in 1964, committed to finding ways of narrowing the divide between rich and poor countries. Next day I spent a frozen, but spellbinding, evening at a young people's concert in Canterbury Cathedral. It was to raise funds for Unicef and I had been invited to give what was hoped would be an uplifting message to the huge assembly. The organizers sent me back to London by car, which just about saved my life. Then I had visited the Hampstead Area Gay Community to speak about development aid. They were friendly and welcoming, but I sensed their feeling of isolation. And there had been the presentation of the Whitbread Community Awards when I served on the panel of judges with Lord Tonypandy and Brenda Dean. To fill any gaps left in the week there had been some important meetings. First the Suzy Lamplugh Trust, established to commemorate a vanished daughter and which aims to protect women in the workplace. And then the meeting concerned with setting up a West End day centre for homeless young people to give them shelter and protect them from the perils of a big city. And another about reclamation and recycling with the Taunton Think-Tank.

No wonder I felt tired. I vaguely wondered – out of curiosity rather than greed – what a professional person might have earned for a comparative amount of work and effort. But I readily accept that those of us committed to supporting the alternative methods conceived to help those who fall through the gaps left by the system do so on alternative terms.

There are times, however, when I return to the conventional mainstream of life. A notable example was a lunch at 10 Downing Street in honour of the Sudanese Prime Minister's visit. I presumed I had been invited because of my work with Unicef and SOS Sahel in Sudan, but was never sure.

The morning leading up to the lunch was less conventional. It had started with reading Robert Kee's book *Trial and Error*, written to prove the innocence of the people who had been convicted of the Birmingham Bomb atrocity in 1974. He maintained that their case should be brought back before the Court of Appeal and, as I had a parliamentary question down about it for the next day, I wanted to get my facts right. (When the case was eventually considered, the appeal was rejected.) Then before my 10.30 European Sub-Committee meeting about consumer education, I helped Henrietta get her Honda Melody moped into the boot of my car on its way to have a puncture mended. This operation removed any shine my appearance may have had and my carefully curled hair drooped in the rain.

But the lunch was enjoyable. Besides the Prime Minister, I was the only woman there, and when I arrived she introduced me inaccurately – 'Lady Ewart-Biggs – she's with Save the Children Fund.' The Sudanese Premier, Sayed Sadiq Al-Mahdi, a double first at Oxford, was in long white djellabah and carried a silver-handled walkingstick. The delivery of his speech was excellent. He spoke the formal words of friendship and referred several times to the brotherhood of man. Tall and impressive, he clenched and unclenched his outstretched left hand while speaking. Mrs Thatcher also spoke of the ties between Great Britain and Sudan, and brought a lighter note into her speech. She referred to the problems of the British in the Sudan political service when learning Arabic. Their text book she understood was called *Thatcher's Grammar*.

During lunch I tried to find out from my neighbour, Hassan El Amin Beshir, previously Sudan's Ambassador to Moscow and presently in the Ministry of Foreign Affairs, what was happening about the war in Southern Sudan and whether the negotiations were progressing. He smiled hopefully and then with a sad look referred to the shooting down of the Sudanese Airline aid plane. Nodding his head towards his Prime Minister he said, in what must have been the understatement of the millennium, 'Yes, he was a bit gloomy about that – but now he has got over it.'

On my way out, I said goodbye to my hostess. The Prime Minister shook my hand and leaning towards me said in rather conspiratorial tones, 'Well, you've got something, haven't you – have you got enough?' Confused as to whether she was referring to my life in general or Save the Children Fund in particular I answered rather lamely, 'Oh yes, thank you... quite enough.'

CHAPTER TEN

Prorogation, the Camera and the Sliding Seat

EACH YEAR, AFTER the two chambers have completed the business of the session, Parliament is prorogued. The ceremony is steeped in tradition, and although it is not necessary for peers to attend, I decided to turn up at the required hour of 9.30 a.m. on Friday 7 November 1986 to see what happens. I had two reasons for doing this: curiosity, and the wish to claim my daily attendance allowance.

In fact there was quite a good attendance and, waiting expectantly on our benches, we saw the arrival at the Throne end of the Chamber of a procession of five peers in their robes and fanciful hats. They sat down in a row at the foot of the Throne. This group represented an all-party Commission which, as Her Majesty never attends in person, is appointed by the Queen to preside on her behalf. The Lord Chancellor then said as much: 'My Lords, it not being convenient for Her Majesty to be personally present here this day, she has been pleased to cause a Commission under the Great Seal to be prepared for proroguing this present Parliament.'

What then happens is a kind of Queen's Speech in reverse, looking back on the dying year. Black Rod is first sent hurrying off to summon the Commons – 'Make way for Black Rod,' cries a tail-coated attendant as the tall, erect figure strides through both Lobbies. The Lord Chancellor, with their added presence, then declares the following: 'In obedience to Her Majesty's Commands, and by virtue of the Commission which has been now read, we do declare and notify to you, the Lords Spiritual and Temporal and Commons in Parliament assembled, that Her Majesty hath given Her Royal Assent to the several Acts and Measures in the Commission mentioned; and the Clerks are required to pass the same in the usual form and words.'

The Clerk of the Parliaments and the Clerk of the Crown, both from the Lords, then take up their positions facing the Throne, on each side of the despatch boxes. From the Temporal side the Clerk of the Crown reads out the short title of each Bill in turn. The Clerk of the Parliaments, grey and grave, turns towards the Bar, where the Commons are assembled, and pronounces the appropriate formula in, what sounds like a faulty French accent but is, Norman French. For a Supply Bill (roughly a finance or money Bill) the words are:

La Reyne remercie ses bons sujets, accepte leur benevolence, et ainsi le veult.

For each other Public or Private Bill and Measure:

La Reyne le veult

and for a Personal Bill:

Soit fait comme il est désiré.

The moment then comes for the Lord Chancellor to repeat the Queen's speech for prorogation. 'My Lords and Members of the House of Commons, we are commanded to deliver to you Her Majesty's Speech in Her Majesty's own words...'

First on this occasion came reference to the state visits made by foreign dignitaries to Britain, then the Royal visits abroad, and a summary of the past parliamentary year, picking out a few legislative landmarks. As I listened to the list – some of it so controversial and hotly contended – my eyes moved instinctively to the face of the Prime Minister standing among the MPs behind the rigid upright figures at the Bar of Black Rod, the Speaker of the House of Commons, the Sergeant-at-Arms and the Clerk of the Parliament from the Commons. Not a trace of guilt crossed her face when the Wages Act, bitterly opposed by Labour for eroding the protection of the wages councils, was baldly described by Her Majesty as a measure 'removing outdated obstacles to the creation of new jobs'; nor did she look at all shifty when Lord Hailsham's solemn voice announced that 'the output of the nation continues to expand, the number of people in work continues to grow...' For a second I felt sure one of the more choleric of my House of Commons colleagues would find that sentence intolerable provocation and stand up and shout, 'But what about the rising number of people out of work? What about all those families who receive the dreaded news of their redundancy and end of all pay packets, the news that will deprive them of the security and dignity provided by a job?' But of course no one did. The only sign of dissent I noticed was one of the Labour MPs standing at the Bar sadly and rather wearily shaking his head. (I saw Northern Ireland's fiery Protestant leader, the Rev Ian Paisley, at the forefront of the Commons group, and he looked as if butter wouldn't melt in his mouth.)

Casting my own mind back I felt the speech gave a selective picture. As I recollected the year, the events which stirred MPs – sometimes also the nation – most had surely been the Westland rumpus about where Britain's helicopters were to come from, the surge of feeling against the Shops Bill allowing Sunday trading, the horror of the American bombing of Libya from bases in Britain, the courage needed to bring about the Anglo-Irish Agreement and the fading away of Mrs Thatcher's front bench Ministers Heseltine and Brittan. However, the Lord Chancellor did not infer that Her Majesty had made any reference to these matters, although, for all we knew, those were the very issues which most enthralled the Queen but which were not matters the Government wanted to include in her speech closing down the 1985/86 session of her Parliament. I wonder if she sometimes complains about the contradictory sort of stuff which is spoken in her name, for after all, the session began on 6 November 1985 when Her Majesty announced her government's determination to curb public expenditure, to diminish its share of national output and open the way for tax cuts, but had effectively closed on 6 November 1986 with the Chancellor's give-away package, exactly the reverse.

The ceremony came to an end at ten minutes past ten o'clock with the Lord Chancellor intoning, 'My Lords and Members of the House of Commons, I pray that the blessing of Almighty God may attend you, and in obedience to Her Majesty's commands, prorogue this Parliament to the 12th day of November, to be then here holden.'

Then we all went home.

Nobody could have called that a hard earned attendance allowance.

Thank God for insomniacs. Without them Channel 4's programme *Their Lordships' House* (now off the air) might have been very short of viewers. It lasted for about fourteen minutes and came on between half past twelve and one a.m., it boasted an audience of half a million. Friends have sometimes told me that they have, or have not, seen me on the telly from the Lords. Either way they express surprise. I ask whether, on the occasions they *have* seen me, they agreed with what I was saying. This invariably brings on a hazy look and they say, vaguely, 'Well, you *looked* very nice.' I began to realize that the programme was appreciated as visual entertainment rather than as a source of information.

Then I became involved with its production and this made me regard the whole thing differently. Walking through the Peers' Lobby one day in about May 1987, Howard Anderson, the editor of the programme, stopped me and said, 'We are thinking of asking one peer from each of the parties to present the programme. Would you agree to be one of them? It will be an experiment. I am hoping to inject the programme with the knowledge you all have of the House of Lords.' He had already asked Lady Young from the Tories and Lord Winstanley from the Liberals. Thinking it might – as my mother used to say about so many things – 'make a change', I agreed to join them.

In the event, the general election intervened and my turn did not come until July. I looked forward to the day and was only sorry it turned out to be such a drenching one. Unable to decide what to wear, I set off armed with three different outfits and my electric rollers in a bag. 'Are you familiar with the autocue?' Howard Anderson asked me over the indoctrination lunch in the St James's Hotel.

'Yes,' I said. 'More or less.'

'Good, then it won't take so much time practising.'

With the Order paper giving the business of the day propped up against the bottle of Beaujolais, we planned what parts to include. 'Frank Beswick has a question down about airport duty-free shops,' I said, 'That might be good – everyone who travels has an interest in "duty frees".' It was agreed as a possibility.

'What about the debates?' said the programme's editor, 'They all look pretty turgid this afternoon; Channel Tunnel Bill and several Northern Ireland Orders. What a tedious lot.'

'But people know very little about Northern Ireland and even less about the legislative process used for the Province,' I said. 'For instance, the Appropriation N.I. Order lays out the entire annual expenditure for Northern Ireland. But as the procedure is by Order in Council rather than a bill, there will be no opportunity to amend any of the clauses or vote as there would be for a bill resolving change in the rest of the United Kingdom.'

'Why not?' asked Howard; proving the point I had just made about people not knowing much about Northern Ireland.

'When the chaos of the early 1970s brought on the dismantling of the devolved Government of Stormont, then the 1974 Northern Ireland Act set up all these Orders. Profound changes are made under their authority. I remember speaking in the debate about closing down the gas industry in the Province by Order in Council. The debate took place at dinner time when there were only a handful of peers in the Chamber. Just think of all those elderly Northern Irish ladies having to break the habit of a lifetime and change to electric cookers – and then imagine removing the supply of gas to every householder in, say, Wales or Yorkshire without allowing an opportunity for discussion. There would be revolution. But the Northern Irish just have to put up and bear with it.'

Question Time seemed different that afternoon. Under normal conditions I am either rigid with concentration because of having to intervene or – if not – most relaxed. I am sometimes amused and other times made angry by the Minister avoiding an awkward question. But on this occasion, with the programme in mind, my concentration was total. At the end of the half hour of questions and with the Channel Tunnel debate booming in my ears I left the Chamber and went to the portakabins in Black Rod's garden which housed – if you can call it that – the Channel 4 unit. Instantly I became part of the team and was reminded of the cohesion and intensity of the working relationship between members of the group from the producer down to cameramen and continuity girls. The objective was to produce a fourteen minute programme and they had from then, about three o'clock, until ten o'clock that evening in which to do it.

A certain divergence showed up immediately we started to write the text for the autocue. My phobia for clarity led me to write in detail and at length. Howard, with the fourteen minutes time limit in mind, removed about three quarters of what I had written from the word processor, leaving only the gist. 'But they won't *understand*,' I complained.

The structure of the programme was emerging. We had learned that the Home Office Minister, Lord Caithness, was due to make a statement to the House early in the afternoon about prison overcrowding and we planned for the programme to include an interview between us both. This would come immediately after my introductory remarks, excerpts from the Northern Ireland Order and the question about the duty-free shops. As a grand finale, the producer intended to include shots from the river where Frank Longford – rather surprisingly – was running a plastic duck race to raise funds for muscular dystrophy.

As the afternoon and evening wore on, I realized how mistaken I had been in my expectation of an easy ride. Drafting the script for the autocue was so difficult. How on earth could I describe the complex legislative system for Northern Ireland in a few lines? How would I manage to be concise and to the point in my interview with Malcolm Caithness? It would require the art, which so consistently eludes me, of thinking on my feet. Finally, at about nine-thirty – we had already had our supper brought in to us – we put the programme together. It was like a jigsaw puzzle with all the pieces strewn around the floor. But in fitting them together, we ran the risk of ending up with either not enough pieces or too many.

I was asked to go and sit on the small chair facing the camera and with the cardboard Palace of Westminster and river as a background. By that time doubting that my dark red dress had been a good choice and knowing how tired I looked, any vision I might have had for a starry career in television disappeared. 'Don't worry, My Lady,' said a production assistant whose job was mainly to see that I didn't get flustered. 'If you make a mistake just start again. We've got all the time in the world.' Having a vague knowledge of the rate of overtime for camera crews, I rather doubted this, but was grateful to him for saying it. 'So when you're ready – and this will be a practice run.'

After the first few introductory lines, the editor's head came round the portakabin door. 'Project your voice more – throw it out,' he said rather alarmingly. We started again. But this time I ran two words together. The girl in charge of the autocue looked sympathetic and taking her pencil separated the merged words with a comma. I set off once more and this time kept going until the end.

Suddenly it was all over and the fact that the whole programme team came tumbling into our portakabin, relief on their faces, proved what I had suspected, that it hadn't been a practice run at all.

'Would you like to watch the whole thing through?' Howard Anderson asked me. He looked tired with shadows round his eyes. In the third portakabin, they were closing things down with the day's work coming to an end. The programme started to appear on the screen. Much as I hate watching myself on television – each line in my face and false note in my voice jarring – I became absorbed in seeing the ragged ends we had worked on all afternoon smoothly joined together and producing such a coherent picture. I went home tired out but grateful to have been given the chance to see the House through the lens of a camera.

'Jack of all trades' might provide a fitting epitaph at the end of it all. But when I looked down into the water at Westminster pier at the long, thin and eminently capsizable boats with sliding seats, I knew I was stretching my luck. Yet, at the time it had seemed the right thing to enter for the Speaker's Summer Regatta in aid of the St Margaret's Appeal for funds to restore the little church by Westminster. I have a special attachment to it because Christopher's Memorial Service was held there. But on the day itself, when I arrived at the assembly point on Speaker's Green below the Speaker's apartment in the Palace of Westminster, in my trousers and shirt, the scene which greeted me made me wonder if I had made a mistake. Everyone looked very professional. Teams of athletic looking young men, jogging up and down in pristine white T-shirts inscribed with the name of the crew on the back: *Hansard*, the Inter-Parliamentary Union, Lobby correspondents, and so on. I went in search of House of Lords Boat No 2 and found a distinguished, although less conventionally attired group, some actually in long corduroy trousers. But the major trouble was that the pinnacle of their athletic stardom was well past. For example, the 13th Viscount of Massereene and Ferrard had been a strong oarsman at Cambridge, but in the 1930s, and the ex-MP from Belfast Lord Fitt had learned a thing or two about the water in his time as a merchant seaman in the 1940s. But those days seemed rather distant. Two other peers, Lord Monson and Lord Milner, were there looking quietly confident. One of the organizers asked us to sit in a long line on the grass as if in a boat to simulate rowing. Rather morosely we obeyed. I started to think of opting out. 'Is it very difficult to row from a sliding seat?' I asked one of my fellow oarsmen.

'Why? Have you never done it?' came the astonished reply.

Grateful that an accomplished cox had been assigned to us (though artistic licence shows otherwise in the cartoon), we set off in the launch from the Speaker's Green pier to be decanted into one of

the lethal looking boats bobbing about alongside the Palace of Westminster. This operation was difficult enough and, to make matters worse, word had got around that the previous Labour prime minister, James Callaghan, had fallen in. This news did nothing to steady our nerves. My place was at bow, presumably because that was where I could do least harm. Very soon I recognized that all earlier errors of judgement paled into insignificance beside the one I had just made. Looking at my fellow oarsmen, I wondered how great were their powers of survival; either from submersion or over-exertion. It was a very hot day and I didn't much like the colour of some of them.

Rowing to the start just the Westminster side of Lambeth Bridge was bad enough. Far worse was negotiating the horrible moving seat without losing my balance and falling in, at the same time keeping the blade of my oar from being dragged down by the water. When this happened the pressure against the oar brought its handle hard up against my middle, threatening to cut me in two. Dislodging it was a near impossibility. Finally we were poised for the start against a journalists' team, and the gun went off. I remember little of the terrible moments which followed except being gripped by a super-human force, a strength which somehow kept me in the boat, hanging on to my oar and not completely sabotaging the efforts of the others. That was the limit of my hopes. We passed – I wouldn't say flashed past – the finishing point and someone in a launch shouted through his loudspeaker, 'The Lords No 2 boat has won against the Lobby correspondents' boat, so must row again in the final heat.' Scrambling out onto the pier and leaving the atrocious contraption behind me, I started running in panic.

'Row again? Never. You have to be joking,' I heard myself mutter as I tried to put as much distance as soon as possible between the nightmare and myself.

When I look back on this adventure – which could so easily have been a misadventure – I still wonder why I did it. I cannot claim that courage is the propelling factor behind such acts of folly. I suppose it must be characteristics such as impetuosity, insouciance and a high degree of optimism.

CHAPTER ELEVEN

Peer and Comrade

THE LABOUR PARTY Conference – or simply 'Conference', as the fraternity call it – is not the most natural setting for noble Comrades. Some of us attend every year in a laudable attempt to keep in touch with the grass roots of the party, others are there to meet the colleagues, journalists, foreign diplomats, trade unionists, pressure groups, etc. who each year congregate at the seaside resorts of Brighton or Blackpool. Some of us go for both reasons and also to have a good time.

I have been attending these explosive annual events ever since I became involved in party politics and have grown to love the occasion, inevitably made up as it is of a heavy consumption of political theories, slogans and sandwiches – all indigestible. My first-ever Conference in the late seventies was in Blackpool and presented the overall picture I always keep in my mind. The constant movement backwards and forwards along the seafront of small groups of delegates, all intent on getting to their next destination: maybe an evening fringe meeting, another party given by the media, the afternoon session in the Winter Gardens when the resolution from their Constituency Party composite will come up, or the proverbial smoke-filled room plotting the National Executive Committee elections. And then there is the jostling throng at the entrance to the Conference Hall where the roped off alleyway is lined by pamphleteers, hands outstretched thrusting sheaves of literature at the arriving delegates. Pamphlets about every subject under the sun; every injustice, national or international, is covered. They chant their slogans, push and jostle for better position. Having run the gauntlet of this outer and extreme fringe of ideology, the delegates pass through the security ring. Handbags are searched, badges examined by the pleasant, good humoured stewards, and finally the inner sanctum is reached.

The vast hall is divided into sections; one for trade union delegates (each one carrying the entire block vote of his union in his pocket), another for the constituency delegates (representing their local parties with one vote each), another for MPs (also with one vote), a section for peers and members of the European parliament who have no vote at all and a last one for the press. People come and go, talking earnestly to each other. Above them all on the platform sit the members of the National Executive Committee with the chairman in the middle behind the microphone. Just below is the rostrum where the delegates make their speeches with one speaker immediately replaced by another, chosen by the chairman from the sea of upstretched hands. Most of them inveigh against all things and their style is confrontational and loud, but there are true orators too.

Although Shadow spokesmen from the Commons are usually called to speak on their particular subjects, members of the House of Lords rarely venture to the rostrum. They keep rather a low profile. After all every Party manifesto until 1987 included abolition of the Upper House which makes us keep our heads down. But in spite of that hang-up I very much enjoy being there and felt less of an outsider at the 1987 conference. On previous occasions surrounded by the sweaters, jeans, trainers and beards I had stood out as a freak in my neat skirt, shirt and jacket. But more formal attire had become the order of the day and there was hardly a delegate not wearing shiny black shoes, neatly knotted tie, etc. This new respectability had not taken over completely. For instance there was the Edwina Currie Joke Wall. This had resulted from her ill-advised and much publicized observation about the people of the North of England needing to pull themselves together and eat healthier food. She claimed this would bring them up to the level of people in the South. Some of the jokes were in remarkably bad taste. But there were exceptions: 'Eat tripe, don't talk it' had a certain succinct charm. But eventually things got to such a sorry state that the wall had to be painted over.

'I would die for my country but I would never let my country die for me'. It was the leader's speech and Neil Kinnock's voice from the platform filled the hall. He has all the qualities required by a great orator: the sense of timing, colourful word play, sincerity and – a final bonus – husky Welsh intonation. He had come onto the platform with his wife, Glenys. They kissed each other and then she took her seat at the back of the rostrum while he went to take his beside the chairman, Neville Hough, at the front.

His speech came straight after the handing out of Merit Awards. Every year, veterans of the party are honoured for long years of loyal service. And each time I listen to their short – sometimes not so short – speeches of thanks I marvel at the old people's fluency and confidence.

I had been watching Neil, wondering if he was nervous, how his stomach felt. But there were no signs of it. He was smiling; he usually does. He appealed to the 'moral majority' in Britain, saying, 'It doesn't expect politicians to deliver heaven on earth. It does expect politicians to work to prevent hell on earth.' He described the Tories as 'rulers who neither see, nor feel, nor know,' and that Mrs Thatcher was 'prepared to leave our children with a legacy of decay and despair.' A get-rich society had been dressed up by the Tories as the 'opportunity society,' he said. 'They have dedicated every policy to making the rich richer and the poor poorer ... They vaunt a commercialized paradise before young people and they give them the purgatory of unemployment and insecurity.' On the thorny defence question, he left no doubt about his party's non-nuclear stand. 'We are the first generation not to have to deal with the existence of weapons of obliteration ... must be faced squarely and honestly by everyone ... I face it as an adult, as a citizen, as a father ... In everything we do, we choose life. In everything we do we refuse to submit to the idea that the present and the future are beyond our control.'

His speech took almost an hour and at the end delegates gave him a rapturous standing ovation. The Kinnocks stood close to each other, the red of Glenys's dress harmonizing with the huge red rose depicted on the background of the platform. They were young, smiling and attractive. Conference loved them.

Sitting in the crowded hall, I thought about the importance of this setting and the platform it gives to people who are not powerful or rich or influential to express their views. A few days given over to ordinary people who are taken up with politics to come together to listen, agree or disagree, drink together, socialize, make speeches and share one week of the year with each other. South Africa featured high on the agenda. A delegate spoke: 'I was there for three days – three days I will never forget ... saw children running away from us because we were white ... I saw what it was like to be black in South Africa ... I saw the courage of the black people ... my time's run out, let's make sure that Botha's does too.'

And then a debate on nuclear power and energy policy brought a packed floor with hands held high waving their agendas trying to catch the chairman's eye. Women speakers were in the majority. Shrill voices from the rostrum; sometimes raised to a shriek as they misused the microphone: 'We have not inherited this earth – we have borrowed it from our children.' But then the deep tones of a trade unionist speaking for the nuclear power industry and putting forward another argument: 'Comrades, the world is going for growth – not only for your prosperity but for Third World prosperity too.'

When the debate concentrated on women's rights and equal opportunities there was a curious lull. The pressmen gathered in front of the platform started reading their newspapers; the photographers put down their cameras and sat down for a rest. The hall noticeably emptied and the remaining delegates relaxed in their seats, thereby providing justification for the strident voices of the women delegates at the podium pouring out their discontent and laying bare the inequalities and injustices to women. 'Fine words and good intentions have not got us far... The fact that women are so badly represented in the Labour Party should be a concern for us all... Women form 52% of the population, yet working women are the most exploited in our country...'

The session given over to international issues saw a much loved and highly respected elder statesman and great proponent of international socialism at the podium. Willi Brandt in his deep voice and perfect English spoke of how the 'Conservatives promise the *majority* what only a *minority* ever get,' and added that social degradation was too high a price to pay for the privilege of a minority. He spoke of the moral strength needed to create policies which do not leave minorities out in the cold and he questioned which was more difficult, to modernize our parties or modernize society. 'Comrades, friends, it is my conviction that the world cannot be a secure place without common security. This will not happen without a British Government playing a constructive part.'

But Conference is not all made up of composite resolutions and speeches. At lunchtime, Tilli Edelman, my regular Conference companion, and I were picked up by a brightly coloured doubledecker bus, with a beaming sun face painted along its side, to take us to the Blackpool pleasure beach. The invitation came out of my being Opposition spokesman for Home Affairs, which covers most leisure activities. First we were shown the rides – 'Ninety white-knuckle thrills' – some still made of wood. My favourite was the flying machine opened in 1904, and designed to give the sensation of flying. The maiden flight was reported at the time in the *West Lancashire Evening Gazette* as follows: 'The sands were black with people all gazing at this strange, umbrella-like structure. Silently and without the least fuss, the machine started. For a few moments the cars hung close to the platform, then the speed quickened and they began to swing out at an astonishing distance and floated far above the heads of the crowds.'

The amusement park is owned and run by a family and the chairman, Mrs L.D.Thompson, aged eighty-three, still tries out all the new rides. 'I used to keep my eyes shut and hang on tight,' she said, 'but then my son said, "You're missing half the fun" so now I keep my eyes open and go round without even holding on.'

I have never understood the craving people have for fear, so it was a relief to discover that three generations of the Thompson family had also tried to provide a good service and to deal fairly with holiday-makers. 'We've tried to get a family bar going where there is a variety of food and drink and things for the children to do,' Geoffrey Thompson told me.

'Good – I made a speech in the Lords once saying we should make our pubs into the sort of places suitable for children, rather than *just* for hard drinking.'

'Yes, I know. I read it.' (This reminded me yet again of how many people read *Hansard*. My mail bag has on occasions even brought me letters from prisoners commenting on something I have said in the Lords. I like to imagine *Hansard* propped up on the Wormwood Scrubs breakfast table.)

I have many Conference memories, and a favourite was when one year the French Socialists joined us soon after their own election victory. Over lunch I asked them what was the major hurdle to their new administration. (I had given up interpreting both linguistically and doctrinely between them and Eric Heffer.) The answer came without hesitation. '*Les banques – nous allons les nationaliser mercredi.*' They settled down again to their lobster leaving their British comrades green with envy.

A less happy memory is of my first Conference. Gaining entry to the hall with a press pass, I spent only one day in Brighton and late in the evening set off back to London, giving a lift to the obliging journalist who had provided the pass. We were in animated conversation about the day's events when all of a sudden a police car stopped us. 'Yes, officer, is there anything wrong?' I asked the short-cropped blond head at the window.

'It seemed you were driving erratically.'

'Do you mean dangerously?'

'No erratically. Would you have had a few drinks?'

Remembering all the highly alcoholic fringe meetings, my heart stopped still. 'Yes, but very few.'

'Then I suppose you wouldn't object to blowing into this bag?'

The next ten minutes turned rapidly into a nightmare. Out of panic and lack of breath, I failed to carry out the exercise adequately. The young policeman then put me under arrest, bundled me into his police car and drove me and my startled friend to the police station. Trying to gather together my shattered wits, I filled in the form they gave me, wondering what the colour of my eyes had to do with it. And then came a poignant moment, from an older policeman: 'You have the right to inform one person of the fact that you are under arrest. You may use that telephone over there.'

'But there's really no one to tell; only my three young children. They must be asleep by now. It would be a dreadful shock to be woken up with the news that their remaining parent is under arrest. So I don't think I'll let anyone know.'

Did I see a miniscule softening in his eye? Anyway they produced the bag again and this time with a sense of hopeless fatalism I blew into it with all my might. A series of despairing pictures paraded through my mind; the beloved Triumph Stag up on blocks – me hanging onto a strap in the underground with garlic eaters surrounding me – me returning home from shopping each arm stretched to the limit by the heavy bags, me deprived of the refuge I loved best, the little car's deep black leather seat and companionable cassette player.

I returned to my senses to hear the voice of the older policeman say, 'Well Jack, there we are – take a look – that's OK. Just under the limit.' Jack, the young gauleiter, didn't seem so sure.

If Party Conferences do not provide the ideal setting for peers, nor do the hustings. Relieved of undergoing the bothersome democratic process of seeking election ourselves, it is a bit embarrassing even to enter the arena. So what with our disinterest in general elections and the tedium of waiting for the Prime Minister to announce the date, the atmosphere in the House of Lords in early 1987 became heavy. We laboured on debating and amending bills which we suspected might well lapse. The wide ranging and complex Criminal Justice Bill had its second reading and amendments were put down for a committee stage which we anticipated – rightly – would not take place, for once an election is called, any unfinished business is dropped. I was reminded of a holiday resort at the end of the season. I even reflected rather gloomily on the similarity between Westminster Palace and the brilliant movie *Death in Venice*. The beach was emptying, the beach huts taken away. Even the old man careering through the empty streets of Venice in pursuit of some unattainable mirage could be compared with the political parties setting off in pursuit of the electorate.

Everything in the Chamber had the feeling of being for the last time. All the well-known mannerisms of colleagues seemed more pronounced. Alistair Kilmarnock, the Alliance spokesman on DHSS subjects, who had the endearing habit of hitching up his trousers over non-existent tummy and hips whenever he rose to intervene in debate. And there was the Tory peer whose name I could never remember who wore a double breasted pinstripe suit which from time to time he smoothed uneasily over his hips when making his speech. Lord Winstanley – from the Alliance front bench – leaned forward speaking fast and lucidly, holding one hand in a cupped position in front of him. And then my dear friend Ted Glenamara who heralded his interventions by loudly clearing his throat. And the specialist adviser for the Criminal Justice Bill with the disarming habit, even in mid-explanation, of lifting both arms and using his index and middle fingers to trace inverted commas in the air to give a word or phrase particular significance.

The most poignant symbol of finality though came when I found Hervey Rhodes sitting in the Bishops' Bar one day. The indomitable ninety-year-old Yorkshireman who had been decorated in the Royal Flying Corps, built his own mill, become a Chinese expert, had tears in his eyes.

'What's wrong, Hervey?'

'It's my wife, she's dead.'

'How – what happened?'

'I just went out for a moment and when I came back there she was in her chair, dead.'

I desperately tried to comfort him. 'But you mustn't ever think of her like that,' I said. 'Think of her as she was all those years – how many was it?'

'Sixty.'

'... sixty years you spent together doing so many wonderful things – you must *never* think of her as she was in her chair.'

'Thank you, Jane – you must know,' he said and went sadly off, on his stick, limping.

There was a lot of minor business to push through before dissolution, some of it Home Office matters, and I found myself in those last days speaking on very different subjects. There was the Crossbows Bill – introduced as a Private Members' Bill in the Commons – which prohibited the sale of these lethal instruments to young people under eighteen. My unstarred question enquired about the funding for voluntary organizations after the abolition of the Greater London Council and the Metropolitan Authorities. A Private Members' Bill had grown out of my original debate about giving people access to their personal files. And finally the Protection of Animals (Penalties) Bill proposed to increase the fine and length of custodial sentences for people promoting dog fights.

I went to the Bishops' Bar for a chat with Wendy Nicol. I admired her great conscientiousness and friendliness. But on this occasion she was far from pleased because of having been stuck on the front bench for several hours without relief. (There is a rota system whereby the team of six Whips take it in turns – about an hour each – to man the front bench.) We then both settled down to supper and talked rather gloomily about the opinion polls: Labour support was sliding.

As members of the House of Lords don't have a real place on an election platform, and indeed in some extreme Labour strongholds their presence might bring the kiss of death to the candidate, only some Labour peers go to the hustings, and they are mainly those previously in the Commons who feel at home being harangued. My first contribution to the 1987 campaign came on the Friday following the announcement of polling day. The date had been planned long before by the Thaxted Labour Party. They had asked me down to speak and join in a social evening, but in the event it turned out a perfect opportunity for the candidate to meet many more of his supporters. A lot of those attending were teachers; and others, the older ones, were the old style supporter. They belonged to the Labour Party not out of ideology or a wish to see a more equal society or to bring about change; but simply because they felt part of it, for better or worse. The evening was typical of the nicest kind of Labour Party event.

A few days later I went canvassing with our candidate for the Chelsea constituency. Wearing very large rosettes and carrying a list of the electoral roll, some posters and packets of leaflets, we descended on Wiltshire Close, a council estate just off Sloane Avenue, and we went along ringing the door bells.

I have a real terror of intruding on people's lives when they are in their homes. Approaching someone either on the pavement, on a bus or in a shop is not difficult, but doing so in the sanctuary of his home takes a great deal of courage. But I shouldn't have worried. Many of the householders welcomed the intrusion, the men especially.

'From the Labour Party? Oh yes, I'll be giving you my vote this time.'

'Thank you very much, Mr A. I see your wife's name is down on the register as well. Do you know if she'll be voting on the 11th?'

'I can't be sure about that. Let's ask her. She's just getting tea.'

Mrs A. appeared and said to the candidate: 'Are you the gentleman who came round a little while ago about our heating problems?'

'Well, yes – that must have been our Labour Councillor. Hope he managed to give you some help.'

'Oh yes – we were ever so grateful. We'd had awful trouble – water never got more than tepid and he had it fixed. I'd like to show him how grateful I am. Yes, I'll be voting Labour.'

The next door was opened by a young Asian.

'Yes?' he said, looking at our rosettes in a bewildered way.

'I've just come round with the Labour candidate, David Ward, to see if you were thinking of voting on the 11th?'

'Yes, but I haven't decided who for yet.'

Here at last was a real live floater. Reading the opinion polls I have never believed they were flesh and blood, but here was the proof. David Ward joined me, scenting the quarry. 'Good evening. Sorry to hear I won't be getting your vote on the 11th. But I think it would be worth your while to know what the Poll Tax will mean before you settle for the Tories.'

'Oh? What's that?' asked the floating voter playing into our hands.

David then gave a lurid description of the new tax replacing rates which the Conservatives had included in their manifesto. Our quarry started to look suitably rattled upon hearing that this charge would have to be met by *each* person in all households.

The next front door remained determinedly shut – then slowly and cautiously it opened, revealing an elderly woman in a wheelchair. Catching sight of us she immediately and vehemently banged the door back in our faces. Why should she place her hopes in the political process? What could it do for her? Her preoccupation was firmly and totally centred on survival, getting through each day and wondering how many more there were before her.

Two little children were playing outside the next door. 'Are Mummy and Daddy in? Would you like a sticker?' Each child thereupon immediately labelled themselves with our Great Party's colours all over their bare tummies. The door opened and a smiling young man came out.

'Don't worry, I'll be putting my cross in the right place on the day,' he said cheerfully. 'We've got to get Thatcher out. She hasn't done people the like of us any good at all.'

The last door we banged on revealed that phenomenon, a first-time Conservative voter. Standing at the door with the squalid dingy interior of the flat behind him, he said, 'No, we're voting Conservative this time.' Here was what many Labour supporters would see as a traitor to his class.

'Fair enough, but why are you doing that, if you don't mind my asking?' came the reply from the entirely pleasant David Ward. 'Mrs Thatcher hasn't done much for you, has she. Look at the mess in the health service, housing policies, crime level and so on.'

'She's for strong government though, isn't she?' came the reply. 'Not like you lot who just want to support blacks, gays, lesbians, out of work layabouts and so on. Labour is only interested in people if there is something wrong with them. Mrs Thatcher thinks of the rest of us. I think she's wonderful.'

A few days later I went with David to a Drop-in Centre for the over 50s in the Earls Court Road. (I wish they had set the age level a bit higher: it made me suddenly aware of my accumulating years.) Although the two women who ran it, one a West Indian and the other a Londoner, were Labour supporters, many of the old people were decidedly not. 'Some of them are ex-nannies, you see,' said the manageress, 'and Tory to their finger tips.' It was a place with an excellent atmosphere and many of the people were busy cooking their lunch.

'Do you often come here?' I asked a dapper old man.

'Certainly in the winter, but in the summer I go for walks too. That takes up some of the time.'

'What do you all talk about when you're here together?'

'We always keep off politics and religion otherwise people get too heated.' He smiled.

The Old Peoples' Home in Dovecourt Street just off the King's Road was functional and efficient. Being there reminded me so much of my old mother who had died only a few weeks before, and I suddenly and hugely missed her. I talked to one old lady who was senile. She had been a nurse, possibly even a Matron, and relived some of the high points of her life with me. Another sitting at the same table was French and in spite of thirty-odd years spent in England her voice reflected every single French intonation. David and I were taken on a tour of the Home and there came the epic moment when two old ladies sitting in armchairs spotted us, rosettes and all, and in an attempt to protect themselves from the evil presence of socialism, closed their eyes. This reminded me of when, still wearing my rosette, I took our dog Milly for a walk in Chelsea Hospital Garden. I was genuinely amazed when I noticed several elderly ladies hastily put their own dogs on leads to avoid the pet having any contact with poor Milly – apolitical though she definitely was.

Television has made public election meetings largely things of the past. I well remember how in the old days halls would be packed out with electors cross-examining their candidate with vigour and humour. But, nevertheless, I had agreed to speak in two public meetings during this campaign. The first was in Chelsea to support David Ward, and the evening started strangely. I was on the point of leaving home when my door bell rang. I found an elderly gentleman wearing a grey suit and apologetic look standing outside wearing an enormous blue rosette. Clutching his electoral list and a pencil poised to tick my name, he asked me if he could count on my vote for the Conservative candidate Mr Nicholas Scott on the 11th.

'Now, you're really out of luck,' I said to him. 'You've happened on the one house in the road where its occupant doesn't have the right to vote.' (I said this on the probability that Radnor Walk did not contain any certified lunatics, convicts, bankrupts or other peers.) 'And the second blow is that even if I did have a vote it would be for Labour.'

The nice old gentleman walked off looking perplexed and even more apologetic.

Crosby Hall in Cheyne Walk was reasonably well filled. Some of the audience did not resemble the standard Labour supporter though, and I realized that many were there only because of their worry about the trunk road due to be built from Shepherd's Bush south to the river. This was a relief road to take away surplus traffic from Earls Court Road, but with the disadvantage of increasing the traffic congestion in Chelsea, polluting the environment and ruining Cheyne Walk and the Chelsea wharf area. This was a concern shared by both Tory and Labour supporters.

The meeting opened with Neil Kearney, the leader of the small band of Chelsea Labour councillors, and his speech related to local issues. He pointed out 'the reality of the situation' in a pronounced Northern Irish accent.

Next came my turn. I know my limitations, and one of them is adopting the right tone for a public meeting. I proved I was not much good at the hustings in the early days. It's not that I haven't got anything to say but I can't say it right. I know my accent is a disaster on a Labour Party platform, but I also know it wouldn't work to try to change it. My speech was about law and order. Speaking as one of the Labour spokesmen on Home Affairs, I presented some of the Party's ideas on crime prevention. I quoted some of the statistics about the rise in crime figures, the most dramatic one being that if you average out the crimes committed in one year in England and Wales it comes to one every seven seconds. The audience looked visibly shaken. The rest of my speech, lasting about twenty minutes, was good, solid, sensible stuff but somehow it didn't sound like a *campaign* speech. I sat down and they clapped politely.

Next came the candidate, who was thirty-one and extremely knowledgeable, having worked in Neil Kinnock's campaign office before the election. He made an excellent speech. In discussion time it was immediately clear that environmental issues and the relief road represented the two major preoccupations of the meeting. The contributions from the floor did not so much come in the form of questions but of statements. They were not seeking information, but giving it.

After a bit Nick Raynsford arrived from the neighbouring constituency of Fulham, which he had won from the Conservatives in a by-election. He spoke about local affairs in a convincing manner and I sensed the audience warming to him. The evening ended at about ten o'clock on a high note. I had noticed an eccentric looking man near the front who had shown no interest whatsoever in the relief road, poll tax or law and order. Finally, unable to contain his impatience any longer, he stood up and cried: 'I thought we'd come here this evening to talk about peace and socialism and there hasn't been a word about either.' Feeling ashamed, we took ourselves home.

Election day, 11 June 1987, was cold and blustery. Quite early the telephone rang and I was asked by the campaign office to give a handicapped lady a lift to the polling station. I rang her. 'Oh, how kind,' she responded. 'About ten-thirty if that's all right and I need to go to Philbeach Gardens. Is that where you'll be voting?'

'Well no, I don't actually have a vote but I'll pick you up.'

Interest crept into her voice. 'May I ask to whom I'm speaking?'

'My name is Jane Ewart-Biggs and I'm in the House of Lords so that's why I don't have a vote.'

Increased interest. 'So you're in the Lords, but you're one of us – that's nice. I'll be waiting on the corner of Hogarth and Knaresborough Roads. Thank you again.'

I set off thinking how much I liked that expression 'one of us'. It gives a feeling of belonging. The French Socialist Party bring about the same thing by using the familiar '*tu*' to each other. The bond was most vividly displayed when once I had a meeting with Madame Soares, wife of Portugal's Socialist President, in Lisbon's presidential palace. Her woman assistant entered the room. 'You can speak,' the country's leading lady assured me, 'she is one of us' – incongruous remark when surrounded by the trappings of power.

The rather stout lady standing on the corner propped up on her stick was obviously waiting for me. She was a music teacher, an ardent Labour supporter and talked local politics all the way. We took several wrong turnings and she rebuked herself each time. Pupils had to come to her house since she couldn't get around easily, and she lived on the fifth floor without a lift. But her spirits were buoyant and I realized what an important occasion elections were for her. 'Will you stay up all night for the results?' she asked me.

'Not if they go against us,' I said. 'I'll get too gloomy.'

'I always stay up. My sister comes round and we have a nice supper of tinned salmon and cucumber. We've done the same every election night for years.'

Later I went to take up my position as a teller at Marlborough School in Sloane Avenue. Already installed in the draughty, cold porch of the school I found the Tory representative, a large, elderly lady who wore her immense blue rosette inside her heart as well as pinned above it. The teller for the SDP/Alliance was smaller, more diffident and male. I took over from Jane Williams, the wife of Charles Williams, Labour Trade and Industry spokesman in the Lords; she had herself taken over from Lord Longford, making quite a noble line of tellers. Armed with pad and biro I started to carry out the mystifying task. The point I finally understood to be was that, during the campaign, results of the canvassers' findings are recorded in each constituency headquarters, revealing the voters who have committed themselves. So the tellers' job is to ascertain who has voted by noting down the numbers of the election cards of voters as they leave the booth. These numbers are then raced back to the different headquarters to give evidence of those who have not exercised their democratic rights. These abstainers receive a visit from a party worker later in the day who will try to entice them to the booths.

Many of the electorate leaving Marlborough School that morning understood this practice and uncomplainingly handed over their cards to the teller wearing the colours of their allegiance. Others, suspicious, walked straight on, hanging on to theirs. My colleague in blue gratefully accepted the vast majority. Some came from people who looked typical Labour supporters and a flicker of anxiety touched me as I saw several young working-class people very deliberately hand their cards to her, averting their eyes from my direction. But occasionally it was the other way round: a man with a couple of days' dark stubble on his chin and wearing a dirty shirt thrust his card at me, 'Here's one for you, luv.'

It was raining quite hard and I got colder and colder sitting on my little stool in the porch of the school. My feeling of gloomy foreboding also grew.

When I arrived home Kate asked me very solicitously what I was doing that evening. She had been to the polling booth in the King's Road and voted Labour, her brother and sister had done the same. But although they were unlikely to vote Tory, their interest in the issues which divided the parties was minimal. Like many young people whose childhood had been saturated with their elders' political talk, they were more attracted by questions of human rights, environmental issues and what was happening in the Third World. I told her I was going to an election party given by the directors of the Independent Broadcasting Authority. 'Now don't get all upset if you lose, will you, Mum. There's no point.'

I tried to follow her advice when the results started coming in that evening. The writing was immediately on the wall. (The story must be true that after the 1970 election Harold Wilson, the Labour Party leader, listened to only the first few counts showing Conservative advances before getting onto the telephone to 10 Downing Street. 'Start packing,' he said.) The improved Labour vote in the marginals prophesied by the media (probably to inject suspense) never materialized. I felt hopeless inside and must have looked dreadful outside. And then I was rude to another guest; a woman wearing a blue dress. I recognized her husband who looked pleasant and was wearing a blue sunflower in his buttonhole. But I had forgotten his name. Unfortunately they greeted me at the height of my incredulity and misery. I drooled on to them lamenting the results until the lady in blue had had enough 'Well, I think it's all to the good,' she said crisply. 'Very sensible,' she added for good measure.

Her husband interceded: 'Sh...' he said, not liking the black look on my face.

I went and watched the television in a corner of the huge room. I met Tom and Maureen Ponsonby also looking a bit grim. The commentators were forecasting more and more dizzy majorities; starting at twenty seats they soon reached 110. Standing alone, I listened to people's conversations. 'What will it mean to broadcasting?' one of the guests asked of our host, George Thomson. 'Mrs Thatcher's radicalism is all very well but it has been directed mainly towards the economy, privatization and so on. She's just not interested in change such as constitutional reform, greater freedom of information, looking at the penal system or setting up a democratic second Chamber.' I felt slightly comforted by hearing there were others who shared my worries.

The first day back at the Lords about a week later was a morbid affair for some of us. The faces reflecting most shock were those belonging to the Alliance peers. And at the bar I overheard one of my colleagues making the cynical comment: 'Well, you've got to hand it to the SDP. They said they would break the mould and they jolly well have. They've changed us from a two-party to a one-party system.'

In each new parliament the Oath of Allegiance has to be taken by every peer before he can sit and vote in the House. I had been to a buffet lunch in the Cholmondeley Room prior to swearing in after Prayers. The lunch was given by the National Environment Research Council to mark the 1987 European Year of the Environment. One of my fellow guests – a cross-bench peer – asked me why I looked so gloomy. 'I really can't bear the thought of "opposing" everything again,' I said. 'I would so much like to be on the creative side of politics for a change; to have a hand in the constructive planning of how to make things work; rather than always pointing out why they won't work. I'm sick of opposition. And anyhow there are so many things which are a mess. For a start, look at our electoral system – a party gets a majority of over a hundred seats in the House of Commons on a 43% vote, and we call ourselves the cradle of democracy.'

My companion, more detached and taking a less tragic view of things, smiled broadly and said cheerfully, 'What do you mean, cradle of democracy? More like the *grave* of democracy.'

Holding my Writ of Summons, I went to queue in the Chamber to take the Oath. The only light relief, as far as I was concerned, was seeing the new conservative Lord Chancellor, Lord Havers, on the Woolsack, wearing his hat the wrong way, with the flat side along his forehead rather than the pointed end. He had a nice look on his face and had gone through his elaborate introduction ceremony carefully. When he finally sank down on the Woolsack he wiped his forehead in a mock sigh of relief that it was all over.

A long queue snaked round the Chamber, but as I have said before, the House of Lords will if nothing else remain the last stronghold of chivalry, and the Bishop of Durham immediately let me into the queue in front of him. Handing in my Writ at the Table and, holding the Bible, I took the oath.

On my way out of the Chamber, like everyone else, I shook hands with the new Lord Chancellor sitting on the Woolsack. 'Congratulations. I hope you'll be very happy here,' I said.

'Thank you. I'm sure I will,' he replied smiling. No one could have predicted that Lord Havers's extreme pallor signalled the shortest period in office of any Lord Chancellor.

Not feeling like hanging around, I went home. The Opening of Parliament was to be on the following Thursday, 25 June and then it would all begin again.

CHAPTER TWELVE

A Real Live Anachronism

THE HOUSE OF LORDS might be seen as one of Britain's most irrational institutions. But yet, it retains the loyalties of its members and the respect of the nation. Why is this so?

In 1867 Walter Bagehot in his *The English Constitution* wrote that 'the danger of the House of Lords is that ... it is not safe against inward decay ... If most of its members neglect their duties, if all of its members continue to be of one class ... if its doors are shut against genius that cannot found a family, and ability which has not £5,000 a year ... Its danger is not an assassination, but atrophy; not abolition, but decline. ...'

Study of the House of Lords in recent years provides clear evidence that it is in danger of neither atrophy nor decline; indeed quite the reverse becomes apparent. Lord Cledwyn, leader of the Labour peers, gave some of the answers in his article in the *House Magazine* at the end of 1987: 'Several factors have combined to increase the significance and the value of the House of Lords as a Second Chamber. These include the consistently heavy legislative workload, the creation of life peers, most of whom resist the notion that bills should be given an easy passage through the Lords, and who believe that its role as a revising chamber should be performed as efficiently as possible. If a bill has been "guillotined" in the Commons, the Lords will today scrutinize it with special care ... The aim is to concentrate on those sections of a bill which have not been fully processed in the Commons and on points of high controversy. Timewasting and filibustering are not favoured although old House of Commons hands on all sides are seen at times to be sorely tempted. It is also well known that Governments with large Commons majorities tend to regard opposition to their measures with impatience tinged with arrogance and this, of course, increases the responsibility of the Second Chamber. ...'

In summing up, Lord Cledwyn presented an inside view: 'There is a reservoir of goodwill in the House of Lords, there is acknowledged ability and experience and a real commitment to perform the job well. But we also have the problem of a comparatively high average age and a part-time chamber where members under sixty-five have to earn their living. Everyone concedes the need for reform of some kind. The view seems to be that the vintage car travels comfortably from Westminster to Brighton and if it does hold up the traffic occasionally that is no bad thing. It is however worth remembering that there has not been a Commission to examine the Lords since the Brice Commission of 1917 which made some sensible recommendations and which were lost in the fog of war. Perhaps the time has come for another Commission, and if it does take a couple of years or more that is nothing compared with the constitutional importance of the centuries old evolution of the Lords.'

Lady Seear, leader of the Liberals, writing for the same publication offered some practical views: 'A revising Chamber needs to get things right. This calls for proper staffing and proper facilities. The library is wonderful, the Clerks are alarmingly intelligent, helpful and hard-working; but this is in no way adequate for the proper preparation and presentation of amendments. Heath Robinsons all, Lords draw on their own considerable knowledge, their contacts, their own private offices – which vary from the grand to the homespun. This is absurd. Merely as an illustration, the Alliance peers, all eighty-five of them, are serviced inside the House by two and a half people, fewer than can be found in the reception room of most Government departments. Maybe the House should be reformed, maybe in God's and Neil Kinnock's good time it will be, but in the meanwhile, there is a job to be done.'

There has certainly been no shortage of ideas about reforming the House of Lords. In 1968 the Labour Government introduced a Bill proposing a two-tier House composed of 230 created voting peers and a second tier of non-voting peers (including existing peers by succession) who would be able to speak, ask questions, move motions and serve on committees, but not vote. Voting peers were to be paid and expected to play a full part in the House. They would be subject to an age of retirement. This Bill was passed by the Lords, but was defeated in the Commons by a conspiracy between the left of the Labour Party and the Tory right-wing backbenchers. This alliance was led by Michael Foot, who opposed the Bill because he wanted the Lords abolished, and by Enoch Powell, who on the contrary wanted to keep it exactly as it was.

Tony Benn, formerly Lord Stansgate, who surrendered his peerage in 1963, also had decided views on abolition. 'The House of Lords', he wrote to *The Times* in 1975, 'like Madame Tussaud's, would be just as good if Ernie, the Premium Bonds' computer, selected those who sat in it.'

Since then both parties have drawn up proposals to reform the Lords. In 1978 the Conservative Review Committee, under the chairmanship of Lord Home, advocated reforms to strengthen the Upper House to enable it to perform more effectively the dual function of revising legislation and acting as a constitutional safeguard. A system was proposed whereby about two-thirds of the 400-member House would be elected by proportional representation and the remainder would be appointed on the recommendation of the Prime Minister plus law lords, bishops and royal dukes. The function of the Chamber would remain broadly the same, but its powers strengthened.

In May 1980 the Labour peers did their bit and produced a paper stressing the need for a second chamber, but rejecting the hereditary principle. Peers by succession would lose their seats, but could be nominated for life peerages. A proportion of voting peers, to reflect the Party balance in the Commons, would be chosen. Moreover, the working group called for a constitutional conference and/or referendum on the issue of the Lords.

Mrs Thatcher, characteristically, had the last word when, on 5 June 1980, she stated in the Commons that the Government had no plans for reform of the Lords as it had more important issues to tackle. So, for the time being, any schemes to ruffle Their Lordships calm have been shelved.

I would like to see our second chamber present less of an anachronism. A committed Francophile, I look across the channel and recognize that France's Senate is well structured. With a function comparable to that of the Lords, it can also claim to be democratically constituted. A third of its 328 senators are elected every three years for a term of nine years. They do not owe their seats, as do the members of the National Assembly, to direct suffrage but to an electoral college. This is made up of members of the National Assembly, the regional councils and the general councils of the Departments; making up 130,000 electors in all. Moreover, it ensures the representation of the territorial entities of the Republic and French nationals living outside France are represented in the Senate. Finally, unlike their British counterparts, French Senators are paid a salary and no doubt, have people to do their typing.

The Conservative Government began its third term with a majority of 104 seats in the House of Commons. Political commentators and members of the public consistently point out that the House of Lords represents the only true opposition to that Government. And, with the votes in the Commons becoming more and more numbingly predictable, there certainly has been a surge of interest in the Lords. But is this new-found confidence in the Second Chamber justified? How does it seem to us who work there? Do we really see ourselves able to make much change to the mass of contentious bills coming our way? And finally, why do we attend so regularly and show so much fidelity to an institution which gives us so little in return?

I believe the confidence placed in the Lords to change things may be over-optimistic. Although in the 1985/6 session the Conservatives lost twenty-two divisions and since 1979 they have been defeated more than a hundred times, this may not continue. The whole character of voting seems to have changed in this 1987/8 session. Various reasons account for this. One may be that Mrs Thatcher intimidates any dissident Tory peers by asking to see the voting lists following a Government defeat. Secondly, the Government Whips have been whipping harder. Thirdly, they have greater numbers at their command, on many occasions a young hereditary peer can be seen at the Table swearing in, which means that the lobby fodder grows. Indeed as I look across the Chamber more and more unfamiliar faces stare back at me from Tory benches. It is becoming clear that if the Government want to win – and in their third parliament they have shown every sign of wanting this – they can always summon up their backwoodsmen from the shires. Denis Greenhill put it in a nutshell one day when the division bells went and we met each other pushing our way into the Chamber to vote. Surrounded by the unfamiliar country members he said, 'You can always tell when the Government want to win. The average height goes up by about a couple of inches.'

Sometimes, unforeseen circumstances bring victory to the Opposition. For instance, two years running the Government were defeated when the Labour peers were holding their Christmas party in the

Cholmondeley Room. For some inexplicable reason these festive annual events take place in March and are so well attended that on these two occasions our superior numbers triumphed.

All Labour peers do their best to attend when there is a three-line whip. But, as speakers can continue for as long as they like, it is difficult to predict the exact time of divisions. 'I really must dash out for a minute and collect my dry cleaning and do a few jobs,' I said to Wendy Nicol, a Labour Whip, one afternoon. 'Will that be all right?'

'We don't think we'll divide until after five o'clock,' she said, 'so you'll be safe until then.'

Imagine my chagrin when at about four-thirty I hurried back with my dry cleaning to find that not only was the division over but the Government had won by a single vote. It was a comfort to find out that my vote wouldn't have made any difference as there has to be a majority to carry an amendment.

I told this story to Philippe Daudy, a friend from France, who was profoundly shocked. 'But that is terrible. I wonder if there is anything we can do to help? Marie-Christine (his wife) does all sorts of charitable work. Perhaps for the sake of the country she could include collecting your dry cleaning!'

An occasion I remember with cynicism was the vote over school meals in the 1986 Social Security Bill. This had such a profound effect on me that I will describe it in some detail. The Bill made a whole range of changes in the Social Security system, including one to substitute the free school meal, to which children of certain needy families were entitled, with a cash compensation. This presented a variety of worries: whether the proposed amount of £2.20 a week was sufficient to cover the whole cost of the meal, or, more likely, whether a hard-pressed mother might be forced to use the money to meet other pressing household needs; or the child might itself elect to buy crisps and a coke with the daily 44p rather than keep it for the healthy school meal.

I went to visit several primary schools in London to see what went on at lunchtime. And what I saw made me realize how much the school meal service had improved. The children made their selection from a whole lot of different dishes and once they had helped themselves they took their plates to sit at little tables where they chattered away happily to each other. The school I remember best was in Lambeth. The head teacher, a Frenchwoman full of warmth and with an obvious love for small children, told me their background. Most of the families lived in the nearby housing estate where there was high unemployment and poverty. The mothers were stretched to the limit in their efforts to make ends meet. She gave me an example of the extreme shortage of cash. One of the mothers, she told me, always borrowed £2 from her on Thursday.

'Why then?' I asked.

'Because that's when the Social Security money has usually run out,' she said, and described how the mother then used the money to buy bread and potatoes and on the Friday, when she got her Giro cheque, she would repay it. The head teacher kept the £2 in her desk, and each week the money wended its way between the two women: until finally, she said, smiling, it had become unclear to whom the money had originally belonged.

Wanting to get things right, I asked if it were possible that some mothers might prefer the cash payment, especially as it was also to be paid during the holidays. Perhaps, I suggested, this might help them with their budget. The head teacher looked at me in amazement. 'People with so little money can't budget. They're always in debt. Any spare cash goes straight to avert crises, crises like the electricity being turned off, the need for a pair of shoes for the child to go to school in, the demands of a bullying husband for the pub. There's always something, and even with the best intentions the poorest mothers might never manage to put the school meal money aside each week. And then what will we do with those children who come to school empty handed? Turn them away, or give them a meal and hope the money will turn up sometime?'

She pointed to a little girl sitting close to us. 'Do you see the way she is eating; piling her spoon as high as she can and opening her mouth very, very wide. That's the way children eat when they are desperately hungry. She probably hasn't eaten anything since lunch yesterday and I've noticed when she arrives at school after the week-end she looks sort of shrunken.' She ended sadly, 'In schools like this we know how much the poorer children depend on their good dinner. I do hope you'll be able to do something to help.'

The day for the debate was 15 July and the sun was out; I remember wearing a summer dress. With the teacher's words still in my mind I introduced the amendment. It had the advantage of having cross-party support; meaning that Lady Vickers, a Conservative, and Lord Kilmarnock, an Alliance peer, had put their names to it along with the Bishop of London. This gave the proposal added weight. The debate started immediately after Question Time which is always well attended, so the Chamber was still pretty full. I noticed to my surprise that some peers were wearing morning suits and vaguely wondered why, but I was so taken up with presenting my arguments that I didn't work out the significance. I ended my speech by mentioning all the support I had received from education authorities, mothers (8 in 10 of whom had voted in a poll for the meal rather than the money), teachers, medical institutions and – my *pièce de résistance* – the WI. 'This morning,' I said, 'I received a tele-message, My Lords, which read as follows: "Eleven thousand Cheshire Women's Institute members are mandated to support the amendment to rescue free school meals. We know when our next meal will be. There are hungry and undernourished children in this country today. There should not be one."' I went on to say, 'Now I am sure no one could accuse the Cheshire WI of being from the Loony Left; they are merely a group of concerned women and their message is proof of this. ... My Lords, may I end by saying that I am convinced our proposal is the best way of helping children of families under pressure. We are not asking for more money; we are simply asking for the present system to be continued and improved. There are many issues for which I have argued in Your Lordships' House, but none with greater conviction and sincerity than this one. I beg Your Lordships to listen to the arguments and support this amendment.'

Although peers from all sides of the House spoke in support, the Baroness Trumpington in replying for the Government rejected the amendment. By that time I had realized why there were so many Tory peers present and why they were looking so smart: it was the afternoon of the Buckingham Palace garden party. Many of them were in London to attend it and had their chauffeur-driven cars waiting outside to take them on to the Palace. I rose to give my final summing up: 'My Lords, I should like to thank those noble Lords who have contributed to the debate. I am most grateful for the support that I have received from all parts of the House. Only two speakers have opposed the proposal, the noble Lord, Lord Boyd-Carpenter, and the noble Baroness, Lady Carnegy. May I say one thing to the noble Lord, Lord Boyd-Carpenter. The noble Lord may have an awful lot of experience, but he cannot have had the experience of being a mother. So he cannot possibly know, amid all the preoccupations that mothers have in their lives, how the removal of one preoccupation – namely, the worry that their children are being properly fed at lunch time – represents a most important factor. I should have thought this was borne out by the fact that 80 per cent of mothers, far from feeling that it was patronizing or that their dignity was at risk, when asked said that they should like to go on with the school meal and not have the cash benefit, even if it was higher. That is surely incontestable.

'The noble Baroness, Lady Trumpington, in my view, left a lot of questions unanswered ... Having heard her I am not really any happier than I was previously. I realize, however, that there is a feeling among certain noble Lords on the other side that they have to get somewhere else –'

'No, My Lords,' interjected the Lord President of The Council, Viscount Whitelaw, in response to this veiled accusation about the garden party.

I concluded, '– So, My Lords, I should now like to test the opinion of the House.'

Watching them file through the lobby opposing my proposal contrasted so brutally with my memory of the small child at Lambeth, eyes intent on her plate, wolfing down her food. The outcome was that the Government defeated our amendment by 154 to 117; a handsome majority. Apart from bitter disappointment, I was left with a greater than ever disillusionment in a system of voting which is so much affected by outside, arbitrary factors.

Not long after this I met Glenys Kinnock at a Unicef gathering and she asked me how things were going in the Lords, and I said although naturally I was grateful for a platform, I often became disheartened by how little there was to show for all the work we did there. 'But you mustn't see it like that, Jane,' she said. 'Good and useful things you do and say are never wasted. They can be put to good use in indirect ways. The ideas Labour peers put forward in debate about, say, education, will be picked up and thought about by teachers all over the country. It will help form their judgement. Even if you don't win the votes, the important things you say and stand for will never be lost.' I was grateful to her.

But now, in 1988, I look back on six and a half years of interest and intense activity. I can think of times when I was proud to belong there, others when I wasn't. And moments when tedium has taken over and the atmosphere created by a surfeit of arrogance and self-esteem has become oppressive. There have been high points as when the House rose to honour its duty as a constitutional watchdog and threw out the GLC abolition clause with the biggest vote ever recorded. And bills removing outdated discrimination: the Family Law Reform Bill for instance rescued children born out of wedlock from being penalized. There have been many debates on matters of public concern which have drawn out not only the wisdom but the very soul of the House. I look back with particular admiration on the work of the European Community Committees and extra-Parliamentary committees such as Roskill and Warnock. Using the abundant experience and humanity to be found among Their Lordships, these committees have worked towards extracting the major benefit from social, economic and scientific changes to the advantage of all people. And there have been many examples of the Lords doing what they can really do well, such as a debate in 1987 on the importance of the English language and the case for making it easier to learn.

In particular I look back on the few times when I have made something happen myself. Once I persuaded the Administration Committee to arrange for a cancer-screening session to be set up for women in the House of Lords. I started the ball rolling with a question in April 1986. 'To ask the Chairman of Committees whether any cancer-screening facilities are provided for women working in the Palace of Westminster.'

The Chairman answered that the House of Commons, having considered doing so, had finally rejected the proposal put forward by the Women's National Cancer Control Campaign for a mobile unit on the grounds that women should go to their general practitioner or local clinic for screening. But there were some important contributions made by two women peers. Baroness Gardner of Parkes pointed out that the women who are in greatest need of screening are often those most reluctant to attend. She added that very effective mobile clinics visit places where a large number of women work and that it would be a simple exercise to have such a mobile clinic for a brief time. The Countess of Mar added to the discussion by saying that 'the majority of women dying from cancer were in the forty to sixty age group, and many of them, hard-working mothers with children, lack the time to see their GPs, and that if a mobile clinic were to come to their place of work, this would encourage a great many women to go who now die unnecessarily.' She finally made the vital point that 'thirty years ago tuberculosis was fairly rife in this country, that mobile clinics were used to x-ray people for tuberculosis, and TB is now a very rare illness in this country.'

Finally – it took a long time – I persuaded the Lords Committee to agree to set up a screening programme independently of the Commons. I argued that in the same way as the House of Lords had experimented by allowing themselves to be televised, we might also experiment with on-site cancer screening and the House of Commons might then follow our example. So the arrangements were made with the Women's National Cancer Control Campaign and on 10 November 1987 a pristine mobile unit, sponsored by the Bingo Association of Great Britain, was parked in Black Rod's garden below the Victoria Tower. Well over half the women working in the Lords made appointments for the test. I went myself and on my way out of the clinic I met some of the women who work in the bars and dining-room waiting their turn. They looked worried and seemed rather embarrassed. However, talking to one of them a few weeks later after I had heard my results, I asked if she had received hers. Relieved and smiling, she said, 'Yes, and it was OK. And having the test wasn't half as bad as I expected. None of us wanted to go, but I'm glad we did because they found something wrong with quite a few of the girls and they were called back for further tests. We're ever so grateful to you for fixing it all up.'

The final stage of my plan failed, however. Delighted as I was at the success of the operation, I wanted the experiment also to provide an example to women all over the country to follow suit and undergo tests. As Lady Mar had said, it's always women under most pressure who neglect their own health, and those who develop cancer of the cervix or the breast are invariably those who have never been screened. So I put another question down asking what the response to the screening session had been. I hoped that the television cameras might focus on this thereby bringing it to the attention of women everywhere. Unfortunately, the rival question that day was about the number of pelicans in St James's Park and how many were male and female. To my fury, this stole the limelight, and the nation was fully informed about pelicans and their idiosyncracies rather than the vital importance of cancer prevention for women.

I also had the privilege of being involved – indirectly – with two people getting married. In these days of one in three couples getting divorced, there is nothing more heartening than to hear about people who want so much to get married that they go to a great deal of trouble and money to do so. There are certain affinities which prevent a marriage between two parties unless they seek special permission from Parliament. These Marriage Enabling Bills used to be debated on the floor of the House, but it was decided that much of the detail was of such a very personal nature that the discussion would be better carried out in private, so they are now referred to a Select Committee, which reports back to the House.

I was invited, together with two other peers and a bishop, to serve on this Select Committee. The relationship of the two petitioners in question was that of a man and his daughter-in-law. A marriage between them would only have been valid if both their original partners were dead. But although the wife of the male petitioner had died, the former husband of the female petitioner, who was in fact the male petitioner's son, was living. So in order to legalize a marriage the older man and young woman were obliged to bring a Bill before both Parliaments – at considerable cost to themselves in legal fees etc. The task of the Select Committee was to satisfy themselves that the relationship between the father-in-law and his daughter-in-law had not, in the first place, contributed to the break-up or termination of either marriage or, in the second place, been damaging to any child of either marriage.

The Committee sat in the intimidating setting of the Moses Room just off the Peers' Lobby, and with the vast mural *The Judgement of Daniel* bearing down on the proceedings, the two petitioners put their case to us. Tremulously they went through each stage of their relationship. The widowed older man and the divorced young woman had kept in touch with each other after the termination of their marriages. They told us how they occasionally had a meal together, and then the father-in-law helped his daughter-in-law to decorate the flat she had moved into after leaving her own husband. Then slowly their relationship changed and two years later a son was born to them and they started living together. They wished to formalize their association for the sake of the little boy.

They gave their evidence separately and then went to sit on a bench at the far end of the room, holding hands and giving each other encouragement. The man's three children – all grown up – were called to give their evidence. Yes, they said, they had been surprised when they realized how far the relationship had developed. Did they think, we asked them, that the marriage should take place? Without any hesitation each one of them, in almost the same words, said, 'Yes, they want to get married because they love each other and we think it should happen.'

The bishop and we three peers then conferred while the petitioners and the witnesses waited outside. It didn't take long to decide and we called them back to hear we would be recommending to the House that the Bill enabling their marriage should be allowed to proceed. With relief on their faces the couple hugged each other. Even the figures in *The Judgement of Daniel* seemed to soften at the sight.

I look back too at all the friends I have made since being in the Lords, and remember with affection so many who have died. One of these was Lord Shinwell. Manny was a very dapper old gentleman; small and neat, his light-weight tweed suits carefully pressed and the black shoes shining. His stiff white collar rode high up his neck and the white cap of hair sometimes overlapped it. The skin of his face was smooth and a pinkish colour; not wrinkled as one might imagine for such an elderly person. He used a walking stick in a businesslike way and got along fast. He didn't smile much and always occupied the same seat in the Chamber at the end of the row behind the bench occupied by Labour Privy Councillors.

At his hundredth birthday, in 1985, television, radio and press all fought to carry interviews with him, and I remember arriving at the Lords several times to see a rugger-like scrum of photographers encircling the small, resolute and utterly impassive figure. Another time he was being frogmarched out between two towering BBC men to the green opposite the Palace which was often used for interviews. Far from becoming exhausted by all this excitement and effort, he seemed to thrive on it and his step took on an extra spring.

It was then his colleagues' turn to celebrate the occasion and they decided to give him a birthday party in the Royal Gallery. This high-ceilinged apartment of State had never before been used for such an occasion. I have already described how it provides a passage for Her Majesty on her way to open Parliament or the setting for a visiting Head of State to address both Houses. On the day we all gathered there and the Leader of the House proposed the birthday toast. Manny replied. He came just about up to Lord Whitelaw's shoulders, but looking alert and fit, in spite of having been on several chat shows that morning and been trailed by squads of photographers and reporters, he first thanked his colleagues for their generosity. Then he commented on the excitement which his birthday appeared to have inspired. Presuming that this was due to his being a hundred, he remarked mildly that it was different for him as the anniversary merely represented the passing of one more year and served as a reminder of all the things he still had to do in the years ahead.

I have several other memories of the old man, who finally died in his 102nd year. One day soon after I came to the Lords I received a note from him. Peremptory in style, it read: 'Dear Lady Biggs. Will you come to lunch with me on –. The Peers' Dining Room at 12.30.' Without hesitation I cancelled the date I had arranged and wrote an enthusiastic note of acceptance. 'Glad you can come,' he snapped as he passed me in the corridor soon after. He immensely enjoyed the role of host and once we were settled down at the table – there were eight of us – he described each course of the meal, the reasons he had chosen them, and then went into great detail about the wines which, again, had been his own selection. I wondered what criteria he had used in the choice of his guests. There was an old crony from the North of England with whom he had presumably shared some challenging stage of his life, an attractive lady from television, a couple and then two other peers, one Tory and one Labour. I asked my neighbour, the Labour peer, if he knew why we in particular had been selected.

'I've no idea about the rest of us, but I do know exactly why he invited you. He came up to me a few weeks ago and asked, "Who's that new woman who has just arrived? She's not bad looking; better than some of the others here." So I can only imagine that was the reason for choosing you.'

And then there was the time he lost his walking stick. This happened at the end of Question Time one day. He had, as usual, taken part vociferously in the discussion following one of the questions. Lady Young who was the Government Minister replying to the question, had made the grave mistake of congratulating him on his 101st birthday of the previous day, prior to answering him.

'What's she saying'? What's she saying'? he muttered to his neighbour. Having been told, he leaped to his feet furiously. 'I don't see what my birthday has got to do with it,' he shouted. 'Will the Minister answer my question?'

Following that, Manny felt he had done his bit and prepared to leave the Chamber. But his walking stick had fallen through the narrow gap at the back of the benches in front, possibly even sent on its way by his feet jerking with irritation. Not only did it elude his grasp but also that of the elegant attendant lying flat on his stomach to the accompaniment of Manny's querulous, 'I want my stick ... I want my stick.' The attendant went off, defeated, and I sensed a crisis looming as Manny left his bench, muttering loudly and clutching at anything to steady him. By that time the attention of the whole House was concentrated on him. The voice at the despatch box continued, but at a slower pace, the Minister's eye flickering anxiously towards the departing figure; the *Hansard* writer's pencil slowed its race across the paper as his eyes too were drawn towards the shambling, complaining figure. The crossbenchers, through whom Manny was making his uncertain progress, were on the alert, like cricketers poised for a catch. Press gallery, the civil servants in the 'box', every neck was craning forward. The proceedings of Their Lordships' House were about to be brought to an abrupt close unless something was done. Moving discreetly – and I hoped unobtrusively – I moved over to his bench, lay flat with my arm down the narrow gap and fingers urgently exploring for the stick. I had it.

Once reunited with his vital possession, Manny, still rather cross, said to me as he resumed his way out, 'You'll be hearing from me.'

'Oh, no, it's perfectly all right,' I said, wondering what on earth he could mean.

Next day, there he was gesticulating urgently at me from the other end of the Chamber. I went up to him. 'Meet me at my locker,' he said. 'I've got something for you.'

I did as I was told and found him as impassive as ever opening up his locker in the Library Corridor. As I arrived he produced out of it a long newspaper-wrapped object. I undid the string and unwrapped layer upon layer of newspaper and finally there was the present – a bottle. 'Nothing like good Scotch whisky,' he said and stumped off.

Now that Manny is no longer with us we feel bereft. Not only do we miss him, but we also miss showing off about him. He had been like a mascot. A memorial meeting for him was held in the Grand Committee Room at the end of Westminster Hall and tributes were paid by former prime minister Lord Home, Labour leader Neil Kinnock, Labour MP Greville Janner and many others. I now look often at Manny's old seat in the Chamber with affection and often reminisce about him.

There are other good friends besides Manny whom I have lost since being in the Lords. Christopher Soames, who died in 1987, featured in both my lives, first as British Ambassador in Paris during our time there and then as Leader of the House on my arrival in 1981. Larger than life and reflecting the spirit and personality of his famous father-in-law, Winston Churchill, he leaves a great void in the Tory benches. I still almost anticipate the arrival in the Chamber of his immensely tall figure, a quizzical look on his face and his long, sensitive hands hidden deep in trouser pockets.

At about the same time, Nicky Kaldor died. I remember first noticing an ominous sign of his illness, when I recognized the cough, which I dreaded hearing from my asthmatic daughter Kate, suddenly coming from right behind me on the back benches.

'What's the matter, Nicky?' I asked him afterwards.

'It's this wretched asthma, I've never had it before in my life.'

I gave him the name of the specialist at the Brompton Hospital who had treated Kate for so many years, but I knew how serious it was at his age. Previously economic adviser to Harold Wilson's government, he took part in debates, in his inimitable Hungarian accent, speaking scathingly against monetarism. He was the kindest and most generous of men. Once he invited me to a Feast at his Cambridge college, to which he, his wife, Clarissa and I travelled from London by car with Nicky at the wheel. His driving soon had me hanging on like mad in the back seat, my eyes closed most of the way, convinced beyond doubt that political economists should never drive cars. But a marriage like theirs was above such trivialities. 'Well done, darling – you drove beautifully,' Clarissa said admiringly as we arrived with a skid, a flourish and a screech of brakes outside their Cambridge home.

There are so many charming and cultivated people on the cross-benches, but I still find myself looking at the places Paul Gore-Booth and John Redcliffe-Maud occupied and recall fond memories. Paul was almost an eccentric; he was much loved in the Foreign Office, when he was Permanent Under-Secretary, and was a well-known authority on Sherlock Holmes. And John, tall, thin and immensely gentle, left his mark in local government, higher education and other areas of our national life. Not least will he be remembered as a remarkable after-dinner speaker.

There are particular moments when the House is at its best. These usually occur at the committee stage of bills. A government Whip proposes from the despatch box 'that the House do now resolve itself into a Committee upon this Bill', and the Lord Chairman takes his seat facing the Clerks at the table. Then it is as if the walls of the Chamber draw inwards, and the atmosphere and discussion take on the intimacy of an after-dinner conversation. Often the bills under review are complex, such as the 1988 Copyright, Design and Patent Bill – not of a party political nature – which after intense scrutiny from all sides of the House, came to the statute-book much improved. Two sessions which enthralled me most were during the Criminal Justice and Legal Aid Bills in 1987 and 1988. In both instances Opposition proposals prevailed. Lord Hutchinson, the SDP peer and distinguished QC, questioned the new clause regarding extradition in the Criminal Justice Bill. This took away from the British courts any judicial examination of the facts on which the foreign state would seek extradition of the person concerned. He gave the example of the Liverpool football supporters involved in the Brussels stadium tragedy. The law up to this point would have allowed for an inquiry in Britain prior to extradition; were the new proposals to be adopted, such defendants would be denied that right and would be sent immediately to stand trial abroad.

The intense debate which followed revealed the strength of the case put by Lord Hutchinson and other Opposition peers. Eventually, the Earl of Caithness, speaking for the Government, conceded that 'It is right that I should look at this again. It is clear that it is of concern to the Committee.' When the bill returned at report stage, the Government had included the required amendment providing for judicial review of extradition decisions. So this change was brought about not by forcing a division but by the power of argument.

A few months later the Legal Aid Bill came before the House and Victor Mishcon in his elegant and lucid style argued that multi-party litigants should be eligible for legal aid. He cited the case of the Zeebrugge ferry disaster, where it would have been to the advantage of relatives to sue for damages collectively. Lord Goodman, another of the country's well-known solicitors, gave an example which had a distinctly black side to it. 'About two years ago,' he said, 'I was called upon to represent some forty or fifty doctors who unfortunately had all been poisoned at a professional dinner – to them it was not a laughing matter, although it has a certain element of humour. Not one of those doctors was eligible for legal aid and not one of them had the means to prosecute an action on his own account. . . .'

Once again the Government Minister was won over by the force of the argument and, at the next stage, the Lord Chancellor introduced a measure enabling the Legal Aid Board to offer contracts to firms of solicitors to handle multiple actions. This rule would, of course, make it easier for victims of disasters and drug injuries to club together and sue for compensation.

Sometimes these complex legal bills have provided the setting for mild acrimony between layman and lawyer. One rather sleepy afternoon the House was jerked awake by an exchange between Lady Faithfull and Lord Hailsham, who by that time had vacated the Woolsack to take his place on the Privy Councillors' bench. Lucy Faithfull wished to ensure that the Legal Aid Bill, still under discussion, should be made more easily comprehensible to ordinary people. The purpose of her amendment was to remedy the fact that the bill lacked a clear statement of principle or purpose. 'There must be more simplicity and understanding in our legislation,' she said, very reasonably.

Lord Hailsham opposed the proposal and said as much, but then went too far. He implied that Lady Faithfull was not experienced enough to know any better. She was, he said, '. . . wholly innocent in these matters, not having held any of the high offices of state to which the amendment relates. . . .'

Lucy wasn't having that and, rising to her feet, she fixed her colleague with a pretty steely look and said, 'I must take issue with my noble and learned friend. I may not have held high office of state but I do . . . understand what people want and need. I am grateful that . . . I should have come to this House in order that I might express the feelings of the people of this country who are vulnerable, who are poor and who need support and help. They do not understand the judges and there have to be people who interpret what the judges mean.' She continued in this vein for several minutes to the accompaniment of rousing Opposition cheers. Then, all indignation spent, she came to a full stop, looked down at her notes and smiling broadly said, 'Now I've quite lost my place.'

But her point was not lost on Lord Mackay, the Lord Chancellor, whose response was clear: 'I shall endeavour to produce, with assistance ... a statement, in the simplest terms that we can devise and which I hope will be comprehensible, on the purpose of the Bill.'

CHAPTER THIRTEEN

Future Uncertain

COMPARING TODAY'S SECOND Chamber with the one I joined in 1981, I wonder how much both the Lords and I have changed since the day of my Introduction such an age ago.

In the Lords there is most certainly increased activity and a higher attendance of peers. We sit later in the evenings and are under greater pressure. The large Government majority in the Commons has increased the responsibilities of the second chamber and, through its proceedings being televised and the press giving it greater coverage, the House of Lords is now better known to the public, who may even have become impressed by what is done there. More and more we are lobbied by organizations and individuals who – disregarding the large majority the Tory Whips are nearly always able to assemble – have a blind trust in the House of Lords' ability to change things when an unpopular measure passes through the Commons. Recent intakes of life peers, in particular on the Labour side, have generated much of the increased activity. Those appointed in the February 1987 political honours list strengthened the Labour group in a variety of fields such as criminal law, agriculture, economics, and education. The new peers have each added their energies and expertise to the work of the House. I remember that when the names of these five specialists were published, one of my more down-to-earth colleagues remarked that they would be better at taking penalty kicks than in the hurly burly on the pitch. The dissolution honours list following the general election of June 1987 brought the House nineteen new members who possibly looked forward to more passive roles. These were all ex-Cabinet Ministers, Privy Councillors or MPs, some of whom, feeling the battle had been hard fought, viewed the Lords as a comfortable resting place.

Another significant change in recent years is the contrast between the two front benches. The Government side is now almost entirely occupied by hereditary peers. Indeed, ordinary citizens may begin to question a system whereby an inherited title is the ticket to becoming a lawmaker. With the exception of Lord Ponsonby, our Chief Whip, the Labour front bench is made up entirely of life peers, with the consequent higher average age and greater experience. This sometimes presents an unbalanced contest between the young earls or viscounts, struggling to master their briefs, and the highly professional voices from the Opposition despatch box.

The confrontational style which has crept into Their Lordships' debates is also new. Rigid positions are more readily assumed and party political point-scoring is not unusual. This is, of course, normal procedure in the Commons, but, representing the cockpit of the nation as it does, aggressive exchanges seem appropriate there, quarrelsome and tedious though the voices on *Yesterday in Parliament* often sound. Nevertheless, elected representatives who see their constituents thrown out of work or suffering human or civil injustices have a right to shout and yell on their behalf. But a non-elected house must be judged for the quality of its work, its powers of scrutiny and reasoned arguments. Confrontation will not assist in the process of bringing about the sound and balanced revision of bills.

I believe this new style reflects the trend in the country as a whole, where confrontation has entered so many parts of our national life. (It is certainly reflected in our steadily increasing mail bag.) We see a greater polarization of the social classes, of the north and south of the country, between those with jobs and those without, the well housed and the homeless, between the very rich and the very poor. We see the re-emergence of an 'under-class'. Inexorably the pendulum is swinging away from a belief that the best way forward is through conciliation of differences and a search for thoughtful and compassionate solutions to complex social and economic problems – proof, indeed, of how far we have departed from the post-war consensus, born out of national unity, to build a more liberal and tolerant society. The Earl of Stockton, previously Harold Macmillan, voiced this fear in his maiden speech in 1984, when he called for 'a kind of moral and spiritual revolution'.

I suppose those dark red benches have always harboured their fair share of bigotry, chauvinism and prejudice, but what has changed is the licence to express such reactionary instincts, which sadly is now more readily assumed. There was ample proof of this during the debate about the controversial and loosely worded clause in the

1988 Local Government Bill preventing local authorities from 'promoting' homosexuality or giving financial assistance or support to anyone doing so, which was debated in the House as I completed this final chapter.

There had been a massive lobby and many of us – myself included – received as many as 200 letters from a variety of correspondents: homosexuals, lesbians, parents, teachers, voluntary workers, university lecturers, actors, writers and so on. They were all worried that the ambiguous wording might lead to discrimination not only against gays themselves but also against those working with them or even writing on the subject of homosexuality. When the Bill came into Committee, Viscount Falkland, from the Alliance benches, introduced an amendment to remove the ambiguity from the clause. He spoke in conciliatory terms, reminiscent of the 1960s, when the trend was towards compromise and tolerance. '... In this country we wish to create a happy, productive community where everyone works together ... where all classes of citizens – whether they are minorities such as homosexuals ... have the best possible life and the ... opportunity of working with everyone else. I do not think this clause helps in that cause.' The following day, Ted Willis, Labour peer and playwright, went further by trying to remove the offending clause from the Bill altogether. Describing it as 'the first breath of a chilly wind of intolerance and the first page of a charter for bigots', he ended his speech, 'I am rather proud of what this Chamber has done in the past twenty years to create a tolerant and understanding society. Yesterday I was saddened because I thought a step backwards had been taken.'

The debate which followed was disturbing because of the highly charged atmosphere and emotive language. One speaker claimed that, if the clause was not passed, an anti-homosexual backlash was quite probable. Another speaker quoted from a letter received – he claimed – from a homosexual accusing his fellow homosexuals of having brought unpopularity on themselves by being too promiscuous, too aggressive and too exhibitionist, and how he (the writer) could not stand the sight of them.

I had planned to describe the anxieties of voluntary organizations working with homeless young people – many of whom were gays and lesbians. The youth workers feared they might be seen as 'promoting' homosexuality with a consequent loss of funding. But I funked it, finding myself unable to summon up enough courage to intervene when so much hostility and intransigence was in the air. When the House divided, the Government majority – retaining the clause – was 202 to 122.

As the vote was announced, three women in the gallery suddenly threw ropes over the brass latticework and let themselves down on to the floor of the Chamber. Shouting obscenities at the peers, they were escorted away by Black Rod. I found the whole episode infinitely depressing. The message the debate brought to the young people in the gallery was one of intransigence and prejudice, so they retaliated. This demonstrates how confrontation can spiral with the expression of one intolerance sparking off a countervailing one.

This incident may have been a signal that on this occasion the House of Lords had moved too far from the consensus and had pushed the pendulum a little further on its journey away from post-war moderation. But, by its very nature, we know a pendulum cannot continue its movement in one direction indefinitely and I believe that the one operating in Britain may soon start its return journey, pointing the way towards a society whose values reflect a greater charity, kindness and good neighbourliness, where human priorities dominate.

I am sure the House of Lords has a role to play in influencing the direction of the pendulum. I know we need a second chamber to provide a constitutional safeguard and to put right things which the parliamentary draughtsmen or the Commons have got wrong, but we also need it as a forum for unbiased and well-informed discussion about the way towards a better society.

I do not think the Lords' present structure makes it possible for those requirements to be met, nor does it enable the many outstanding men and women who serve there to perform to the best of their ability. So, after seven years of intensive involvement with the work of the House – part of which was a very necessary apprenticeship – I have come to the conclusion that Parliament now needs a modern, more professional second chamber in keeping with most other western European democracies. I am not suggesting the demise of the House, but I am suggesting the need for reform to remove outdated elements from the present system whilst retaining what is good. I would like to see its members treated as people with jobs rather than people with titles; they deserve the same working conditions as their colleagues in the Commons. This would mean the House no longer need rely on the services of the rich, whilst at the same time the frustrations of hard-pressed working peers might be relieved. If it were decided that the role of a peer required democratic legitimacy, then I have earlier given examples of different systems of election to be considered – there is no shortage of options.

Although such changes might well receive broad agreement in the country, the fear of the Commons that a stronger and more efficient second chamber would be to the detriment of its own unchallenged position of authority will doubtless continue to be the stumbling block. So, until forces and events coincide to make reform possible, I have no doubt that members of all parties in the House will continue to show it commitment and loyalty. This is because, in spite of all its idiosyncracies, we are united in our determination to make it work. Perhaps, too, we feel compelled to show the Commons that we can.

Finally, what part have I played in this anomalous but respected institution and how different am I from the person introduced to her peers on that day in June 1981? There is little doubt that I was one of its rawest recruits. But now that has changed and I have a place in the inner circle of the Labour group as one of the six Whips responsible for organizing and directing the work of the Opposition.

Besides this, I still speak on Home Office subjects and most recently was responsible for piloting through its different stages the Licensing Bill allowing pubs extended opening hours. I have in addition taken up the portfolios of Overseas Development and Consumer Affairs. Such wide ranging subjects bring me a lot of work and with the help of the Labour peers' only, but highly intelligent, researcher, Andrew Bold, I try to become sufficiently informed. I look back on the time I contented myself with a starry-eyed belief that social responsibility comes just with being alive, but now I make use of my position to add substance to the ideal.

Yet in spite of my increased experience and higher status, I still find the Chamber an intimidating place. Sometimes, on the days I am due to take part in a debate I practice my speech as I drive to the House. Speaking aloud to the windscreen the words come out lucid and clear, but when I try to repeat this in the Chamber my old lack of self-confidence and childhood shyness reassert themselves. At other times, during the committee stage of bills, through listening carefully I recognize a relevant point but dare not intervene. This takes me back to the lunchtime agonies at school when, sitting round the big table, I used to work out an intelligent contribution to the conversation. Not brave enough to interrupt, I waited patiently for a pause. Then, inevitably I gloomily heard my intervention being made by somebody else and greeted with general approval.

I most envy my colleagues who can 'think on their feet', those who never miss an opportunity to drive a point home or find an instant response in debate. Sometimes there are days I feel I have made a little progress when boldly I rise to my feet and interrupt. 'If the noble Lord will give way ...' and make my point. But it does not often happen.

My personal life has adapted to my increased parliamentary involvement and this, in turn, has filled the void left by my three children growing up. Henrietta and Robin, who are now in their early twenties, live independently and Kate, a student at Edinburgh University, is only at home for holidays. Because of his office moving out of London and his frequent business trips abroad, I see less of Kevin, my dear friend of so many years. I have never, at the best of times, had the benefit of a large all-embracing family of my own, but now I am the only member left. My mother died at Easter 1987, in her 95th year, at peace and still very beautiful, and the previous year, Dick, my only brother, died when he was only in his fifties.

So many of the people who were nearest me are not around any more. For the first time in my life I often face returning to an empty house. I know this happens to most people at some time in their lives, but I do believe the degree to which we are all affected by solitude depends so much on our natures. I am a gregarious person, so find solitude provides no stimulation, whereas others, who are more self-sufficient, use such time to charge their batteries. I thought I could cope with the problem by delaying my return in the evening as long as possible, but soon found that it doesn't make any difference. However late you come home, the house is just as empty. And it's the same thing waking up in the morning; I immediately sense whether the house is empty or it is a day when some warm presence is inhabiting it somewhere. So now I fully accept that a house cannot be a home unless used by a group of people to lead their lives collectively. But none of us can change our nature, so instead of sitting at home trying to persuade myself I *ought* to feel all right, I accept that this may never happen and instead keep very busy. Besides my greater involvement with the work of the House of Lords, I also accept more invitations – both social and professional – either at home or from abroad. There is the danger that fear of being alone brings on un-natural hyperactivity and removes the freedom of choosing what to do. This reminds me of the time I asked a mini-cab driver how many hours he worked each day.

'About sixteen,' he said.

'Why so many?'

'To pay off my debts – I owe money for the car, the insurance, the washing machine. . . .' I think of him still, hunched over the wheel with debt at his heels compelling him to drive on and on and on.

But I hope fear of being alone will not always dictate what I do, and I have even set myself a modest aim. I remember clearly how during those dark days after Christopher was killed the weekends were the worst. My ambition then was to attain the point of recovery where an empty weekend with nothing to do held no fears. Now I aim to become sufficiently self-reliant to look forward to getting home in the evening and regard it as a pleasure and relaxation. After all, I have one domestic responsibility left, because Milly is there; with her huge spaniel eyes welcoming me and saying how pleased she is I have returned to feed her.

I often have supper in the Bishops' Bar, where Mary serves out eggs, bacon, sausages, etc. Everyone is very friendly and we talk about everything under the sun. It makes me feel I have found an extended family and, although it is comprised of Lords and Ladies, they are people like everyone else. So I believe Kevin was right that evening years ago at the Festival Hall when we looked through the rain at the blurred outline of the Palace of Westminster and he said he was sure I would be very happy there.

Index